Mandolin Man

MUSIC IN AMERICAN LIFE

*A list of books in the series appears
at the end of this book.*

Mandolin Man

The Bluegrass Life of Roland White

BOB BLACK

UNIVERSITY OF
ILLINOIS PRESS
Urbana, Chicago, and Springfield

Publication of this book was supported in part by a grant
from the Judith McCulloh Endowment for American Music.

Library of Congress Cataloging-in-Publication Data
Names: Black, Bob, 1949– author.
Title: Mandolin man : the bluegrass life of Roland White /
    Bob Black.
Description: Urbana : University of Illinois Press, 2022. |
    Series: Music in American life | Includes bibliographical
    references and index.
Identifiers: LCCN 2021054597 (print) | LCCN 2021054598
    (ebook) | ISBN 9780252044335 (cloth) | ISBN
    9780252086403 (paperback) | ISBN 9780252053320
    (ebook)
Subjects: LCSH: White, Roland. | Mandolinists—United
    States—Biography. | Bluegrass—United States—Biography.
Classification: LCC ML419.W414 B53 2022 (print) | LCC
    ML419.W414 (ebook) | DDC 787.8/41642092—dc23
LC record available at https://lccn.loc.gov/2021054597
LC ebook record available at https://lccn.loc.gov/2021054598

Hold fast to dreams
For if dreams die
Life is a broken-winged bird
That cannot fly.
Hold fast to dreams
For when dreams go
Life is a barren field
Frozen with snow.
—Langston Hughes

It's hard to beat a person who never gives up.
—Babe Ruth

Contents

Acknowledgments

Thanks to Kristie Reynolds Black for her invaluable editing help, her love, and her support all through the writing process, especially during the latter stages when things got really tough. Thanks as well to Diane Bouska for her generous sharing of information about her and Roland's musical life together and for helping me with a myriad of details while putting this book together.

My greatest appreciation, of course, goes to Roland White for unflinchingly telling Kristie and me his life story, especially the part about his brother Clarence's death; for arranging interviews with Vic Jordan, Alan O'Bryant, and Marty Stuart; for putting me in touch with many of the other interviewees in this book; for taking Kristie and me backstage at the *Grand Ole Opry* and introducing us to the Steep Canyon Rangers; for jamming with me down through the years; and for being a major source of inspiration for the last fifty years.

Thanks also to LeRoy McNees for sharing his memories and photos; William (Billy) Smith for sharing his memories; Jim Lauderdale for sharing his memories; Marty Stuart for taking the time on a busy tour to talk with me about Roland; Richard Bailey for contributing his thoughts about Roland; Jim Renz for sharing his memories; Alan O'Bryant for sharing his thoughts about Roland and about music in general; Vic Jordan for sharing many stories; Alan Munde for providing information about Country Gazette in addition to sharing his stories about Roland; David Grier for his touching written tribute to Roland; Jody Stecher for sharing his memories of Roland and the Kentucky Colonels; Doc Hamilton for sharing his memories and providing a wonderful photo of Roland with the Blue Grass Boys; Rick Gardner for sharing his Country Gazette photos; Jon Weisberger for sharing information about the 2018 *Tribute to the Kentucky Colonels* album, as well as his thoughts about Roland; Stuart Duncan for sharing photos from his collection; Rosemarie White for her fond thoughts about her brothers Roland and Clarence; Woody Platt for his information about Roland's part in the Steep Canyon Rangers' video "Tell the Ones I Love"; Kenny Wertz for his recollections of playing with Roland (and for the banjo inspiration he gave me back in the 1960s when he played with the Scottsville Squirrel Barkers); Tom Ewing for the years of work he spent in researching Bill Monroe and bluegrass, and for the column he wrote in *Bluegrass Unlimited*, "Thirty Years Ago This Month," which was of invaluable help in putting this book together; Roline Hodge for her affectionate childhood memories of Roland and her mother, Arline; Lawrence LeBlanc for his stories about Arline, Country Gazette, and debuting with Lester Flatt on the Opry; Doug Green (Ranger Doug) for telling me about living next door to Roland and his family, playing bluegrass together every day.

Additional thanks to Mark Kuykendall and Art Rosenbaum. That music is still out there, somewhere.

Mandolin Man

Introduction

Seventeen years had gone by and things had really changed. I hadn't been at the *Grand Ole Opry* since 1998 (when I performed there with Rhonda Vincent). Now, in March 2015, Kristie and I were roaming the same backstage halls once again, as guests of Roland White. The Opry House had been remodeled since the flood of 2010, when Tennessee's Cumberland River was the highest it had been since 1937. But the place somehow didn't seem the same—the brightness and gaiety were gone. The dressing rooms all looked darker, and the general décor had a more subdued feeling. It certainly didn't feel the same as it had back in '74, when everything was brand-new and I was performing there regularly with Bill Monroe. Everything was fixed up all right, but it all seemed different somehow. I suddenly realized it was me that had changed. I had grown older, somewhat more disillusioned with things in general and the music business in particular.

Inspiration was what I needed. Our return to Nashville was ostensibly to conduct some interviews for this book, but another reason—unknown to us at that time—was to rekindle some of the enthusiasm that had been lost over the years. I think Roland knew this as well, and he was willing to help.

Musically, things were going okay for me. My wife, Kristie, and I had been performing together with our band, Banjoy, for over thirteen years.[1] The members of our group are all friends who support one another. It's the only band I've ever been with whose members have stayed together in a "forever" sort of way. What a blessing!

But I was craving some of the excitement of the old days. A pilgrimage to Music City always leaves a mark of some kind, and this time the mark was left by Roland White. I had received a phone call from Roland a few weeks earlier. He told me he was enjoying reading my book *Come Hither to Go Yonder: Playing Bluegrass with Bill Monroe*.[2] I had known Roland since 1974, and I had enormous respect and admiration for him. We hadn't talked in several years, and I was quite surprised when he unexpectedly called to pay me a compliment. I couldn't believe it; here was a world-class musician going out of his way to let me know he liked what I had written. I didn't often get calls like that. It made me feel really good, like I was somebody who mattered.

I was just a plain old country boy from Iowa. Kristie and I had been living in an old-fashioned farmhouse since 1990, on a gravel road eight miles from the nearest town, unless you count Kinross—population seventy-two.[3] We had restored the house; it was once abandoned and used to store bales of hay. There had been snakes in the walls. The power often went out during storms. It was a great place to practice bluegrass music, though, since there were no neighbors to disturb. We're still there and we still love it.

During my phone conversation with Roland, I told him he needed to have a book written about him. I asked him if he had ever thought about writing an autobiography. He quickly said no. It might have been because he was too humble and believed that writing a book about himself would be too much like bragging. Maybe it was a hasty decision on my part, but I told him I wanted to do a book about his life in bluegrass music. Would I be going down an ill-chosen path? I didn't know yet, but I knew a book was needed. It would be a record of a rare person, a truly generous and sincere individual who happened to play the mandolin and who had influenced thousands of players worldwide. It would also be a source of inspiration for me, and Roland White was just the person to give it. After all, he has inspired countless others.

So here we were in Nashville, Kristie and me. A Red Roof Inn near the airport was our home for several days—room number 123—and Roland White was our guest each day as he told us his life story. He had also arranged a visit to the home of Vic Jordan (1938–2016) for an interview about their shared background as members of both Bill Monroe's Blue Grass Boys and Lester Flatt's Nashville Grass.

In addition, we visited Alan O'Bryant at his home near Pegram to talk about the Nashville Bluegrass Band (NBB), of which Roland was a member for twelve years. Alan was someone I had also met in 1974, on my very first night in Nashville, just before leaving to play in Black Mountain, North Carolina, with Bill Monroe and the Blue Grass Boys. He became one of my best friends in Music City. He still writes, sings, and teaches and also performs with the Nashville Bluegrass Band. He was a founding member of the NBB.

Our trip to Nashville had also included several jam sessions. I borrowed a banjo for those jams since I had taken my own banjo to Ed Weber's Nashville shop to have it re-fretted during our Music City stay.[4] Ed was a fellow Midwesterner and had spent many years working in the Nashville Gibson factory constructing banjo necks. He is now a freelance scrimshaw artist and finish craftsman for Recording King banjos. He can really pick a five-string too!

On our final evening in Nashville, Roland had taken us to the *Grand Ole Opry* as his guests. He wasn't playing that night, but all of the personnel knew and loved him, and any guests of Roland's were welcome backstage. He knew many of the Opry staff band members. Guitarist Jimmy Capps (1939–2020) smiled and said hi to Roland right from the stage as he backed up a singer. I remembered hearing Jimmy back in the '70s when I played the Opry with Bill Monroe.

In one of the dressing rooms, we listened to Bobby Osborne singing "Rocky Top" as he rehearsed with his band. In another dressing room, we listened to the bluegrass group the Steep Canyon Rangers. Together since 2000, they are perhaps best known for their collaboration with actor/comedian/banjoist Steve Martin, who often joins them on their shows. Martin wasn't there that night, so the Rangers were free to show off their own talents. The group was getting ready to perform on the Larry Gatlin portion of the Opry, and they greeted Roland warmly. He introduced us to the band, and some of them remembered me for my recordings with Kenny Baker.[5]

The Rangers were thanking Roland for being a part of a music video they had recently completed. Later I talked to Woody Platt, the guitar player, about that video. He told me:

The name of the song was "Tell the Ones I Love." We needed a guy just like Roland to play the role of a grandfather. It was a great endearing story about a grandfather presenting a gift to his grandson, and there was this camaraderie between the two. The video went kind of back and forth between that and us playing. It starts with him in the attic, opening up this gift that he's going to pass down to his grandson. There were several scenes where they were bonding, playing ball, et cetera. He's such a sweet guy, so it made sense. We've been huge fans of the Kentucky Colonels [Roland's early, now-iconic bluegrass band, which we'll talk a lot about in chapter 4]. It was an honor for us. We're kind of new on the bluegrass scene, relatively speaking. Roland is sweet and kind, and I'm glad he dropped by to visit tonight.[6]

Later it occurred to me that the role Roland White played in "Tell the Ones I Love" is a perfect fit. He's just like a grandfather to all the young pickers in the family of bluegrass. Roland is now at the stage of life where he's passing on his musical gifts for later generations to study and admire. At the end of the video, he gives his grandson a great big hug. It's like he's giving all of us a hug too—and this book is my hug back.

There are lots of overlooked figures in the field of bluegrass music, people who have made enormous contributions that are known only to a few passionate followers of the music and its history. Joe Stuart comes to mind immediately.[7] He played on many landmark recordings with Bill Monroe, including Monroe's first album, *Knee Deep in Blue Grass*,[8] but his name has been all but forgotten by the general public. A Joe Stuart biography has yet to be written. Roland White is another person who should be written about. His life in bluegrass stands out as an example of the steadfast determination and creativity of an artist who has never given up on his dreams.

And so I've decided to proceed with this book. I hope Roland's story will provide as much inspiration to others as it has to me and that the telling of it will fill a gap in the history of bluegrass.

1

Doing It for Real

I've always thought of Roland White as a pro who was just as much a part of the world of bluegrass as any of the other major pioneers. His name wasn't out front much, however. He was a trench fighter, a lower-ranking soldier bearing the burdens without getting much recognition. He lived to play the music. It was his passion. Recognition didn't matter; his ego could handle that. What mattered most to Roland was "doing it for real"—that's his description of the rare musicians who actually try to make a living with music. It wasn't just a hobby, or something to be talked about, or become an expert on.

It seems like I've known Roland White all my life. We share the same musical interests and background. I was first drawn to bluegrass while listening to Lester Flatt and Earl Scruggs and the Foggy Mountain Boys. I was trying to copy Earl's banjo licks. I grew up admiring that band and buying their records. I listened to their early morning Martha White show whenever my old-fashioned radio could pick it up; AM 650 in Nashville was a long way from Des Moines. Shortly after Earl left Lester in 1969, Roland White joined the group, which was renamed the Nashville Grass. All the same members remained in the band except Earl, who was replaced by Vic Jordan. In effect, Roland was actually playing with the Foggy Mountain Boys minus Earl, and that put him on a pedestal in my mind. I continued to buy Lester's records when Roland White was with him. His name became part of my bluegrass vocabulary.

Later I found out that Roland had also played for the "Father of Blue-grass," Bill Monroe, and in my eyes that elevated his stature even more. After a little research, I learned he had been a founding member of the Kentucky Colonels, a legendary bluegrass band that existed from 1962 to 1966, but I couldn't find any of their records in the Des Moines area, so that band remained mythological to me.

Marty Stuart, a member of the Country Music Hall of Fame in Nashville, is deeply rooted in bluegrass. He has taken it upon himself to be a historian and ambassador of genuine bluegrass and country music, and he shares a personal musical background with Roland White. I interviewed Marty in Winterset, Iowa, in May 2016 at the grand opening of the John Wayne Birthplace and Museum. In speaking about Roland White, Marty took an unusual conversational approach. Here's part of what he said:

> We toured out in California two or three years ago, and it was very successful, and when I got home, I picked up the phone and called Merle Haggard [1937–2016]. I said, "I just want to thank you and the Strangers and Buck and the Buckaroos and all you guys for what you did to set up a trail for us, because those people still love it." Merle said to me, "Hey, we all owe the debt to the Maddox Brothers and Rose because they were the first ones to bring the sound out here."[1]

Haggard was right. The Maddoxes had brought their hot, honky-tonk music from Alabama to the West Coast in 1933, when Rose was only seven. Nearly penniless, they hitchhiked and rode in boxcars, staying in migrant communities, and eventually wound up in Modesto, California. They performed at dances, fairs, rodeos, bars, and on radio programs.[2] Later they became known as "America's Most Colorful Hillbilly Band."[3]

The Maddox influence lives on in the "Bakersfield sound," which started in the honky-tonks around Bakersfield, California. It was a reaction to the overproduced music coming out of Nashville, and the sound was popularized by Buck Owens, Merle Haggard, Tommy Collins, Wynn Stewart, Jean Shepard, and many others.[4] Modern-day artists influenced by the Bakersfield sound include Dwight Yoakam and Marty Stuart. Even the Beatles were influenced by the Bakersfield sound when in 1965 they recorded "Act Naturally," originally a Buck Owens hit.

Marty then came to his point by comparing Roland White and his musical family to the Maddox Brothers and Rose, who sowed the seeds of the Bakersfield sound: "The same can be said for the Kentucky Colonels. If you go back to bluegrass in California, they were among the very first people there. They played in bowling alleys and anywhere they could get a job. Roland White and his brothers, Eric and Clarence, lit the fuse and opened the door for everything that has happened since."[5]

Vic Jordan—who had played with all the greats, including Wilma Lee and Stoney Cooper, Jimmy Martin, Bill Monroe, Lester Flatt, Jim and Jesse, and many others—agreed with Roland on the subject of doing it for real. In our conversation of March 2015, this is what he told me:

> What I call a professional musician is not how good you are but whether you make your living at it. That doesn't mean guys who play excellent but don't make their living aren't professional grade—they certainly are—but that's how I distinguish professional from non-professional. People used to ask us all the time, "What do you guys do for a living for the rest of the week?" I said, "I don't do anything [except music] for the rest of the week."
>
> "Well, you can't make your living playing music, can you?"
>
> "You see me here, don't you? You know how many years it took to get here?"[6]

I joined Bill Monroe's Blue Grass Boys in 1974. I'm so glad I took the opportunity to do that when the chance came along. Moving to Nashville taught me a lot. There are musicians there who have come from all over the country, and most know all about the disappointment involved and the perseverance required in doing it for real. That's why they all admire Roland White. He's never given up on his dreams, and he's made count-less life adjustments in order to fulfill those dreams. You can't just take what life gives you and sit back and complain about the unfairness of it all. You have to turn things around yourself and step it up and go. That's what Roland has always done.

When I first entered the Nashville bluegrass music scene, Roland had only recently lost his brother Clarence, who was an original member of the Kentucky Colonels and later became lead guitarist for the Byrds. I wasn't even aware of Clarence's passing. Roland was always at the Sta-tion Inn,[7] Nashville's longtime bluegrass music gathering place, singing and playing as though nothing was even wrong or missing. The tragedy of losing his brother had put an end to the New Kentucky Colonels, an exciting and promising rebirth of their earlier band.

Nothing ever seemed to stop Roland. He was coming from a totally different perspective than I was. I'd arrived in town with a job already in hand, and I figured I'd just keep that job forever, not knowing about the dangers lurking ahead. When I lost the job with Monroe, I stayed around town for a couple of more years, but my attitude never really bounced back like it should have. I should have stayed around like Roland did. The importance of mental toughness was the greatest life lesson I learned from having lived in Nashville. I never regretted my four and a half years in Music City, but I also had good reasons for moving back to Iowa. I felt more at home among Midwesterners. Kristie, the girl I married in 1990, is a fellow Iowan, and we share many of the same common, down-to-earth values that make our state so wonderful.

By contrast, Roland White spent the first part of his childhood in rural Maine and the second part in teeming Los Angeles. Growing up at both ends of that spectrum resulted in a worldview characterized by enthusiastic receptiveness to change. Being the oldest in a musical group of siblings brought responsibility to him, and he was energized by a restless desire to succeed. Early exposure to some of the greatest country music stars in the LA area was the flame that ignited Roland's dream of making a career out of performing on stage. Eventually that dream led him to Nashville.

Playing music is something many people can do well, but that's only a small part of doing it for real. Perseverance is the key, and Nashville requires a level of perseverance that is way beyond what most people have. Roland has been there for many years, in the thick of it, steady and enduring. He's been an inspiration to many musicians, past and present, and he's passing along an unmatched tradition to the incredible talent coming up.

The name Roland White stands on its own. Though he's been a part of several of the most influential bands in the history of bluegrass, his legacy isn't tied exclusively to any one of them. Many exceptional singers and musicians make a name for themselves while performing with one certain group, and when that group runs its course—however successful it may be—those performers are remembered only as a part of that one particular band. It's kind of like an actor becoming stereotyped in one role or character; truly great actors don't allow themselves to fall into that trap. And so it is with top-notch musicians like Roland White: his career has spanned the entire panorama of bluegrass, and he has achieved enviable success in every setting.

The story of Roland White is a fascinating one, with an uplifting central theme. He made a childhood commitment to playing bluegrass music for a living—something that is very nearly impossible to do—and he has stuck by that commitment all through the years. It hasn't always been easy, but his love of the music has carried him through in a very inspiring way. He doesn't give up on his dreams.

Roland is a man who has done so many things, played with so many people in so many places and influenced so many lives, that to document and chronologically arrange all of these elements is a great challenge. However, through it all runs a constant thread: everyone who has ever come into contact with Roland loves him as a person as well as a musician. I first got to know him in the 1970s, playing and jamming with him a handful of times, attending many of his concerts, and feeling a sense of kinship with him that countless other musicians have also felt. We all love him. "Who wouldn't?" says Alan Munde, a banjo player who has performed, traveled, and recorded with Roland for many years.

For over six decades Roland has been blazing trails, making elemental contributions to the evolution of a musical style that is unique and unforgettable. Unlike most other genres of music, bluegrass has not yet become totally homogenized (intermingled with other styles of music to create a hybrid sound that offends no one but is bland and unexciting as a result). It's a special kind of music, to be cherished and treasured like a gem handed down from one's ancestors. Roland's contributions to bluegrass are some of the most notable to be found. Indeed, he's an enduring part of the foundation; his style, technique, approach, and attitude are fundamental elements of bluegrass today. His improvisational and creative touches are always present while remaining within the framework designed by the music's acknowledged creator, Bill Monroe.

Roland is gracious, humble, and genuine—full of twenty-four-carat qualities that no faker could possess. Easygoing, composed, and self-assured, he displays his gifts and shares himself without reserve. He lives with memories of triumphs and tragedies that define who he is. He's a product of nearly seventy years of traveling, performing, and relating with loyal listeners who share his artistic passion. A musical master, he has crafted a style that is warm, unique, and intensely personal. He has performed and recorded with many of the most celebrated and renowned bluegrass groups to ever grace the genre: the Country Boys (1953–1961), the Kentucky Colonels (1963–1966), Bill Monroe and the Blue Grass Boys (1967–1969), Lester Flatt and the Nashville Grass (1969–1973), the New Kentucky Colonels (1973), Country Gazette (1973–1987), the Nashville Bluegrass Band (1989–2000), and the Roland White Band (2000-present).

There are countless mandolin players who can play swarms of notes guaranteed to blow the listener away. It's sometimes said of these types of musicians: "I wish I could do that, and then not do it." But Roland is different. He's been around long enough to differentiate between musical bluster and the real thing. He's grown up with an instrument in his hands. It's a part of him. He's not out to prove anything; he's just doing what he's always done.

Silence is often more profound than words, just as the silence between notes is an important element of music. Listen to Roland's playing—and what he *doesn't* say. He's not telling you, "Listen to me; you won't understand what I'm doing, but you'll marvel at my technical ability." Instead, he shares his music with you, *including* you in the process. He doesn't make you feel stupid. Truly great music is collaboration between artist and listener. No one understands that better than Roland.

Mike Compton, one of the foremost mandolin players around, had this to say about Roland's playing:

> I remember sitting with him in the Station Inn one night and watching a band play; I think it might have been the Johnson Mountain Boys. We were talking about playing music, and he said something about the space between the notes—they don't feel like they have to be playing all the time. He's the first person that I ever heard say anything much about the space being as important as the notes. At that point in time all I was thinking about was how to play the notes. He asked me if I had ever listened to any jazz players, and I told him, "Not that many." He said sometimes whenever they stop playing, they won't come back for about twelve or fourteen

bars before they start playing again. When they come back, it really sounds like something.[8]

Diane Bouska, Roland's wife and singing partner, has described his mandolin playing as much like watching a dancer[9] performing different movements. This is a very apt description. His playing ornaments the melodies with graceful movements and flourishes and serves to remind us that all of the arts—visual, musical, and literary—are connected by a creative flow that comes from virtually the same wellspring. Roland sees his playing as like climbing a tree. "The melody is like the tree trunk," he told me. "I'll start down here at the bottom, then go out on a limb a little bit, fall off, and then I'll climb back up and test another limb."

Roland's singing is also something that I've always had enormous respect for. His singing voice isn't high, and it isn't low—it's mid-range. Roland *can* sing high harmony if he wants to, or if the group he is performing with needs a high harmony part, but he stays mostly in the middle of the vocal realm. He has the range of voice that a majority of singers can identify with. His study of classic bluegrass vocals is evidenced by his many recordings featuring songs by the masters he has performed with, such as Bill Monroe and Lester Flatt.

Roland has been a mainstay in the Nashville bluegrass scene for over fifty years. He moved there in 1967. He often performs at the Station Inn, which first opened in 1974 and is now known the world over as *the* place to go in Nashville to hear bluegrass. Top bluegrass names, as well as new and promising groups, often perform there. Roland White has been a supporter of the establishment from day one. He can be found quite often at jam sessions around town—places like the Fiddle House (fiddler Brian Christianson's violin repair, sales, and rental shop) and the Authentic Coffee Company in White House, just outside of Nashville, where old-timers as well as young folks gather to jam and have a good time on Thursdays and Fridays. Jam sessions take place every Sunday evening at the Station Inn, and at the time we were visiting, Roland himself was organizing jams at Phat Bites restaurant on a semi-regular basis.

Roland's playing is an extension of his personality: inclusive and supportive. He treats his fellow musicians with respect, not as though they were competitors. He has played a huge role in turning the bluegrass music scene in and around Nashville into a friendly cadre of pickers who, though they occupy a modest niche in the larger country music scene, are loyal, passionate, and caring about one another—qualities that are frequently missing from the impersonal, oftentimes cold Nashville music industry.

Marty Stuart, in the 2016 interview I had with him, spoke of the help he received from Roland when he first came to Nashville in 1972:

Had it not been for Roland, I don't know how things would have worked out. He allowed me to live with his family. He was the guy that picked me up at the bus station in Nashville. He was the guy that gave me his phone number.

We played all the time when I first moved to Nashville. The instruments cooled off just long enough for us to get some sleep. People jammed all over Nashville, and there was the Bluegrass Inn and later on the Station Inn. We picked all the time. Roland never seemed to quit.[9]

Marty's enormous respect for Roland White shines through whenever he talks about him:

Roland has a true gift of mentoring—that's Chee Chee [the nickname given to Roland by Lester Flatt]. Regardless of the individual style, Roland has the uncanny ability to bring it to order and inspire people to go on and do what they do. I think the liberties that he and Clarence took in the Kentucky Colonels followed him through his whole life. As Waylon [Jennings] said, "There's one more way to do it—and that's how *you* feel it." Roland always encouraged me to play it the way I saw it and felt it. That's what a great teacher does.[10]

Bluegrass is here to stay, though it may not always be in the mainstream. The musicians who create it do so out of love, often living on the fringes of the country music establishment, because they know it's something real, not manufactured according to a "star" formula for the sole purpose of making money. Bluegrass is much like country music was seventy years ago. The musicians are allowed to interpret the music in their own way. They're not held in check by corporate overseers who want everything to have a certain predictable sound, again for the sole purpose of making money.

During Roland's entire career, he's managed to hang on to his dreams and keep on the upside, not letting things get him down. Going on after the tragic death of his brother Clarence in 1973 is a definitive example. Working nonmusic jobs to make ends meet is another example. He has always dealt with setbacks that would devastate many other musicians who try to do it for real.

"I was always fortunate, you know," says Roland. "Somebody would always say, 'Hey, we're doing this—you want to do this?' and I would say, 'Okay.' If I hadn't gone to Lester Flatt, I wouldn't have gotten that job." (He went to Lester and asked him if he would consider adding a mandolin player to the Foggy Mountain Boys. Later, after Earl Scruggs left the band, Lester hired Roland for his new group.)

Whenever new opportunities have come along, Roland has always been able to adapt to them. He's willing to take risks and undergo hardships, which make up 90 percent of success in music and life. In his quiet way, Roland is a virtuoso of both.

And now let's go back to the early days.

2

Birth of a Dream

Roland Joseph White was very fortunate to be raised in a music-loving family. His mother, Mildred, would kick off her shoes and dance when she heard her favorite songs. Her dream was to become a dancer, but kids and family were more important to her. There were several live country music shows that could be picked up on the radio where they lived in Madawaska, Maine. On clear nights they could tune in to the WSM *Grand Ole Opry* from Nashville, the *WLS Barn Dance* from Chicago, the *Wheeling Jamboree* from West Virginia, and the *Old Dominion Barn Dance* from Richmond, Virginia. WCKY from Cincinnati also played lots of country music that the White family's radio could pull in.[1]

Of French-Canadian descent, the Whites' family name was actually LeBlanc. Their town was just across the border from Edmundston, New Brunswick, Canada. Roland's father, Eric LeBlanc Sr., was born in Rogersville, New Brunswick. His mother, Mildred Cyr, was born in Maine and was also from a French-Canadian family. Roland was their first child, born at home on April 23, 1938.

They all spoke French until Roland was eight years old, at which time the kids were switched to an English-speaking school. The school told Mildred that she would have to start speaking more English at home so that her kids could communicate better in class. Three of Roland's siblings also understood French, since Eric Sr. and Mildred spoke it around the house a lot. Many of Roland's relatives still speak French, but he has mostly forgotten it now.

Roland's grandfather, Jacques LeBlanc, moved his family into Madawaska because he built houses and there was a lot of work available in that area. Roland thinks his father was around ten or eleven at the time. The whole family started using the name White, though Roland isn't sure when. He thinks it was around 1949 or 1950. As far as he knows, nobody ever made a legal name change, though.[2]

Roland's mother, Mildred, had grown up around music. Her father tried to convince her to learn to play the *violon* (he said it in French), but that dream never came to fruition. Collecting records was a serious hobby for her. She had lots of country music, and young Roland was lucky enough to grow up listening to the sounds of Vernon Dalhart, the Delmore Brothers (Alton and Rabon), Roy Acuff, Gene Autry, the Sons of the Pioneers, Lulu Belle and Scotty, Wilf Carter (aka Montana Slim), and the Blue Sky Boys (Earl and Bill Bolick).[3]

Eric Sr. was also interested in music and he often brought instruments home. One of Roland's aunts told him that one day Eric's dad saw a truck hauling a piano to the dump in Madawaska. He followed the truck, and when it stopped, he told the drivers, "Don't throw that out. Could you deliver it to my house?" The piano needed strings and the soundboard was cracked, but he was good with wood and he fixed it, tuned it, and played it a little bit.[4]

Eric Sr. played fiddle, guitar, tenor banjo,[5] and harmonica. Two of his brothers, Albert and Eddie, played boogie-woogie piano tunes like "In the Mood." Two of his other brothers, Gerard and Johnny, could play guitars and sing. Family get-togethers would always include music making. These gatherings usually took place at the home of Roland's grandparents, Jacques and Marie LeBlanc, in Madawaska. French-Canadian tunes were often played, but old-time American tunes were also in the repertoire. Eric Sr. played melodies like "Rubber Dolly," "Ole Joe Clark," "Soldier's Joy," "Liberty," "The Old Spinning Wheel," "St. Anne's Reel," "Wednesday Night Waltz," and "Over the Waves."[6] He also played an old Scottish reel called "Money Musk," which was quite popular in New England and along the eastern seaboard.[7]

Every time "Ragtime Annie" was played, those present would roll back the carpet and dance. Eric Sr. played mostly Irish jigs on the harmonica. He had a collection of harmonicas in various keys, including push-button types. He was also good at strumming a guitar and singing sad country songs like "Willie Roy, the Crippled Boy" and "The Story of the Lawson Family," a folk song that tells the true story of a tobacco farmer from North Carolina who, on Christmas Day 1929, killed his children, his wife, and then himself.

Roland remembers his dad getting up every morning before going to work and playing a few tunes while Mildred fixed breakfast. Then in the evenings he would come home and—if he wasn't too tired—play his fiddle before supper (or sometimes after). He went to bed early because he had to get up at 4:00 a.m. to go to work. He had many types of jobs, including carpentry, construction, and road building. He built houses with a few of his brothers and sisters. He worked in power plants, building wooden cooling towers, and he also worked in shipyards as a pipefitter.

Roland's family moved to Lewiston, Maine—approximately thirty miles north of Portland—when Roland was still quite young. Some of Roland's musical uncles and aunts followed them there, bringing their instruments with them and continuing to play and dance. Once a year, around the Fourth of July, Roland's family would return to Madawaska to visit. They would leave after supper on Friday and drive all night, arriving on Saturday afternoon. It was over three hundred miles and there weren't any interstate highways.

Three of Roland's four siblings were born in Lewiston. His younger sister JoAnne came along in 1939, and his brothers, Eric Jr. and Clarence, were born in 1941 and 1944, respectively. Music continued to be an important part of life for the White family in Lewiston. At first the only playable instruments they had were a guitar and a fiddle. They also had an old tenor banjo, but it stayed in a closet because it had a broken head (the part of the banjo that resembles the playing surface of a drum).

When Roland was six, he tried playing chords on the guitar to accompany his dad's fiddling. One day he tried his own luck on the fiddle. He was too small to manage the bow, and it squeaked and squawked. Eric Sr. told him, "Keep trying; it'll get better—you'll grow into it." About a week later, Roland came home from school, and his dad's car was in the driveway. This surprised him because his dad didn't usually get home until about 6:00 p.m. When he went into the house, he heard a new instrument being played. He wondered, *What is that?* Entering the living room, he found his dad playing "Ragtime Annie" and "Soldier's Joy" on a stringed instrument he had never seen before. It was like a small guitar with a rounded, bulging back. Finally his dad stopped playing and Roland asked him, "What is that instrument?"

"This is a mandolin," answered his father. The mandolin was a bowl-back, sometimes disparagingly called a "tater bug" or a "chili dipper." Dating back many centuries—at least as far back as the violin—the bowl-backed version of the mandolin was brought to America by immigrants from eastern and southern Europe. Though beautiful visually, the instrument was difficult to hold while playing, and Orville Gibson, founder of the Gibson Guitar Company, redesigned it with a flatter back, somewhat in the image of the fiddle. This is the style of mandolin that most people play today.

Roland asked his dad, "How did you learn to play it so fast?"

"Well, it's tuned like my fiddle," replied his dad. "It has frets and you play it with a guitar pick." He played another tune, and then he said, "Here, it's yours," handing the mandolin to Roland before walking away.

Roland learned some tunes after that. First he worked out some melodies he had heard his dad play, starting with "Soldier's Joy" and "Ragtime Annie," and then graduating to "St. Anne's Reel" (a little bit harder). Occasionally his dad would take the guitar and accompany him, and then Roland, with the guitar, would back up Eric Sr.'s fiddle. They went back and forth like that.[8]

When he was eight years old, Roland was listening to a country radio station while helping his mother in the kitchen. She knew a great deal about many of the singers whose records were being played, and Roland asked her lots of questions about them. He told her that he wanted to sing on the radio someday, and Mildred told Roland that if he practiced diligently, he would indeed be performing on the radio, making his living by singing and playing. Even back then, that's what Roland wanted to do. His lifelong dream had already taken root.[9]

After living in Lewiston, the family moved to Bath, Maine—approximately thirty miles southeast, on the coast—where Eric Sr. once again worked on power plant cooling towers. From there the family moved several other times: to Kittery, at the southernmost point of Maine; Portsmouth, New Hampshire, just south of Kittery; back to Kittery; back to Portsmouth; and then to Waterville, Maine. Roland's dad would move his family into houses rent-free in exchange for fixing the places up.

JoAnne began to join in the singing at around the age of ten. Roland was eleven at the time. They sang in unison and memorized the lyrics to many of the songs they heard on the radio.[10] Clarence began to show an interest in making music at the age of five. Roland describes how his younger brother's enthusiasm was sparked:

> I remember it vividly, a cold day just before Thanksgiving, 1949. JoAnne and I were singing and I was strumming the guitar in the living room. Clarence and Eric were running through the room, and Clarence suddenly stopped and backtracked, standing in front of me. When we finished the song, Clarence pointed at the guitar and said, "I want to do that." So I invited him to get up on his knees on the sofa at my right side. I handed him the flat pick to strum with his right hand, and I made the chords with my left [on the neck of the guitar]. I had a harmonica next to me, so I grabbed it and played "Bile 'Em Cabbage Down." He strummed right in time. [His rhythm was perfect from the start—he was a "natural."] Well, every time I had the guitar, he wanted to try it again. I told Dad about this, and soon after he brought home a ukulele. Each time I played, Clarence would strum along on the ukulele.[11]

Clarence didn't chord the ukulele too much, but he strummed it a lot, getting his timing down. (At the time of this writing, Clarence's daughter Michelle, who lives in Nashville, still has the ukulele.) After that, every time Roland picked up the mandolin or guitar, Clarence was right there, wanting to play with him.

Finally, at the age of eight, Eric Jr. got into the act. He told Roland, "I want an instrument to play too." Roland said, "Okay, let me talk to Dad about it." When he mentioned it to his father, Eric Sr. said, "I've got that old tenor banjo in the closet. I'll replace the head and strings and get it set up [playable] for him." A couple of days later he had the banjo all strung up. Eric Jr. started strumming on it, and that's how the family band got started. Since the boys were still a little bit shy about singing in public, JoAnne did most of that. They learned as many songs as they could and played for free about once a month at Grange Hall functions and family gatherings.[12]

Before long, Roland started insisting on having band rehearsals every day. Eric Sr. was supportive in that regard. He encouraged Roland's musical ambitions all the way. In our interview, Roland said, "If he [Eric Sr.] was doing something around the house, I would hang out with him

White family photo, 1952. Background (L-R): Roland White (holding Blackie the dog), Mildred Marie Cyr LeBlanc (White), Eric Joseph LeBlanc (White) Sr., JoAnne White. Foreground (L-R): Clarence White, Eric White. From the White family collection.

and ask to help. He'd say, 'Well, I'd rather you be working on your instrument.'"[13] In a very short time, music had become a primary passion with Roland, and it was rubbing off on his siblings. The stage was thus set, and the family was about to make an exciting move—to the epicenter of the entertainment industry: Burbank, California. That move would crystallize Roland's musical ambitions and forever shape his life and career.

The Country Boys

Off to California

In August 1954, when Roland was sixteen, the family loaded up the trunk of the new Nash Rambler with instruments, clothing, and photo albums and headed to California. Eric Sr.'s brother Armand and his sister Alma had already moved out there the year before and had been urging Roland's parents to make the move too. They said work was plentiful, and "they told of an end to the bitter cold, and the short, dark Maine winter days!"[1]

After saying their good-byes to Grandmother and Grandfather LeBlanc, and a stopover at Uncle Leo's and Aunt Irma's home in Connecticut, Eric Sr. drove the whole way to Wheeling, West Virginia. There they had supper at a restaurant where they experienced air conditioning for the first time. It was a welcome relief from the heat, which had been increasing as they moved farther south. The next day they made it to Amarillo, Texas, with a stop in Joplin, Missouri, for fuel, haircuts, and lunch. The Texas landscape made them think of cowboy movies and the Wild West. That helped to ease the discomfort of the exhausting journey. There were no interstates beyond the Pennsylvania Turnpike, and the late summer heat was almost intolerable for a family of New Englanders. Finally they made it to Burbank, California. The palm and orange trees, wide streets, and stucco homes were an exciting contrast to their former Maine surroundings. Drive-in restaurants were something they had never seen before. Air pollution was the only thing they disliked about their new world.

The family made their base of operations at Aunt Alma's for the first few days and then found an apartment on Bethany Street. The kids registered at school, and when Roland and JoAnne walked to Burbank High on their first day, they were astonished to see the kids mingling around outside, "dancing to Bill Haley's 'Rock Around the Clock,' blaring from school loudspeakers."[2] Roland found a job sacking groceries at Alexander's Grocery market, and Eric Sr. once again started working on cooling towers. Their new home had lemon trees growing in the yard, so lemonade became a routine drink for the family. There were also avocado trees in the backyard, but they didn't know about avocados. They thought the green fruits were ugly things that fell off the trees and had to be scooped up with a shovel and thrown away. That's what they did until a neighbor kid told them they were to eat. Soon, "mashed avocado was showing up among the bologna, peanut butter, tomatoes, and bacon of Eric Sr.'s Dagwood-style sandwiches."[3]

After they had been in California for a couple of weeks, Eric Sr. found a music store in Burbank where he purchased a Martin D-18 flat-top guitar. He knew that Martin flat-tops were considered the best guitars for folk and bluegrass music. They produce a loud, bright tone that is suitable for both rhythm chords and playing lead melodies.[4] They had a couple of archtop guitars that had come with them from Maine, but those weren't as good as flat-tops for the kind of music they were playing. (Archtop guitars have carved wooden tops and are used more often in jazz than in folk music.)

A friend of Eric Sr.'s, Leo Cannon, had loaned them an acoustic upright bass, and JoAnne rapidly learned to play it. She started taking part in the practice sessions then, contributing her strong, clear voice to the family band. She emulated some of the popular singers she had been hearing since the age of four or so, taking much of her phrasing of lyrics from those sources.[5] The band was growing and evolving.

The family was growing too. In 1955 Roland's sister Rosemarie was born. Being the youngest, she was the sweetheart of the family. They all loved rocking her, feeding her, and playing music for her.[6]

One day Roland's aunt Alma told them about a local radio talent contest. She said to Roland's father, "Bring the kids down to the Riverside Rancho and get them on the show—I think they could win."[7]

The Riverside Rancho was a large dance hall in Glendale just across the city line from Burbank. It featured western swing dance bands like

Tex Williams and His Western Caravan. Tex Williams, whose real name was Sollie Paul Williams (1917–1985), was born in Ramsey, Illinois. In the early 1940s he became a popular western swing performer in the Los Angeles area. Tex was well known for his "talking blues" singing style. He worked in Spade Cooley's band for a while, and his voice is featured on Cooley's hits "Shame on You" and "Detour." After leaving Spade, Tex formed his own band, Western Caravan. He performed at the Riverside Rancho in Los Angeles for ten years. He had a major hit in 1947 with "Smoke, Smoke, Smoke (That Cigarette)," which was written by Merle Travis,[8] who we'll talk about later in this chapter.

Bob Wills and the Texas Playboys were also featured quite often at the Riverside Rancho.[9] They were one of the favorite dance bands to perform there. The venue was a beautiful redwood building with wagon-wheel-framed pictures of country music stars on the walls. On Sundays a talent show was presented. Chairs were placed on the dance floor, and the venue was opened to the public, free of charge. The show was broadcast live over a 50,000-watt country music station, KXLA, located in Pasadena.

Eric Sr. took Alma's advice and drove the kids to the dance hall on Sunday. They introduced themselves to the host, Carl "Deacon" Moore, known as "the Squeakin' Deacon."[10] In addition to being the host at the Riverside Rancho, the Squeakin' Deacon was also a country music DJ. He had an hour-long radio show on KXLA that was broadcast five nights a week during the evening rush hour. It could be heard all the way down to San Diego. He had a high-pitched voice with an Arkansas accent, hence the nickname "Squeakin' Deacon." Deacon and his wife, Marge, were there at the Rancho that day, tending to the details of the program, and they were both "good-humored and gracious."[11] When he heard that the White kids played music, Deacon told them to bring in their instruments so that he could hear them perform. Unfortunately, they hadn't brought them that day, but Mr. Moore told them, "Bring them next week—I'm sure you'll get on."[12]

They decided to stay and watch the show, which ran from 1:00 p.m. till 3:00 p.m. The radio program started with an announcement: "Enoch Chevrolet presents the Squeakin' Deacon Talent Hour, followed by one hour of some very special guest stars."[13] The house band played, and then Deacon started telling jokes before the talent contest got under way. The first thirty to forty-five minutes were devoted to the music competition,

The Three Little Country Boys with JoAnne at the Riverside Rancho, 1954. L-R: Eric White, Roland White, JoAnne White, Clarence White. From the White family collection.

and the rest of the time featured entertainment by popular country and western stars.

The first guests were Joe and Rose Lee Maphis. Often called "Mr. and Mrs. Country Music," they became one of the most successful husband-and-wife duets of all time. Otis Wilson (Joe) Maphis (1921–1986) was born in Suffolk, Virginia. His wife, Rose Lee (1922–2021), was born in Baltimore, Maryland. They moved to Southern California in the late 1940s. When television came along, they were featured on numerous TV shows in addition to their performances at the Riverside Rancho. One of those shows was *Town Hall Party*, which began in 1951 as a radio broadcast.[14] It took place in the Town Hall building at 400 South Long Beach Boulevard, Compton, California, and was broadcast over KXLA in

Pasadena. One year later it was being televised on KTTV in Los Angeles. It became the most popular country and western program in Southern California and continued successfully all through the 1950s.

Joe and Rose Lee Maphis were a huge part of the West Coast country music scene. Joe played anything with strings, but his high-energy electric guitar playing was what he became best known for, influencing many guitarists, including Roland White's brother Clarence. Joe was a session guitarist until his death in 1986, supplying backup for such artists as Wanda Jackson, Tex Ritter, and Ricky Nelson.[15]

Eric Sr. and his kids saw another star at the Riverside Rancho that day: Mac Wiseman, who was accompanied by Joe and Rose Lee and the house band. Malcolm B. "Mac" Wiseman (1925–2019) was a singer and guitarist who played or recorded with Lester Flatt, Bill Monroe, the Osborne Brothers, and many others. In 1953 he joined the cast of the WVRA *Old Dominion Barn Dance* in Richmond, Virginia. In 1957 that show was taken over by Carlton Haney,[16] who changed the name to the *New Dominion Barn Dance*.[17] Early on, Mac had a bluegrass band and was one of the first to use twin fiddles. One of his most famous releases was his 1954 recording "Love Letters in the Sand," which became a hit for Pat Boone in 1957. Wiseman also had a hit in 1969 with an RCA Victor record called "If I Had Johnny's Cash and Charley's Pride (Then I Wouldn't Have Buck Owens on My Car)."[18] In 1993 Mac was inducted into the Bluegrass Hall of Fame.

At the Riverside Rancho show, Eric Sr. and his boys were quite impressed with how Mac held his acoustic guitar up high, close to the microphone, so that the instrument could be heard. The White boys went home later that afternoon and worked hard on recreating the single-note guitar runs used by Mac to transition from one chord to another. Clarence was especially motivated by this technique, and a new and important ingredient was added to the family band as a result.

The Country Kids

The next Sunday saw the White brothers back at the Rancho again, ready to compete in the talent contest. JoAnne didn't want to participate in the audition, so it was just the three boys.[19] Deacon said, "Come on up here, kids. Get those instruments out and let me hear y'all."[20] Roland,

Eric Jr., and Clarence had played about half of the first part of "Ragtime Annie" when Deacon interrupted them, saying, "Okay, boys, that's enough—you're on. The show starts in about 15 minutes. Marge will give y'all a number."[21] He asked them what the name of their band was. They hadn't taken on a name yet, so Deacon suggested the Country Kids. That was the name they used. They were contestant number four, and they played "Ragtime Annie" with Roland on mandolin, Clarence on guitar, and Eric on tenor banjo. Although he had never played in a talent show before, Roland wasn't nervous.[22] It came naturally for him; he just did what he always did and didn't worry about it.

After all the contestants had performed and a commercial was aired, judging took place, using an applause meter. The Country Kids won! They returned to the stage and accepted their prize (which was a wristwatch), and then they played an encore, "Under the Double Eagle." They stuck around for the rest of the show, which featured, among others, the Maddox Brothers and Rose. Roland's mother, Mildred, was there too, and when she heard Rose's vibrant, energetic performance, she said, "That woman can *sing*!" They were real crowd-pleasers with their lively songs and lots of whooping and hollering.

After the show was over, the boys were asked to return to the Rancho "every other Sunday or so" to perform with the big stars.[23] It had been an exciting day for the Country Kids. Before they left, Deacon gave them a telephone number, saying, "I want you to call this man—Ralph T. Hicks. He's comin' out with a new country music TV show called the *County Barn Dance Jubilee*,[24] and he's got a group called the Three Little Country Girls."[25]

Three Little Country Boys

On Saturday afternoon they went to see Mr. Hicks, who asked them to play a couple of tunes. They performed part of one tune, then part of another. "That's great—do you sing?" They told him no. They were too bashful. Mr. Hicks then told them, "You know, I want you boys to wear some straw hats, bib overalls, matched shirts, and no shoes." He explained to them that he had found three sisters who sang and would be called the Three Little Country Girls, and Roland and his brothers would be called the Three Little Country Boys.[26]

The boys were excited to be doing the TV show. They weren't bothered at all by being barefoot and having to wear straw hats and bib overalls. They thought it was funny. They left two hours early to make it to the first show because of the traffic and the distance. During the show, the Three Little Country Boys appeared right after the Three Little Country Girls. They sat on the side of the stage and played a couple of tunes. Among the guests were Bob Wills and Lefty Frizzell. Born in Texas, Lefty (1928–1975) was a frequent guest on the *Town Hall Party*. His hits included "If You've Got the Money, I've got the Time"; "Always Late (With Your Kisses)"; and "Saginaw, Michigan." His vocal style influenced Merle Haggard's singing. Lefty was notable for his tendency to bend notes and add syllables to words.[27]

Located in Baldwin Park, California, the *County Barn Dance Jubilee* TV show featured emcee Les "Carrot Top" Anderson. In addition to the Three Little Country Boys, there was a large cast of regular performers, including Eddie and Hank Cochran, Johnny Mosby, and Skeets McDonald. In order to be paid TV scale, Roland—being sixteen—had to join the musician's union. All three boys planned to save their money for purchasing band outfits and paying travel expenses. Roland opened a savings account at the Bank of America in Burbank.[28] He was already taking his music career seriously.

Eric Sr. drove them to the performances most of the time (the kids were still too young to drive), but sometimes their uncle Armand would take them. They continued doing the show for several more weeks but then had to give it up. In Roland's words, "Baldwin Park was east of downtown LA and to travel there in bumper-to-bumper traffic every Friday afternoon would take us an hour and a half. It was hot, so we had the windows down, and in those days of leaded gasoline LA's air was thick with fumes and soot. . . . It was too much of a trip to make every Friday for the adults, who also had to work, so we gave it up."[29]

JoAnne had appeared with the Three Little Country Boys on some of the Riverside Rancho and *County Barn Dance* shows. She helped them win a TV talent contest too, by singing the Hank Williams number "Kaw Liga." That show was called *Bob Yakel Oldsmobile's Rocket to Stardom*. Oftentimes JoAnne enhanced the band performances by helping out at store grand openings and fund-raisers for various causes like the March of Dimes. In all, JoAnne played with her brothers for about a year—until she got a boyfriend.[30]

The Three Little Country Boys at the Foreman Phillips County Barn Dance, Baldwin Park, California, 1954. L-R: Eric White, Clarence White, Roland White. From the White family collection.

Uncle Armand came by the house one day to listen to the boys play. He asked Roland if he'd ever heard of Bill Monroe. Roland told him no. "Well, he's a mandolin player," Armand said. "He's on the *Grand Ole Opry*, and he's *fast*."[31]

This piqued Roland's interest because they had been playing dance music up until then, medium tempo—nothing too fast. He went down to the same music store in Burbank where his father had purchased the Martin D-18 guitar and asked Mr. Corradi, the proprietor, "Where can I buy some records?"

"Who're you looking for?"

"Bill Monroe," Roland answered.

There was a big yellow catalog on the counter, and Mr. Corradi said, "Well, he's probably in there if he's on a major label." Roland looked and found listings for Bill Monroe, on the Decca label, seeing dozens of titles he had never heard of. Then he saw a song title with the word "breakdown." He asked Mr. Corradi, "What's a breakdown?"

The music store owner told him, "That usually means it's a fast instrumental."

"Oh, really?" Roland said. "Well, I'll take this one right here."[32] He had chosen a record with "Pike County Breakdown" on one side and "A Might Pretty Waltz" on the other side. Although Roland didn't know it at the time, both of these selections featured (in addition to Bill Monroe) Jimmy Martin on guitar, Sonny Osborne (1937–2021) on banjo, Charlie Cline on fiddle, and Ernie Newton on bass. Owen Bradley played piano on "A Mighty Pretty Waltz."[33]

Every day after school, Roland would stop by the music store on the way to his job to see if his record had come in yet. Finally one day Mr. Corradi said, "Your record's here," and handed him a 45 rpm disc. Roland thought to himself, *How did they get two songs on this little disc?* At home they had nothing but 78 rpm records. Most 78s are approximately ten inches in diameter, and 45s are approximately seven inches in diameter.

"I just talked to your dad," Mr. Corradi told him. "And I'm sure you don't have a phonograph that plays 45 rpms."

Roland said, "No, we don't have one."

"Well, your dad gets home from work after I close," he said, "but you tell him to call the store this evening and I'll open it back up for him. I've got this little Magnavox record player, a table model." He had ordered it ahead of time because he knew the Whites were going to buy it.

Roland's dad purchased the phonograph and brought it home before supper. When the family finished eating, he brought the Magnavox in and set it on a chair, because they didn't have very much furniture yet. Roland could hardly wait! Eric Sr. put the 45 on and played "Pike County Breakdown." Roland's jaw dropped. "Wow, that's fast!"[34] Bill Monroe's mandolin set the pace as the tune charged forward, and the fiddle break by Charlie Cline was nothing short of terrific (Eric Sr. loved that!).[35] The banjo break by Sonny Osborne made the needle nearly jump out of the grooves.[36] When the record was over, Roland's dad played it several more times while the whole family listened intently. That recording inspired them all so much that their music took off in a new direction: bluegrass.

But it didn't come easily. Roland had a hard time learning "Pike County Breakdown" from the 45, until his dad suggested that he listen to the record for a couple of weeks before trying to learn the tune. That was good advice, and it was easier for him to learn lots of music after that. Jim Renz, a St. Louis musician who's been a friend of Roland White's since 1972, told me, "That's Roland's advice to others to this day: listen to a piece for a while before actually trying to play it."[37]

The next Bill Monroe 45 Roland ordered had "Poison Love" on one side.[38] The other side featured "On the Old Kentucky Shore." Again, Roland didn't know the names of the sidemen (Jimmy Martin, guitar; Rudy Lyle, banjo; Joel Price, bass; and Red Taylor, fiddle).[39] Bill's tenor singing was so high that Roland thought it was a woman's voice.[40]

The boys began to work on their harmony singing. At first Clarence sang tenor, Roland sang lead, and Eric Jr. sang baritone. However, after Clarence had his tonsils removed, he couldn't sing as high, so he switched to baritone, Eric Jr. switched to lead, and Roland learned tenor, which was somewhat out of his vocal range but, with practice, he learned to do it.[41]

Back at Mr. Corradi's music store, Roland saw an issue of *Country Song Roundup*, a monthly magazine that had started in 1949 and covered the post–World War II era of country and hillbilly music, remaining in publication until 2001. On the back cover of the issue, Roland saw a whole list of Bill Monroe recordings available from the Jimmie Skinner Music Center,[42] a Cincinnati mail-order and retail store. Soon Roland started ordering lots of records.[43]

Roland turned on the radio one morning to listen to Jolly Joe Nixon on KXLA. Jolly Joe was a DJ whose program ran from 5:00 to 7:00 a.m. Every once in a while, he'd sneak in a bluegrass song, and on that morning Roland heard a great banjo tune. He wasn't familiar with it, so he called up the radio station and Jolly Joe Nixon himself answered the phone. Roland asked him what the banjo tune was that he had just played, and Jolly Joe told him, "Oh, that was 'Dear Old Dixie' by Lester Flatt, Earl Scruggs, and the Foggy Mountain Boys."[44]

"Lester who?" asked Roland. Jolly Joe spelled out the names for him.

Roland bought the record, and a few weeks later, after seeing Flatt and Scruggs on a TV show, he went to Mr. Corradi's music store and bought a Gibson Mastertone five-string banjo. He wanted to sound like Earl Scruggs, often sitting up late at night practicing in the bathroom. He didn't use his fingerpicks like Earl, because his playing would be quieter without them and he wouldn't wake up his sleeping family.[45] His brother Clarence was also very interested in the banjo and would also practice without picks. Roland believes Scruggs's banjo style was one of the greatest influences on Clarence's later music.[46]

About four houses up the street lived a fellow named Sam Tester, from North Carolina, who had a watch repair shop in his home. He played the banjo, both frailing and Scruggs style. Frailing style, sometimes called "rapping" or "clawhammer," is a method of playing the banjo by picking a melody note downward on one string with the index or middle finger, then plucking the fifth string with the thumb, then strumming downward across several strings before picking the fifth string once again with the thumb. This is the basic technique, but frailing style can be very complex and exciting to listen to. Scruggs-style banjo playing involves the use of the thumb and first two fingers of the right hand to play the strings, using certain repetitive patterns or "rolls."

One cool evening when the windows were open, Sam overheard Roland practicing. He came by and knocked on the door. "I hear some banjo pickin' in there."

Mildred said, "Oh, yes, that's my son—he's trying to play the thing." At that time he really *was* only trying; he couldn't actually play a tune yet.

Sam introduced himself and asked, "Could I talk to him?"

Mildred called to her son, "Roland, come on out here."

When Roland came to the door, Sam told him he played the banjo.

"Really?" replied Roland. "I need some help!"

Sam came inside and frailed the banjo a little bit. Roland thought that was really cool. Then Sam asked to borrow Roland's fingerpicks. The picks were metal, and Roland had bent them to fit his fingers. Sam had to unbend them slightly because his fingers were bigger. Then he played a little bit in Scruggs style.

"Oh, yeah—that's what I've been trying to learn!" So Sam showed him "Cripple Creek," a tune almost all banjo players start out on.

Roland practiced "Cripple Creek" for a couple of weeks, and Sam came back to tell him he was sounding really good. He invited the family to come up to his house on Sundays. He would get out his five-string banjo, Eric Jr. would play his tenor banjo, and Roland and Clarence would bring their mandolin and guitar. They looked forward to those jam sessions, because Sam Tester's wife always had milk and cookies for them. Sam always told lots of stories about the players he knew from North Carolina.[47]

Roland's interest in Scruggs-style banjo grew, and he later ordered all the Flatt and Scruggs 45s available. He still has them to this day.[48]

On Christmas Eve 1955, the White family watched Bill Monroe and the Blue Grass Boys on the *Town Hall Party* TV show. Roland and his father had purchased an audiotape recorder, and they taped the television performance.[49] By watching that TV show, Roland was able to see how Monroe played his mandolin chords, especially the four-finger chord used for the off-beat "chops." (Monroe used the chop technique a lot because it gave the music more drive, working like a snare drum.[50]) Clarence paid close attention to Arnold Terry's style of bluegrass rhythm guitar playing, taking notice of the important G- and D-runs.[51]

The Country Boys

By 1955, after having played at the Riverside Rancho for over a year, the Squeakin' Deacon talked the boys into getting rid of the hillbilly outfits and shortening their name to the Country Boys. They went to Nudie's Rodeo Tailors in Hollywood and got themselves decked out in the best Western wear ever.[52] Nudie's was famous for the sequin-spangled outfits worn by many celebrities, including Hank Snow, Ray Price, Porter Wagoner, Tex Williams, and Lefty Frizzell.

During the next couple of years, the Country Boys continued to polish up their act. They would perform on weekends, playing whatever gigs they could get in the area, such as county fairs and store grand openings.[53] Except for the Riverside Rancho, the places where they played were not really "listening" rooms; the audiences talked a lot, and the music served mostly as background.

Practice sessions would take place almost every night at home, and they would work up songs from the records Roland had. During that time they listened to more music by Bill Monroe, as well as people like Joe Maphis, Jim and Jesse and the Virginia Boys,[54] and Don Reno and Red Smiley and the Tennessee Cutups.

One weekend in late 1957 or early 1958, Roland went into a music shop in downtown Los Angeles to talk to Milt Owens, a guitar repairman. Roland had broken the neck off of one of his mandolins and wanted to know if it could be glued back together. It was a fairly standard fix, and Roland left the instrument there to be worked on. Later, when he went back to pick it up, he took it out of the case and played it a little bit to see how the repair job had gone.

There was another person in the shop who was trying out a Gibson Mastertone banjo. He turned to Roland and asked, "What kind of music do you play with that mandolin?"

"Well, we play Bill Monroe, Flatt and Scruggs. . . ."

"You do?" the stranger interrupted. "I do that kind of music too. You have a banjo player?"

Roland replied, "Well, I play a little banjo, but we're looking for a banjo player. You play that style of music?"

"Yeah, I do."

"Where do you live?"

"I live in Glendale." Glendale was a neighboring town, very close to Burbank. It turned out that the banjo player lived only two miles from Roland's house.

So Roland gave him his address, saying, "Well, come on over; let's pick some!"

Billy Ray Latham (1938–2018) was the banjo player's name,[55] and when he came over to the house for dinner, they had a music session, after which they invited him to join their family's band.[56]

Billy Ray was destined to occupy a large part of Roland's musical career. He was born in a cabin in Wild Cat Corner, Arkansas, but Billy Ray Latham's father moved the family to Michigan when Billy was about ten years old.[57] A friend loaned him a banjo and he made some fingerpicks out of an old Prince Albert can and taught himself how to play.[58] Later he and his brother moved to California and Billy Ray got a job at a gas station in Los Angeles. He augmented his income by giving banjo lessons.[59] One of his banjo students was a little girl named Barbara Mandrell,[60] who later became a leading country music star.

Billy opened the White brothers' minds and ears to bluegrass performers they had not been aware of. J. D. Crowe, the banjo player for Jimmy Martin's Sunny Mountain Boys, was a big favorite of Billy Ray's, and he told the boys about how Jimmy Martin had recorded with Bill Monroe and worked as one of Monroe's Blue Grass Boys from 1949 until 1951, and again from 1952 to 1954.

It was right about this time that the Country Boys first met Bill Monroe in person. When I asked Roland about his first initial encounter with Bill, he said he no longer recalled the location or circumstances, but he knew it was in 1958. However, in a 2010 interview in Mandolin Cafe,[61] Roland stated that he and the rest of the Country Boys met Monroe for the first time at Rose Maddox's 101 Club in Oceanside, California, in 1958. They got up on stage and played a few tunes while Bill and the Blue Grass Boys were taking a break, and as Roland said, "He seemed to like what we did. It probably amused him."

Bill was touring the West Coast at that time and had a day or two off during his busy schedule. The boys invited him to their home one evening for dinner. That's when they got to know him better. Later, while touring Southern California again, Bill came over for some more of Mildred's home cooking.[62] He especially liked the banana bread they had for dessert.[63] They invited him several more times after that, and after dinner they would always play music.

One day in 1959, Roland received a phone call from a banjo player and luthier by the name of Walt Pittman. He said, "Roland, you know, I was down on Melrose Avenue in Hollywood at this beatnik club called the Ash Grove, and I met the owner, Ed Pearl. I told him that you guys had a bluegrass band, probably the best bluegrass band around." In reality, the Country Boys were virtually the *only* bluegrass band around Southern California at that time. It wasn't until 1962 that the West Coast bluegrass scene really began to blossom. That was the year the Dillards moved there from Missouri, later becoming one of America's best-known bluegrass bands. That year also saw the formation of the Scottsville Squirrel Barkers in the San Diego area, as well as Don Parmley and the Golden State Boys in the LA area.[64] In addition to playing bluegrass, Parmley was driving a Greyhound bus back and forth from Los Angeles to Las Vegas at the time.

The Country Boys had been to the Ash Grove before; they were already "Groveys," a name given to fans of the club.[65] It was a big coffeehouse full of chairs and tables. On the menu were things like cheese and crackers, tea, and, of course, coffee—but no full meals. On previous visits to the club, the White kids had seen people like Jean Ritchie, Bukka White, and Odetta. The Ash Grove first opened in 1958 and later become the primary West Coast venue for folk, bluegrass, and blues music, having featured artists like Bill Monroe, Lester Flatt, the Stanley Brothers, Muddy Waters, Mississippi John Hurt, Odetta, Ry Cooder, Buffy Saint-Marie, Taj Mahal, the Reverend Gary Davis, and many more. Ed Pearl, the proprietor, even included stand-up comedians as featured entertainers.[66]

Roland called Pearl, who said, "Come on down." They played a couple of tunes for Mr. Pearl, who said, "Okay, I'm gonna hire you guys." He offered them a weeklong engagement as an opening act. On their first night, they opened for Sonny Terry and Brownie McGhee. The place was almost full, and Roland noticed all the faces looking at them and smiling, and he heard so much applause that it scared him. That was the first time he ever got nervous on stage. (The Riverside Rancho had been different in that they played only a couple of tunes during every show and, although the audience members were listening somewhat, the place had a much more casual and low-key atmosphere.)[67]

The Ash Grove stage had three microphones—one for the guitar, one for vocals, and one for any other instruments. The bass didn't need any microphone, because the acoustics were so good and it was a "listening" room. The sound booth was upstairs, looking down over the stage. They had monitor speakers facing them, which the Country Boys had never even seen before, let alone used. They could actually hear their music clearly for the first time, and as a result, Clarence began to play lead solos on the guitar. His first solo was on the Carter Family song "Wildwood Flower." The second was on "Jimmy Brown, the Newsboy," also by the Carter Family.

The next time they played at the Ash Grove, still in 1959, they opened up for the New Lost City Ramblers, a group that was at the forefront of the folk music resurgence at the time. Formed in 1958 in New York, the New Lost City Ramblers consisted of Mike Seeger (1933–2009),[68] John Cohen (1932–2019), and Tom Paley (1928–2017), who was replaced in 1962 by Tracy Schwarz (1938–). They brought genuine traditional string band music into the folk boom that occurred during the late 1950s and 1960s, appearing several times at the Newport Folk Festival (founded in 1959 in Newport, Rhode Island). Large audiences were made aware of the group through their many TV appearances and live performances. In 1962 Tom Paley expressed his beliefs about the legacy of the New Lost City Ramblers. He said the music they loved had become all but extinct before the Ramblers gave it a new lease on life and helped to make it an important and lasting form of expression.[69]

Ed Pearl continued hiring the White boys at the Ash Grove, where they honed their performances.[70] Their appearances at the club opened the door for them in a lot of ways. College students were really beginning to enjoy and appreciate string band music and bluegrass. Lester Flatt and Earl Scruggs, whom the Whites had met at the Ash Grove, were making inroads at colleges and music festivals around the country. The Country Boys, as an offshoot of their performances at the Ash Grove, began to make connections with a few of those same folk venues.

Successes were piling up, and before too long an additional member was added to the group, a Dobro player. Dobro is the brand name of an acoustic guitar that has a metal resonator cone. Invented by John, Rudy, and Emil Dopyera, the name "Dobro" is a contraction of the words "Dopyera" and "brothers." The generic name for such an instrument is "resonator guitar." In bluegrass the Dobro is played horizontally, using a slide bar on the strings.

LeRoy McNees, aka LeRoy Mack, was the Dobro player who joined the White brothers. He told me how his involvement with the group came about:

A friend of mine asked me to come over to his house; he'd just bought a record and he wanted me to hear it. So when I got there, I sat down and listened to it—and it zapped my brain! It was Flatt and Scruggs, their first Mercury recording ["We'll Meet Again Sweet-heart"], and I thought, "Man, that is unbelievable!" After that I was looking to hear more of that music. One Sunday afternoon I was listening to the radio and there was a live broadcast taking place. It was a talent contest put on by a local DJ [the Squeakin' Deacon]. I heard that sound again—I thought, "Oh, man, I've got to check this out." So I went down to the Riverside Rancho, where the show was taking place. There I saw the Country Boys, and I went over to talk with Roland. I said, "Man, where else are you guys playing? I'd love to come and hear you." Roland answered, "We don't have any regular place to play, but we rehearse every night at my house, and if you'd like to come over, that would be okay."[71]

It turned out that LeRoy lived in Glendale, which was only about five miles from the Whites.

> I was like, eighteen years old at the time and had no real obligations. I was at their house every night, just listening. It was Roland, Clarence, Eric, and Billy Ray. I kept hanging out with them, and after a while Roland said, "You know, we need a Dobro player in this band, so why don't you get a Dobro and learn how to play it and join the band?" I said, "Great—what's a Dobro?"[72]

They showed him an album cover photo of Flatt and Scruggs with the Foggy Mountain Boys. Josh Graves was holding his Dobro in the picture.[73] LeRoy told them that his dad had a similar instrument, only it was all metal. They knew exactly what it was: a National resonator guitar. The next evening LeRoy brought the instrument over. Although it wasn't a Dobro brand of resonator guitar, which most bluegrass musicians preferred at that time, it was perfectly adequate for the job, and LeRoy could see that the others were reacting quite positively to it. His enthusiasm was kindled, and by the end of the rehearsal he found himself going home with a borrowed stack of Flatt and Scruggs records. (By the way, LeRoy still has the National resonator guitar, which is hanging on the wall in his living room.)

After trying the National for a little while, LeRoy realized he wouldn't be satisfied until he had a Dobro just like Josh played with the Foggy Mountain Boys. So he went on the hunt, searching pawn shops with the hope of finding one. He had no luck at first, but finally, in one of the shops, another customer overheard him asking about a Dobro. The stranger said, "Well, I've got one of those." Hopeful, LeRoy told the man he would be interested in looking at it, so they went to his house: "He wanted fifty dollars for it," LeRoy told me. "I said, 'Oh, man, I can't afford that,' so I let it go and went home. Later I started thinking about it and I told myself, 'You idiot! Where else are you going to find one?' So I went back to his house. He was gone, but I bought it from his wife for fifty dollars. That's the one that I learned to play on."[74]

Roland was very encouraging to LeRoy in learning the art of the Dobro. Billy Ray was also quite helpful, showing him some banjo-type licks and finger rolls. LeRoy also pored over records, slowing them down from 33⅓ rpm to 16 rpm. In doing so, the pitch remained about the same but an octave lower, half as fast, and easier to hear and duplicate. That's exactly the way I taught myself to play the banjo—destroying many classic bluegrass LPs in the process by getting them so scratched up they wouldn't play anymore!

LeRoy kept playing with the Country Boys but at rehearsals only, and then one night they tricked him. They went out to perform and LeRoy tagged along, bringing his Dobro. When it came time to go on stage, they said, "Come on, you're going with us." He said, "No way, no way!" But they talked him into it and he ended up playing with them—mostly backup, little fills, licks, and chords.[75]

That was how LeRoy received his on-the-job training, and he soon became an indispensable part of the band. He was a little bit nervous at first, and at one performance he dropped his heavy slide bar onto the stage, making a loud clunk as it hit the floor. He was a huge addition to the Country Boys, and he wrote several songs that Roland still plays today.[76] Many of those numbers were included in their first album, *The New Sound of Bluegrass America*, but let's not jump ahead to that yet.

As their band got better, the Country Boys continued getting more jobs. One was a two-night-a-week gig at the Frontier Club in Pomona, about forty miles east of Burbank. Roland and his family had moved to Pomona, and the band members all stayed at that house. They made eight dollars apiece per night at the club, and they each gave Mildred five dollars out of that to cover their room and board.

One night at the Frontier Club, a gentleman walked up to the stage and said to Clarence, "I will give you all the money in my pocket if you will just smile." Clarence, who never smiled much, shot the guy a quick grin and the guy emptied his pocket. It was about eight dollars. The band began encouraging the audience members to do that more often and they would split the take.[77]

The Country Boys made a couple of 45 rpm discs around 1959. One of them included "Kentucky Hills" and "Head Over Heels in Love with You," and the other contained "On the Mountain (Stands My Love)" and "The Valley Below."

L-R: Earl Scruggs, Roland White, and Lester Flatt at the DJ Convention in Nashville, 1959. Photo by LeRoy McNees (with his Brownie camera). From the White family collection.

That same year, 1959, Roland and LeRoy decided to take a trip to Nashville. LeRoy had a new El Camino he wanted to break in, and what better way than to take it to Nashville? They had heard about Music City's annual DJ Convention, where lots of bluegrass and country artists would be performing. Disc jockeys from all over the country would be there, schmoozing with the artists.

Starting in 1952, the DJ Convention was conceived as a way for country music performers to thank disc jockeys for playing their records and

The Country Boys outside their traveling vehicle. Standing (L-R): Roland White, Clarence White, Eric White; kneeling (L-R): LeRoy McNees, Billy Ray Latham. From the collection of LeRoy McNees.

promoting their concerts. In succeeding years, it became more successful, extending over several days, and included receptions, formal and informal parties, and *Grand Ole Opry* concerts. Later, because so many fans were coming to Nashville for the convention, a festival concert was created just for them, called Fan Fair.

When Roland and LeRoy got to Music City, they found a boarding-house in Donelson (close to Nashville). LeRoy remembers that it cost them only five dollars a night. The boardinghouse became their home away from home for the next week and a half. Before going to the convention, the boys drove up to Cadiz, Kentucky—just north of the Tennessee state line—to see a Flatt and Scruggs show. Part of the price of that show ticket was a backstage pass to the *Grand Ole Opry* show at the Ryman Auditorium back down in Nashville.[78] They went to both the Friday and

Saturday night Opry shows, seeing many of their favorite entertainers and getting to meet them close up. They went to the Ernest Tubb record shop for the *Midnight Jamboree* after the Opry.[79]

At the DJ Convention they got to hear Lester Flatt and Earl Scruggs perform a second time. With his little Brownie camera, LeRoy took a picture of Roland standing with Lester and Earl after the show. Even more exciting, LeRoy got to talk to his Dobro hero, Josh Graves. They also met Luther Perkins, Johnny Cash's guitar player. "He was deadpan on stage," LeRoy said, "but he was really a character—an up and lively type fellow."

They listened to Flatt and Scruggs on the *Martha White Biscuit Time* radio show every morning and noted the places where Lester announced they would be performing locally. Over the next few days, Roland and LeRoy followed Lester and Earl around to several of those venues (little schoolhouses, etc.). Soon they became familiar faces to the Foggy Mountain Boys, and Earl invited them to his house, where he gave them an album and a band photo of the group standing in front of their bus.[80] They even attended a taping of the Flatt and Scruggs Martha White TV show at the WSM studio, where Lester announced on the program, "Two fellows all the way from California are here with us today."[81]

"It was magical," said LeRoy in our interview. "We had listened to the records [at home], but then we were actually able to see music being played. It was unbelievable—to hear that music coming off of the instruments. It just blew our minds."

The boys were totally fired up by their Nashville adventure. All the meeting and greeting was to leave a permanent mark on them. They had been introduced to Stringbean (Dave Akeman), Grandpa Jones, the Foggy Mountain Boys, and many other famous performers. Bill Monroe was a prominent figure at the convention too. It was like going to hillbilly heaven.

They returned to California with renewed energy and enthusiasm. Roland's bluegrass dream was now firmly implanted and there was no turning back. As always, his energy rubbed off on the other Country Boys. They found more playing jobs at folk and country music venues, as well as on local TV shows, including *Home Town Jamboree* and *Town Hall Party*. By this time, Eric Sr. had gotten to know Merle Travis, who was a regular on *Town Hall Party*.

Merle Robert Travis was born in 1917 in Rosewood, Kentucky. His father was a coal miner, which inspired Merle to write one of his greatest hits, "Sixteen Tons." One of his neighbors was Ike Everly, father of Don and Phil, the Everly Brothers. He developed a guitar style called "Travis-picking," which is copied more than almost any other style of picking. Even Chet Atkins was greatly influenced by Merle. A popular vocalist and hit songwriter, Merle could also do impressions and draw cartoons. Other Travis hits included "No Vacancy," "Dark as a Dungeon," "Fat Gal," and "Smoke! Smoke! Smoke! (That Cigarette)."[82]

Jim Renz, Roland's longtime friend, told me, "Sometimes Travis would have problems. He'd start drinking and one thing and another, and he'd lock himself in a motel room somewhere in LA—probably in the San Fernando Valley—and he wouldn't come out. Eric Sr. would go to the motel room and talk Merle into opening the door and coming out."[83]

Travis really liked the Country Boys. He enjoyed their music and later helped finance their first album. A few other *Town Hall Party* regulars chipped in on that project too. We'll discuss that in the next chapter.

A lucky break came for the Country Boys in a 1961 appearance on the *Andy Griffith Show*.[84] LeRoy said in a 2012 interview, "We made a little record and they were playing it on the radio, and my understanding is that Andy heard the song on his way to the studio one morning, and there was an episode coming up where they needed a bluegrass band to back Andy up."[85] Steve Stebbins from Desilu Productions called the Whites' house and Roland's mother answered. She passed the phone to Roland, who talked to him and arranged for an audition. Roland thinks Stebbins may have called Ed Pearl first, and Pearl had recommended them.

Roland had seen the *Andy Griffith Show* only once, and he thought it was a local TV program. The boys showed up at the studio wearing ordinary clothes, nothing fancy. They were waiting in a dressing room, and pretty soon Andy Griffith walked in with his guitar, saying, "Hi, boys, I'm Andy." He played only a few bars of "Whoa Mule Whoa" with them and then stopped, saying, "That'll do boys." That was their audition! They played the song once during the filming, but the studio had a problem with it, so they all went out to lunch and came back later and did it again. They never did play the whole song. They performed on the set by themselves during the production, but when the final broadcast was completed, the studio had spliced in pieces of film showing various characters, including Barney Fife (Don Knotts), coming in to Floyd's barbershop to listen.[86]

The Country Boys, 1959. Standing (L-R): Clarence White, Roland
White, Eric White; kneeling (L-R): Billy Ray Latham, LeRoy McNees.
From the White family collection.

The episode was named "Mayberry on Record." The plot was about a
record executive who comes to Mayberry seeking local folk talent, but
Andy believes him to be a con man. The promoter records Andy and
the Country Boys in Floyd's barbershop. The group also performed an
instrumental, "Cripple Creek." A *Grand Ole Opry* fiddler named Curley
Fox also made an uncredited appearance on the show. He was shown
as a local musician recording "Sally Goodin" for the record promoter.[87]
(Spoiler: the agent turns out to be honest after all, and Andy is proven

The Country Boys on the *Andy Griffith Show*, "Mayberry on Record," 1961.
L-R: Andy Griffith, Roland White, Eric White, Clarence White, Billy Ray
Latham, LeRoy McNees. From the White family collection.

wrong.) Several weeks after filming the episode, some of Roland's cousins
called them from Maine and said, "We saw you on the *Andy Griffith Show!*"

LeRoy added this in the 2012 interview: "Back in those days we were
poor. We didn't have much money at all, and every time that episode
aired—for six times—I received ninety dollars. Our house payment was
a hundred and five dollars at the time, so it just about covered that."[88]
LeRoy thinks the Country Boys were the first bluegrass band ever to
appear on national TV. (They were certainly among the first: Flatt and
Scruggs had appeared on the CBS network *Folk Sound* show on June 16,
1960. They performed "Salty Dog Blues," "Earl's Breakdown," and "Before
I Met You.")[89]

The year 1961 was a pivotal one for the Country Boys. That was the
year Roland married Arline Melanson, whom he had met at the Frontier

The Country Boys. L-R: LeRoy McNees, Eric White, Roland White, Billy Ray Latham, Clarence White. From the White family collection.

Club in Pomona, California. Clarence introduced Roland to Arline. She liked Clarence first but she found out he was only fourteen, and she was nineteen.[90] LeRoy also got married that year. He had met his bride-to-be, Janice, when she was working for the owner of the Ash Grove. Clarence was best man at their wedding. LeRoy and Janice are still together to this day. Also that year, Eric married Carolyn Jordan and left the Country Boys. Carolyn had been the daughter of a traveling musician and hadn't liked that lifestyle very much, so she talked Eric into quitting.[91]

There had always been a little bit of sibling rivalry between the three White brothers. The music was great and they worked together really well, but as time went on, a few attitude problems began to develop with Eric. He was a little jealous, and his oppositional demeanor began to show itself. Roland and Clarence were really tight, and relations between them were much smoother. Eric could sense that and didn't like it. He was like a square peg in a round hole.[92]

Eric's contrariness can be seen in the following amusing incident: One time Roland, who had been financially supporting the band by working on the assembly line at Lockheed Aircraft, bought some shoes for the band and had trouble getting Eric to reimburse him. "Eric wouldn't pay me, so I took the shoes to the backyard behind the garage door, poured lighter fluid on them, and set them afire. Eric saw that and said, 'What's that smoke out there?' He went out there and saw that and said, 'Those are my shoes!' I said, 'Yes? Go out and buy yourself a pair.'"[93]

Roland took the band very seriously. Being the prime motivator of the Country Boys, one of the many things he took care of was buying the outfits, which all matched. "Roland was the band leader and director of the whole endeavor. He would call practices and bring the records to learn from."[94]

Soon after Eric left the County Boys, the bass position was filled by a musician they had met at the Frontier Club, Roger Bush. Roger grew up in the San Gabriel valley. He played a wide range of instruments, including banjo, guitar, and some piano. He was about nineteen when he started playing with the Country Boys. "I was a banjo player," Roger told me in an interview,[95] "and nobody I met needed a banjo player. I was in a band with Don Parmley called the Smoggy Mountain Boys; smog was then becoming a big huge thing in the LA/Southern California area." Other sources say that band was called the Green Mountain Boys, but I prefer Roger's memory of the group being called the Smoggy Mountain Boys.

"Don played the banjo and I learned to play the Dobro, my brother played the mandolin, and I had a friend I had known since the second grade named Larry, who played the rhythm guitar,"[96] Roger told me in our interview. Another friend, Ronny Vokes, came into the group, playing bass.

The Smoggy Mountain Boys were just getting started when a friend, Walt Pittman, came over to El Monte, where Roger lived, and asked them to go with him out to Pomona to see a live bluegrass band. Their enthusiasm was triggered, and they drove twenty-five miles to watch the Country Boys at the Frontier Club. A husband and wife were singing duets when they walked into the club, but after they got seated the Country Boys were introduced. "They came out on stage," said Roger, "and started playing all this music we'd never seen the like of before."[97]

Roger and his friend Larry had grown up in a town with a large Mexican population. "He [Larry] looked at Roland and Clarence, and leaned over to me and said, 'I didn't know Mexicans played bluegrass.' We found out later that they were French Canadians by ancestry. [Billy Ray also thought the White brothers were Mexicans when he first saw them.] That was our introduction to live bluegrass. We went and talked to them and told them that we were trying to play bluegrass too."[98]

After making friends with Roger, the Country Boys came to his house and played music quite often. At that time Roger lived with his parents, but he had a big room in the back of the house with a separate entrance. When it became apparent that Eric was going to leave his brothers' band, Roger became the prime candidate to replace him:

> I forgot who made the actual phone call, but I believe it was LeRoy. He said, "Eric has quit the band, and we need a bass player." I said, "Well, I never played one in my life. If you're talking to me about that, what's going on?" He said, "Well, we can't find a bass player and teach him bluegrass. You already know how to sing tenor, baritone—whatever we need, and we can teach you to play the bass in probably five minutes good enough to go on stage with us. Are you interested?"[99]

Roger was interested, but he was still playing with Don Parmley and the Smoggy Mountain Boys. He felt really guilty about quitting his current band to join the Country Boys. "I could just feel Parmley breathing down my neck."[100]

Don wasn't exactly happy about Roger taking the new job, but he accepted it. There was still a problem, though: Roger didn't have a bass fiddle. The solution to that came when Roland was at the musician's union one day, looking at a bulletin board. He noticed an advertisement for a used Kay bass. The asking price was $200—high for those days—but it was a good brand, so he thought it might be worth looking into. When they went to check it out, they were pleased; it was in excellent condition. They offered $150 and got it for that. Roger Bush still plays that same bass today.

LeRoy started showing Roger how to play the bass, and he soon developed his own signature style: high-energy, jazzy, and with a good deal of slapping, a style in which the strings are plucked and released in such a way as to make them slap against the fingerboard.

Roger quickly found out that Roland was the spearhead of the group. He was very particular about staying in time, not speeding up or slowing down. "We'd be playing along, onstage, and all of a sudden I'd hear

THUMP-THUMP-THUMP and Roland was stomping his foot. Roland's sense of timing was impeccable, and Clarence's was every bit as good."[101]

Though Roland wasn't naturally bossy, his love for the music and desire to get it right sometimes made him seem that way. "Roland's always been a feisty customer," Mike Compton said in my interview with him. "For the size he is, he's not afraid to get in your face if he feels like he's right or if he feels like you're doing something you ought not to. He doesn't mind stepping up and saying, 'Hey, knock it off.'"[102]

Roger brought a new energy into the band, and jobs started coming in at a quicker pace. They found themselves traveling a lot more. Mike Seeger was instrumental in getting the Country Boys connected to folk clubs and folk festivals around a wider area. Ed Pearl and Ralph Rinzler also helped in that regard.[103] Things were really looking up.

One night in San Bernardino, the Country Boys played on the same program with Johnny Cash. During a break, Johnny appeared backstage. "He came in the dressing room, and he was just soaking wet; he was sweating so much. He went into another little part of the dressing room, and he was trying to get the window open, but it was painted shut. So he picked up a chair and threw it through the window so he could get some air."[104]

The Country Boys were delighted to get another invitation to perform on the *Andy Griffith Show*. That episode was to be called "Silent Sam." But Roland received a setback—in the form of a notice from the draft board. He was to report for a physical. The day the filming took place was the very same day Roland entered the army. It looked like he was going to have to put his dreams on hold.

After the Country Boys (minus Roland) filmed the "Silent Sam" episode of the *Andy Griffith Show*, the White family moved and the Desilu studio lost their contact information. Later the studio put an ad in *Variety* stating they were having auditions for a country band. By then the Dillards had arrived in LA, and they answered the ad, ultimately becoming the group portraying the Darling Family on the show. The Dillards were probably a better choice for the role; they had more of a comic persona than the comparatively serious Country Boys.[105]

When Roland got drafted, the Country Boys never took on a permanent replacement for him (though they temporarily hired mandolin players for certain jobs). But when he did return, one of the most important and consequential groups in the history of bluegrass came into existence: the Kentucky Colonels.

4

The Original Kentucky Colonels

Joining the army hadn't been in Roland's career plans, but he was drafted in 1961 and stayed in the service until 1963. He went to basic training at Fort Ord, an army post at Monterey Bay on the California coast (approximately three hundred miles north of LA).[1] A friend of Roland's was also at Fort Ord: Brooks Otis. He was a fellow musician (banjo and fiddle, mostly) and a big fan of folk and bluegrass music. He had recorded the Country Boys several times at the Ash Grove. Back in the 1960s, recording live bluegrass shows was a passion for Brooks. "That's how it was in the old days," he told me. "You recorded everything. That's the only way you got it and hung on to it. . . . You just had to record wherever you could. A lot of it was really funky but we loved it. . . . The harder it was to get, the more we loved it."[2]

Roland and Brooks were standing in the chow line for breakfast at the army base when they noticed each other. "Roland! What are you doing here?"

"I've been drafted."

"So have I."

That was only the first of several times Roland would cross paths with Brooks during his stint in the army. Ultimately the two would play music together overseas.

While still in basic, Roland was talking on the phone one day to his wife, Arline. She told him that Flatt and Scruggs were scheduled to perform at the Ash Grove the following weekend. Roland's ears perked up.

"Really?" he said. He remembered getting together with Lester and Earl at the DJ Convention. That experience had turned him into a devoted fan of the Foggy Mountain Boys. He wanted very much to catch up with them again.

"Yes. Do you think you can get a pass to come down here for the show?"

"I'm gonna try!"

"How are you going to get here?"

"I'll hitchhike."

Roland got the pass, but he had to be back at Fort Ord by midnight on Sunday. After leaving the post, he thumbed a ride on the main highway. The driver apologized that he wasn't going very far, but he told Roland, "You GIs always get rides real quick."

Fifteen minutes later, another car pulled over. They took Highway 101 south for a little way, and then Roland noticed the smell of liquor. The man behind the wheel had been drinking. When he stopped at a traffic light in a small town, Roland opened the door, saying, "Thanks for the ride, sir," and took off. When the light changed, the car roared away.

Roland stuck out his thumb again and about four or five cars went by. Then a semi stopped and Roland climbed aboard. After an all-night journey they arrived in Oxnard, California. He used a pay phone there to call his dad, who came and picked him up. They drove straight to the Ash Grove just in time for Flatt and Scruggs's second set. Roland went into the dressing room afterward, where Lester and Earl recognized him. They were somewhat amused by his dress uniform and short hair.[3] Later Roland hitched a ride and made it back to Fort Ord with only half an hour to spare.[4]

After basic, Roland went home for Christmas and then traveled to Fort Sam Houston in San Antonio, Texas, to go to medic school. He was surprised to run into none other than Brooks Otis again, who was also attending medic school. After that, Roland was flown to Fort Dix, New Jersey, and was put on a boat with a lot of seasick GIs. Roland was lucky; he didn't get sick, because he was in the center of the ship and was therefore subjected to less tossing and turning on the waves than those closer to the fore or aft. (It's like riding or sleeping in the middle of a tour bus; it's a much smoother ride than at the front or back.)

They landed in northern Germany, where he boarded a train bound for Sandhofen, near Mannheim. He was assigned to a dispensary in Coleman

Barracks, where he gave soldiers their shots. Many times big, tough GIs would pass out just looking at the needle, and there were others assigned to catch them so they wouldn't hit the floor. Roland gave shots to himself too (he never passed out).

He crossed paths once again with Brooks Otis in Sandhofen, and they formed a little hillbilly band. Roland had brought a mandolin with him, and Brooks had his banjo sent over. (It got there all in one piece, by the way!) Roland played the banjo too. Another member of their band was Jack Martin, from Paducah, Kentucky, who sang and played both guitar and Dobro. (Years later, Jack Martin took Josh Graves's place in Lester Flatt's band when Josh left.)

Their band was called the Southern Mountain Boys. Three other fellows sat in occasionally on bass, guitar, and fiddle. Roland can't recall their names today. The Southern Mountain Boys played bluegrass and old-timey music. A lot of times they just sat around and picked together informally. The band performed occasionally at a little club on the post. One time they played in a town on the French border. Otis had a small car and all five of them crowded into it to get to the gig.

There was a captain on the post named Natkin, also part of the medical corps, who liked their bluegrass music. He had often listened to them playing in the lounge. One day he asked Roland, "How do you like working in the dispensary?"

"Well, it's kind of boring," Roland told him.

"I can assign you to the Jeep. You'll be traveling around to different army hospitals in West Germany to deliver medical records."

That was more to Roland's liking; he loved traveling. It was lots of fun driving around Germany. Roland was by himself, except on the occasions when he had to drive officers wherever they needed to go. He had a little Jeep, and he knew about four or five small *gasthauses* where he could go to eat German food. These were mostly family-owned, and the proprietors usually lived upstairs. They would open the restaurants for lunch and dinner. The food was inexpensive and exceptionally good.[5]

Meanwhile, back in California, the Country Boys continued playing shows without Roland. They often rehearsed at the Ash Grove. Ed Pearl would let them go in and use his sound system during their practice sessions. It helped them learn to work the microphones more effectively. Occasionally they played shows there when other groups canceled out.

In Germany, 1962. Jack Martin (who later played Dobro with Lester Flatt and the Nashville Grass) and Roland White. From the White family collection.

The band also used to practice two or three times a week at LeRoy's house. Timing was something they very much tried to perfect. According to Roger, they sometimes got Clarence to play along with a metronome, and then they would leave the room, taking it with them. When they returned ten minutes or so later, Clarence—amazingly—was still right in time with the metronome.[6]

Clarence continued to get better and better. He played lots more lead guitar on the shows to make up for Roland not being there. He played solos on everything—instrumentals as well as vocals. He began to develop a personal style that was very pleasant to listen to; it was spontaneous and free without being overbearing. Supported by the other band members, Clarence was taking his guitar into uncharted territory.

Roger, Billy Ray, Clarence, and LeRoy worked several day jobs to supplement their band income. For Roger these jobs included installing brakes on cars and packing mail-order shipments in a warehouse. Billy Ray worked at a few different gas stations, and LeRoy drove truck shipments to the post office. Clarence gave guitar lessons, and Roger also taught both banjo and guitar.[7]

The Country Boys were big fans of Joe Maphis, who was still performing on the Saturday night TV show *Town Hall Party*. Clarence would struggle to learn guitar licks that Joe played on the show. It must have been tough, because Joe was a lightning-fast picker and he played mostly electric guitar, while Clarence was using an acoustic. There was a brother-sister act on the show too—the Collins Kids, Larry and Laurie—who were unbelievably talented. Larry was much younger and shorter than Laurie, but he played like a maniac. "Larry had a big double-neck guitar about his size," says Roger, "and he played the heck out of it. And Laurie was cute [she could really sing too]." Sometimes Larry would be introduced as Joe Maphis's sidekick, and the two of them would play a twin guitar number that was fast, flashy, and flamboyant. "I don't know who taught Larry—I guess Joe did—but he learned real quick."[8]

By the fall of 1962, the *Town Hall Party* was no longer being broadcast. Joe and Rose Lee Maphis moved to Bakersfield, where they had joined the cast of a TV show called the *Big W Roundup*. The Country Boys also got a job playing on that show, which was broadcast on Sunday mornings. Roger Bush recalls, "I remember at the *Big W Roundup* one day Billy Ray was so sick he couldn't get out of the bed, so we went there and we played anyhow. I played the five-string banjo. . . . We just did it without the bass."[9]

The band carried on, hoping to maintain their momentum until Roland got back from the service. They would drive to Bakersfield every weekend. Joe and Rose Lee Maphis had jobs lined up all over that town. The couple had a brand-new Dodge bus, almost like a motor home. There's a picture of it on the cover of a Starday record album titled *Mr. & Mrs. Country Music: Joe and Rose Lee Maphis*.[10] The Country Boys and the Maphises would play at drive-in theaters on top of the snack bars during intermission, at church sales and yard sales, or at square dances; then they would play the *Big W Roundup* on Sunday mornings.

Roger became a great front man and told lots of jokes and stories. LeRoy, Billy Ray, and Roger often performed country-style comedy routines together on stage—little gags and sketches that Billy Ray had heard on the *Grand Ole Opry*. One routine went like this: Billy Ray would tell LeRoy or Roger that he had been to college and taken biology. He said he took a test and they had a questionnaire for him to fill out.

"What kind of questions?" they asked him.

Billy Ray would say, "Well, one of the questions was, 'Why is mother's milk better for babies than cow's milk?'"

"What was your answer?"

Billy Ray would say, "'It's more nutritious, it helps the baby's immune system, and it comes in the cutest containers you've ever seen.'"

Joe Maphis, Merle Travis, Johnny Bond, and Tex Ritter all took a liking to the Country Boys during their association with them on the *Town Hall Party*. The country stars encouraged the boys and even provided some financial aid.

Tex Ritter cohosted the *Town Hall Party* from 1953 to 1960. Born in Marvaul, Texas, in 1905, Maurice Woodward "Tex" Ritter moved south with his family when he was teenager, graduating from South Park High School in Beaumont in 1922. He later attended the University of Texas in Austin. He was interested in theater, which he studied in both high school and college.[11] During the 1930s and 1940s he starred in more than eighty western films. His greatest music hits included "I'm Wastin' My Tears on You," "There's a New Moon Over My Shoulder," "Jealous Heart," "You Two-Timed Me One Time Too Often," and "I Dreamed of a Hillbilly Heaven." (Ritter was inducted into the Country Music Hall of Fame in 1964.)

Johnny Bond cohosted the *Town Hall Party* with Tex Ritter. Born in Oklahoma in 1915, Cyrus Whitfield "Johnny" Bond wrote lots of classic country songs, including "Cimarron"; "So Round, So Firm, So Fully Packed" (a hit for Merle Travis); and "Divorce Me C.O.D." He also played in many western movies and worked a lot with Tex Ritter, Jimmie Wakely, Merle Travis, Johnny Mack Brown, and Ray "Crash" Corrigan. He was a member of Tex Ritter's studio band, the Red River Valley Boys. Bond helped to keep the singing cowboy image alive during a time of chaotic change in the music business.[12] (He was inducted into the Country Music Hall of Fame in 1999.)

Bond, Ritter, Travis, and Maphis helped to pay for the Country Boys' first album. It was recorded in the fall of 1962 and was titled *The New Sound of Bluegrass America*.[13] The group was given a new name for the project: the Kentucky Colonels. Johnny Bond didn't like the name Country Boys, possibly because that was the name of Little Jimmy Dickens's band, and he didn't want to infringe. The Kentucky Colonels name was conceived by Merle Travis, who himself was a member of the Honorable Order of Kentucky Colonels, a philanthropic organization.

Roger Bush told me, "They made us a list of names, and they were all so bad that we picked the Kentucky Colonels as the least objectionable. I never did like Kentucky Colonels as a band name. Here we were, two guys from Maine [including Roland], one Arkie, and two guys from California."[14] Merle's primary justification for the name was "It's Kentucky music."[15]

The New Sound of Bluegrass America contained some great material, and Roland loved the album the first time he heard it. Clarence's guitar picking had shown dramatic improvement. He had started using a new style (for him) called cross-picking. That was a technique of picking the strings in a repetitive pattern that involves jumping over or crossing certain strings. It sounds a little bit like a finger roll on the banjo. Examples of Clarence's cross-picking can be heard on "I Might Take You Back Again" and "Won't You Call Me Darling." The album contained excellent traditional bluegrass harmony, and there was a comedy number on the recording called "Howdy Hoss," which was reminiscent of an earlier Stanley Brothers recording, "How Far Is It to Little Rock?" There was an instrumental called "Banjo Picking Fever" that featured Billy Ray Latham playing bits and pieces of "Cripple Creek," "Ole Joe Clark," and "Cumberland Gap."

Most of the songs had been written by LeRoy McNees: "I'll Be Coming Home Tomorrow," "Cabin in the Sky," "LeRoy's Ramble," "Howdy Hoss," "Won't You Call Me Darling," "Rainbow Shining Somewhere," "420 Special," "To Prove My Love for You," and "Memphis Special" (which was later recorded in 2007 by a Southern rock band called Blackberry Smoke). LeRoy had also cowritten two of the songs with his new friend Josh Graves: "I Might Take You Back Again" and "If You're Ever Gonna Love Me."

Joe Maphis and Johnny Bond had brought in a guest fiddler for the album, Gordon "The Mule" Terry. His nickname had been given to him because he made his fiddle "bray" whenever he played and sang "Johnson's Old Grey Mule" (which he recorded in 1957). He first started doing that imitation on the *Town Hall Party*, where he was a regular. Terry had already done two stints with Bill Monroe and the Blue Grass Boys before playing with the Kentucky Colonels on their debut album. The only thing missing was Roland, yet his influence was always present. He had been the primary motivator, and his return to the band upon discharge from the army was taken as a given.

Shortly after recording *The New Sound of Bluegrass America*, LeRoy got married and left the band. That was quite a disappointment for the others, for they had grown partial to the bluesy sound he added to the band with his Dobro, and they were also going to miss LeRoy's good humor. (He didn't quit playing, however. He soon started another group, the Born Again Bluegrass Band, which stayed together for thirty-one years and recorded twelve albums.)[16]

After the loss of LeRoy, the Kentucky Colonels did some touring with just Roger, Clarence, and Billy Ray, hoping to maintain the group until Roland came back. Additional musicians were sometimes hired on a temporary basis. Roger said, "We'd get to where we were going, and we'd say to the bluegrass folks in town, 'Hey, we need either a rhythm guitar player or a mandolin player—or maybe a fiddle player.' That's how we met David Grisman.[17] He was just a kid. I don't think he was even twenty-one years old."[18]

When Roland was finally discharged from the army in the fall of 1963, he was reunited with the Kentucky Colonels and one of the first shows they played was at the Ash Grove. They were joined by left-handed fiddler and bass player Bobby Slone.[19] By that time the Ash Grove had become part of a circuit of coffeehouses. The entertainers would play on Tuesday through Saturday at one place, then take Sunday and Monday off and move to the next establishment for another Tuesday through Saturday run. Ed Pearl was the primary organizer, and he booked the Colonels at many of the venues in San Diego, Los Angeles, Santa Barbara, Palo Alto, Berkeley, and even Phoenix. Ed also started booking the Kentucky Colonels at lots of little colleges around Southern California. They would play during lunch hours and put on afternoon concerts in auditoriums.

The college kids loved the music; many of them had heard Flatt and Scruggs, who also toured colleges. The Colonels received $100–$150 per show, which was a lot, because they traveled in just one car and gasoline was only twelve to fifteen cents per gallon. They could buy quite a few hamburgers with the amount of money they were pulling in.

Later on in 1963 Clarence's guitar playing really started taking off, blazing new trails. Elements of the great Gypsy guitar player Django Reinhardt started appearing in Clarence's playing, and he adapted many of the guitarist's astonishing techniques to his own style. Joe Maphis had also been listening to Django Reinhardt recordings for years, and Clarence soon realized that many of the licks he had copied from Joe were really Django licks.[20]

Jean "Django" Reinhardt (1910–1953) was born in Belgium. He was of Romany descent and spent most of his childhood in Gypsy encampments. He learned the violin at an early age, and later the six-string banjo, tuned like a guitar. Reinhardt was making his living playing music at the age of fifteen, usually by busking. At the age of seventeen he got married to Florine "Bella" Mayer, a girl from the same Romany settlement. By 1928 he had made several recordings and was gaining wider attention. Late in 1928 he suffered an accident in the wagon he shared with his wife. A candle was knocked over, so the story goes, igniting some celluloid used by Florine to make artificial flowers. A huge fire resulted, and the couple narrowly escaped with their lives. Django suffered burns over half of his body. The third and fourth fingers of his left hand were rendered practically useless, but he reinvented his style using only the first two fingers to fret the instrument. Eventually he became a legendary and much-admired jazz guitarist, playing and recording with the likes of Stéphane Grappelli, Louis Armstrong, Duke Ellington, and Dizzy Gillespie.[21]

A high point for the Kentucky Colonels came in September '63, when they helped celebrate the tenth anniversary of Cousin Herb Henson's much-loved *Trading Post* TV program. The event took place in Bakersfield, California, at the brand-new Civic Auditorium. Two performances took place with a total attendance of six thousand. A live album with some of the best performances from the two shows was released called *Country Music Hootenanny*.[22] The Kentucky Colonels joined some of the leading pioneers of the Bakersfield sound on the show, including Buck Owens,

Rose Maddox, Tommy Collins, Glen Campbell, Roy Clark, Merle Travis, and Johnny Bond. Roland and the Colonels performed "Green Corn" on the record, and they backed up Johnny Bond on the bluegrass standard "Blue Ridge Mountain Blues."

In early 1964, Dick Bock, a producer who had put out a great many jazz albums, came into the Ash Grove to listen to the Kentucky Colonels. Affiliated with World Pacific Studios, he offered them a record deal: an album of instrumentals. He told them that the budget was limited and that instrumentals would require less studio time than vocals. That was how the Kentucky Colonels came to make the now-famous album *Appalachian Swing!* The producer chose the name of the album; it was a play on the title of Aaron Copland's ballet *Appalachian Spring*. The groundbreaking record spotlighted Clarence and Roland. (It is now available on CD after having been out of print for many years.) Instrumental versions of songs were included on the album as well as several bluegrass standards. The selections were recorded by playing each tune for as long as ten minutes (no easy feat) and taking the best portions of the tapes and splicing them together. Once they visited Dick Bock while he was editing the album, and they were surprised to see pieces of audiotape hanging all around the room.

The album, though short, was a masterpiece with unmatched interplay between the instruments. Clarence's guitar was a full-fledged lead instrument as well as a rhythm instrument—something that had never really been done before in a bluegrass setting. The album started off with a Ralph Stanley banjo tune, "Clinch Mountain Backstep." Roland played his mandolin solos using some of the archaic mountain scales of early old-time music, giving the tune a timeless feeling. The second tune, "Nine Pound Hammer," was a mandolin-guitar duet. Clarence's solos started out bluesy and then became more straightforward with each successive turn he took, whereas Roland's mandolin solos started out in a very traditional manner and became bluesier on later solos. Clarence took "John Henry" in a new direction with several blues guitar licks that put a personal stamp on the old folk tune, making it a fresh and exciting experience for both player and listener. There were some traditional fiddle tunes played as mandolin-guitar duets, showcasing Clarence's phenomenal guitar style: understated, adventurous, and full of possibilities yet to be explored. *Appalachian Swing!* was truly a landmark album.

In March of that same year, Clarence and Roland met Robert Arthur "Tut" Taylor (1923–2015) at the UCLA Folk Festival. An innovative Dobro player from Possum Trot, Georgia, Tut was a musician's musician whose distinctive trademark was the use of a flat pick instead of fingerpicks. He had recently appeared on an album with the Folkswingers titled *12 String Dobro!*[23] Tut was about to make his first solo album, and he recognized great talent when he heard it. The White brothers agreed to join him on the record project, which was cut three days later and titled *Dobro Country*.[24] Here's what Louise Scruggs (Earl's wife) had to say in her liner notes to the album: "I would like to call the listeners' attention to the almost classical interplay between Roland's piercing mandolin, the amazing guitar of Clarence and Tut's unique Dobro. How well these three instruments weave their spell . . . always blending, each subtly alternating melody and rhythm, and each adding its own meaning to the mood of *Dobro Country*."[25]

Louise was right about Tut Taylor's creative talent. In 1971 he participated on John Hartford's iconic album *Aereo-Plain*,[26] along with Norman Blake and Vassar Clements. His 1972 record, *Friar Tut*,[27] put him in the Dobro Players Hall of Fame. Another memorable recording featuring Tut Taylor was *The Dobrolic Plectral Society*,[28] which included such illustrious musicians as Sam Bush, Butch Robins, Curtis Burch, and Norman Blake.

In May, Ed Pearl, Mike Seeger, and his first wife, Marge (an excellent guitar player, by the way), booked a tour of folk clubs on the East Coast for the Kentucky Colonels. These venues would include the Unicorn in Boston; Club 47 in Cambridge, Massachusetts; the Foghorn in Baltimore, Maryland; the Ontario Place in Washington, D.C.; and Gerde's Folk City in New York City. The Colonels would have the chance to meet and pick with some of the East Coast's finest bluegrass musicians, including the Country Gentlemen, Bill Keith,[29] Jim Rooney, Frank Wakefield, and the Charles River Valley Boys.

San Francisco–area musicians Jerry Garcia and Sandy Rothman tagged along with the Colonels on part of that trip. Jerry was a big fan of the Kentucky Colonels; he had made the journey to LA several times to hear them at the Ash Grove. He especially loved listening to Billy Ray and Clarence. Garcia (1942–1995) had been a banjo player before eventually switching to electric music and becoming guitarist and leader of the Grateful Dead. The five-string banjo was one of Jerry Garcia's early loves. He spent many hours in the 1960s slowing down bluegrass records and learning from them. Garcia had lost part of one of his fingers on his picking hand during a childhood woodcutting accident, which made his finger rolls very different and his sound distinct. Roland White once said, "It always seemed like he was about to miss his roll because of the fingertip, but he would get it." His guitar playing with the Grateful Dead was heavily influenced by his banjo-playing years. He liked hearing single notes clearly, an important component of banjo music.[30]

Rothman was a bluegrass bandmate of Garcia's. The two had been playing together in a group called the Black Mountain Boys since early 1964. Sandy went on to perform with a wide variety of notable bluegrass groups, including Bill Monroe, Larry Sparks, Earl Taylor, Red Allen, Jimmie Skinner, the Kentucky Colonels, and the Jerry Garcia Acoustic Band.[31]

For the 1964 bluegrass trip back east, Garcia and Rothman took Jerry's 1961 Corvair down to the San Fernando Valley to meet the Colonels, who were riding in Roland's station wagon, with the bass on top. They caravanned east; sometimes Clarence rode in the backseat of Jerry's Corvair, and Sandy occasionally rode in the station wagon. Rothman recalled, "We'd pull up at some truck stop with each car going to a different pump, sometimes really far from each other, and we'd agree to play the same tune in each of our cars in hopes of freaking out the guys at the gas station. But nobody ever said a thing. We tried that endlessly and thought it was just so entertaining."[32]

In the fall of 1964, Marge Seeger got them some more work up and down the East Coast. The band relocated to Boston for several months. By coincidence, Arline, who was in the later months of her pregnancy with daughter Roline, wanted to be near her sisters who lived in the area, and to give birth there. Clarence, Roland, and Arline stayed with her sister,[33] and Billy Ray and Roger rented an apartment above a Portuguese market.[34] Roland had this to say:

> Our band played the Second Fret in Philadelphia, and all the venues we'd played on our previous tour, and topped it off with performances at the Newport Folk Festival. At the request of Ralph Rinzler, Clarence sat in on Doc Watson's guitar workshop, which made Clarence very nervous. I assured him that no one noticed and he played great. There's a CD of our performances at Newport,

The Kentucky Colonels, ca. 1964. L-R: Billy Ray Latham, Roland White, Roger Bush, Clarence White. From the White family collection.

titled *Long Journey Home*, and some of the songs Clarence and Doc played together are on Doc's album *Treasures Untold*.[35]

Clarence had every reason to be in awe of Doc Watson, who was already revered in the folk music world for his flat-pick guitar playing. His style was unmatched in clarity, spirit, and vitality. Born in Deep Gap, North Carolina, Arthel "Doc" Watson had a deep knowledge of American traditional music. He also played banjo in an authentic, old-time frailing style. From the early 1960s until his death in 2012, he played a huge part in introducing many to the folk genre of music. In 1972 he appeared on the Nitty Gritty Dirt Band's groundbreaking album, *Will the Circle Be Unbroken*. He won several Grammys, including two with his son Merle (1949–1985).

Doc's workshop with Clarence White at the 1964 Newport Folk Festival was a significant event in guitar history. Clarence's progressive style was a perfect complement to Doc's more traditional approach, and together they won many new admirers. The festival itself had been going since 1959, when the event drew thirteen thousand people. That year featured performances by the Kingston Trio, Joan Baez, and Pete Seeger. Seeger was also on the bill in 1964, and the Kentucky Colonels came onstage right after him during one of their performances (no pressure there!). "Back then," said Roger Bush, "Pete Seeger was God."[36] The Kentucky Colonels had a tough act to follow, but they came through with flying colors, getting several standing ovations.

During that tour the Colonels got together every day to practice. Roland was a real stickler about rehearsing. All of them found bluegrass to be a demanding and exacting music, requiring dedicated effort to stay sharp. Roger wanted to keep up his banjo-playing skills, so he practiced often, sometimes working out twin banjo breaks with Billy Ray. On some shows the two would play "Sally Ann" together. They had both learned the tune almost note-for-note the way Earl Scruggs recorded it on the 1961 Flatt and Scruggs album, *Foggy Mountain Banjo*.[37] As a stage trick, Roger would fret Billy Ray's banjo and Billy Ray would fret Roger's banjo, and they would play the tune in harmony together. Another of their twin banjo numbers, "Wild Bill Jones," can be heard on the *Appalachian Swing!* album.

In October of that year, Roline was born and Roland took some time off to be with his wife and their new daughter. While he was gone, David Grisman filled in for him on the mandolin at a New York club called the Gaslight. The Kentucky Colonels played there for a week.[38]

One evening during that eastern tour, Clarence was loading up their station wagon. He set his two Martin guitars down behind the vehicle and went back to go get something else. (Can you guess what happened next?) Coming out, he forgot about the instruments, got in the station wagon, and backed up—hitting the guitars. His D-18 was smashed to pieces, and his D-28 was also damaged but still playable. They moved on to the next show location in Ann Arbor, Michigan, where Clarence took his D-18 guitar to the Herb David Guitar Studio for repair. He carried some of it in the case and the rest of it in a sack. A few days later Herb had it glued back together, and it sounded better than it had ever sounded before.[39]

After the tour was over, the Kentucky Colonels went back home to California and continued perfecting their act. Lots of times when Clarence was playing solos on his Martin D-18 guitar, especially at the Ash

Grove, Roland would walk over to him and press the pointed tip of his mandolin peg head against the top of Clarence's instrument, behind the bridge. That would mute the guitar, and the sound vibrations would travel into the mandolin—you could hear that D-18 coming right out of the mandolin.[40]

One time the Kentucky Colonels performed at Knott's Berry Farm in Buena Park, California. The stage in the outdoor amphitheater had a large tree growing over it. A bird flew down and made a deposit on Clarence's guitar during the show. The audience laughed, and he stepped off to the side of the stage and flicked it off with his finger. Roland said he wishes he had a picture of that![41]

The Kentucky Colonels traveled hard and far. Roger Bush recalls, "We flew to Dulles Airport [west of D.C.] and rented a car—mileage free for a certain length of time—and drove it as far as western Oklahoma. We drove it all over the place. I remember we were down in North Carolina. There were a ton of miles on that sucker when we got through."[42]

Jody Stecher,[43] a singer and multi-instrumentalist with whom I had the pleasure of working in a bluegrass band called Perfect Strangers (during the mid-2000s), had this to say about Roland and his performances with the Kentucky Colonels:

> His solos in the Kentucky Colonels (at gigs), were the freest, least-formulaic I had heard at the time. What especially impressed me was that he would start his solo before the "official" melody began. As his solo approached he'd start playing as he walked up to the microphone. He arrived at the mic just before the downbeat at the start of the song or tune. And then sometimes as he backed away from the mic he'd keep on playing. This caused a natural "fade-out." Clarence was great of course but what he played seemed more predictable (since I had heard the band many times). He was careful. Roland was less safe, more risky. My hero back then was Sonny Osborne because he constantly took chances on the stage. Sometimes his spontaneous banjo explosions blew up in his face so to speak. But that almost made it even better. He was fearless. But he had a large personality on stage. Roland was modest. He never said (in his music) "Look what I'm doing. Did you hear that?" He just did wonderful things and left it to the listener to notice it or not.[44]

Jody's personal recollections of the Kentucky Colonels are priceless. Here is more of what he said:

In the shows I saw of the Kentucky Colonels Roger Bush did almost all the talking. Billy Ray Latham talked a bit, mostly as part of comedy skits. The White brothers never spoke. Neither did fiddler Bobby Slone. This was typical of bluegrass bands at the time. It was not expected that every band member would speak. But Clarence and Roland appeared particularly taciturn somehow. They were a bit mysterious up there on the stage especially when they stood beside each other to sing a duet. In contrast to Roger Bush and Billy Ray they did not put on an outgoing performance. It was rather solemn. This is in strong contrast to Roland's off-stage personality in later years when I got to know him a bit. He was always friendly and good-humored and full of stories of musicians he had worked with. Funny stories, sad stories, amazing stories, and always full of details.[45]

For a few months in 1965, the Kentucky Colonels acquired a unique fiddler by the name of Scotty Stoneman, who had been playing with his family band, the Bluegrass Champs (later just called the Stoneman Family). Inspired by fiddler Chubby Wise, Scotty's playing was unrestrained, wildly imaginative, and unequaled to this day. Calvin Scott "Scotty" Stoneman (1932–1973) was born into a musical family in Galax, Virginia, and grew up in the Maryland suburbs. His father, Ernest Van "Pop" Stoneman, started his commercial recording career in 1924 with a song he had written himself, "The Sinking of the Titanic." He and his wife, Harriet "Hattie" Frost Stoneman, had twenty-three children. In 1927 "Pop" was signed to Victor Records, and he included his wife and many family members on the recording sessions. Pop Stoneman and the Little Pebbles was one of the band names used before it became the Bluegrass Champs, which included Scotty, his sisters Ronnie and Donna, and his brothers Jimmy and Van. Banjo player Porter Church was also in the group. They moved for a while to the Washington, D.C., area before relocating again to Nashville. Scotty left the family band in 1964.

He joined the Kentucky Colonels at the Ash Grove and the Cobblestone Club, and some of these live shows have been released down through the years: *Livin' in the Past*, *The Kentucky Colonels Featuring Roland and*

The Kentucky Colonels with Scotty Stoneman, 1965. L-R: Roland White, Scotty Stoneman, Roger Bush, Billy Ray Latham, Clarence White. Photo by Dave Spencer. From the White family collection.

Clarence White, 1965 Live in LA, and *The Kentucky Colonels Onstage.* "He was totally amazing," Roger told me. "I got to room with him, got to make sure there were sliced pickles to lay on his eyes to get rid of the bags every morning. There are great fiddle players like Byron Berline, Chubby Wise, Kenny Baker, Bobby Hicks, and so forth, and then—there's Scotty Stoneman. He was just a show all by himself."[46]

Jerry Garcia was also greatly impressed with Scotty's fiddling. He described watching him with the Kentucky Colonels at the Ash Grove, captivated by the endless improvisations of the fiddle master. Scotty often took long, uninterrupted solos while Roland and the rest of the Colonels practically stopped playing altogether, just looking at him with fascination like everyone else in the room.[47]

Plagued by alcoholism all his life, Scotty died of alcohol poisoning after a period of sobriety in the early 1970s. His fiddle playing was unlike anything else ever heard—unsurpassed in the annals of bluegrass music.[48] Today Scotty is a cult figure in bluegrass.

In June 1965 Roland was included on an album called *The Beverly Hillbillies*,[49] featuring Flatt and Scruggs along with the cast of the TV show: Buddy Ebsen, Donna Douglas, Irene Ryan, Max Baer, Nancy Kulp, and Raymond Bailey. Lester wasn't featured on any of the songs except "The Ballad of Jed Clampett," which was simply a reissue of the original Flatt and Scruggs recording from their *Hard Travelin'* LP.[50] Roland's only mandolin solo on *The Beverly Hillbillies* album was on a song called "Jethro's a Powerful Man." His picking transcends the silliness of the lyrics and illustrates his signature style: a melody statement in strong, clear notes followed quickly by a rambling improvisation. The song melody is reminiscent of an old-time tune, recorded by many, called "Cornbread, 'Lasses, and Sassafras Tea." Of special note on the LP is Earl Scruggs's rapport with the drummer, perhaps a foreshadowing of his later work with the Earl Scruggs Revue.

The Colonels provided music for a movie in 1965. It was a low-budget "hicksploitation" feature called *The Farmer's Other Daughter*, obviously influenced by *The Beverly Hillbillies* TV program. Besides providing music for much of the background of the film, they appeared on a stage for three numbers, supplying vocal and instrumental backup for Opry star Ernest Ashworth. Ernie, a very good singer, performed "Pushed in a Corner," "Love Has Come My Way," and the song that made him a *Grand Ole Opry* star, "Talk Back Trembling Lips." He was wearing one of his distinctive suits ornamented with lips and musical notes. Behind him, Roland could be seen, always smiling at Clarence, who provided guitar kickoffs on every song as well as turnarounds (short musical phrases) after the choruses. Roland and Clarence split a full solo on "Love Has Come My Way." Billy Ray didn't play much banjo at all during the stage performance with Ernest Ashworth, but he could be heard playing some great banjo parts in the background during the rest of the movie. Richard Greene played fiddle on the soundtrack too, but he was on rhythm guitar for the stage portion. Ernie Ashworth sang the theme song, "The Ballad of Farmer Brown," at the start and finish of the movie, with vocal and instrumental backup by the Kentucky Colonels. In conjunction with the movie, the Colonels released a single that featured "That's What You Get for Lovin' Me" and "The Ballad of Farmer Brown."[51] Things began to slow down in late 1965, and by 1966 the folk scene had pretty much dried up. By that time Roland, Arline, and their little baby, Roline, had moved back in with Mildred and Eric Sr.

It became increasingly difficult to find work playing acoustic music. Ever dedicated and faithful to continuing at any cost, Roland and the Kentucky Colonels began playing electric dance music Tuesdays through Saturdays at a bowling alley lounge in Azusa, California. ("Everything from A to Z in the USA" is how Roger remembers the name of the town.) Roland had an electric mandolin that his father had built, and Clarence had a 1950s Fender Telecaster electric guitar. Billy Ray got an archtop Gibson rhythm guitar with a pickup and amplifier, and Roger Bush brought in a new electric Gibson bass and amp. They also hired a drummer named Bart Haney.

They sang popular country music hits of the time by people like Merle Haggard, Jim Reeves, Buck Owens, and other traditional country singers. Clarence began bending (or "choking") strings on his guitar to get a pedal steel effect. One of the tunes he started playing was "Buckaroo," by Don Rich, leader of Buck Owens's band and champion of the Bakersfield sound. Clarence played "Buckaroo" all through his later career. Around 1967 he figured out a better way to get the pedal steel effect. While playing with a group called Nashville West, Clarence and bandmate Gene Parsons developed a special mechanism that used spring-loaded levers to allow the second, or B-string, to be raised to a C-sharp note by pulling downward on the neck. At first they called it the Parsons/White Pull-String but eventually renamed it the StringBender. Later that name was shortened to the B-Bender. During Clarence's later association with the Byrds, "Buckaroo" was one of the numbers he played that showcased his invention, along with "You Ain't Going Nowhere" and "Lover of the Bayou." (Other examples of his B-Bender can be heard on the Everly Brothers' "I'm on My Way Home Again," Joe Cocker's "Dear Landlord," and Arlo Guthrie's "Coming into Los Angeles.")[52]

At the bowling alley lounge in Azusa, the Kentucky Colonels would take out their acoustic instruments and play about twenty minutes of bluegrass midway through the evening. The dancers, who had had quite a bit to drink by that time, would get increasingly rowdy and start whooping and hollering and jumping around. One time a couple of people fell down and hurt themselves, so the band decided to play only slower ballads and waltzes, songs like "Kentucky Waltz" and "Tennessee Waltz." They also sang many of the slower Flatt and Scruggs and Reno and Smiley songs.[53]

Word started getting around that they had a very good country music group. Many musicians would come in to hear them play, including James Burton, who was Ricky Nelson's guitar player as well as a recording session musician.[54] He liked the band a lot, especially Clarence's guitar playing. During a break he talked to Clarence and said he wanted to give him some of his session work because he was too busy to handle it all. He passed along Clarence's phone number to several record producers, and soon Clarence found himself doing session work for nearly every artist on the West Coast. He eventually got so busy recording that he had very little time to do anything else.[55]

Inevitably, by mid-1966 the Kentucky Colonels disbanded. Their families were growing and needed more money. To supplement his music income, Roland took on a job as a breakfast cook at a nursing home. Clarence was married and had a new baby. Roger was also married (he met his wife at the bowling alley) and was working as a machinist. Billy Ray moved back to Arkansas and got a job playing on Lee Mace's Ozark Opry.[56]

A real diehard, Roland tried to start up another Kentucky Colonels band. It was a part-time band that included Eric on bass and vocals, a guitar player and tenor singer named Dennis Morris, Roland on mandolin and vocals, and a banjo player named Bob Warford.[57] There was no fiddler, since they couldn't find a replacement for Scotty, who had gone back to Virginia. They played the Ash Grove, and Roland tried to book a tour up the coast, but nobody could go, because their day jobs interfered. Bob Warford was going to law school and he could only play locally. It just wasn't working.

5

The Blue Grass Boys

In 1967 Roland got a job playing electric bass in a dance band, six nights a week, union scale. He was doing okay, but it wasn't really fitting in with his dream of playing bluegrass for a living. By now, music was in his blood and he couldn't quit playing, even if it wasn't the particular style that he liked the most.

One day in May 1967, Ed Pearl got a call from Bill Monroe, who told him his bus was broken down in Dallas. He planned on leaving his Blue Grass Boys there to get it fixed and wanted to know if Ed could round up a band for him at the Ash Grove until his own band could bring the repaired bus to LA. The "Bluegrass Special" broke down lots of times, probably because it was driven so much and had so many miles on it. It was secretly called the "Bluegrass Breakdown" by the Blue Grass Boys. This time it was the transmission. A custom bearing was going to have to be built for it.[1]

Monroe was planning on flying out to Washington state for a couple of shows with only one of his Blue Grass Boys, Doug Green.[2] Doug played guitar and was able to sing duets with Bill,[3] so he was the most useful to Monroe in that situation. (Today Doug is well known as "Ranger Doug, Idol of American Youth" in the cowboy group Riders in the Sky.)

Monroe asked Ed Pearl, "What about those White boys?" He didn't remember any of their names, but he did remember going to their house for dinner back in 1959, after he had performed at Rose Maddox's 101 Club in Oceanside, California, near San Diego. Maddox had asked the White brothers to play a guest set, and Bill liked it, telling them, "That's mighty fine, boys."[4]

"I'll call Roland," Pearl told Bill.

"Is he the one that plays the guitar?" asked Bill.

"No, he's the mandolin player, but I'll give him a call. We'll get you a band."

Pearl then called Roland, explaining the situation. "Do you think Clarence would play guitar with Bill?"

"Well," said Roland, "he could, but he's really busy. I'll ask him, though."

When Roland put it to his brother, Clarence told him, "You know I'm not gonna do that—even if I had the time. I'm not a good lead singer, and I have too much session work. You know how to do a damn G-run on the guitar, don't you?[5] That's all you need to know—you could do it."

"Well, . . . okay."

Roland called Eric, who jumped at the chance to play bass with Bill Monroe at the Ash Grove.[6]

After Monroe and Doug Green played their shows in Washington state, they took a Continental Trailways bus down to LA. As it turned out, members of the Dillards performed with Bill on the first night, May 12.[7] On the next night, Roland played guitar, Eric was on bass, and Bob Warford was the banjo player. After finishing the show, Bill told them, "Well, the Blue Grass Boys are on their way in. They'll be here tomorrow night. Let me settle up with you." He paid each one of them separately, and when he got to Roland, he said, "Roland, could you stay on?"

"You've got a guitar player, don't you?" answered Roland.

"Yeah, but we need help."

Roland didn't know what he was saying. "What'd you say?"

"We need some help."

"Oh, okay. I'll be back."[8]

So Roland played guitar the next several nights with the Blue Grass Boys: Lamar Grier on banjo, James Monroe on bass,[9] Doug Green on second guitar, and Byron Berline on fiddle.

Berline (1944–2021) would be an important figure in Roland's musical career, and the two were destined to perform and record a lot together. Byron also knew Brooks Otis, Roland's friend who had been drafted at the same time as White. Otis had given Berline a tape he had made of some Kentucky Colonels live shows when Scotty Stoneman was in the group.[10] Byron had some pretty impressive credentials: he had recorded with the Dillards in 1964; won the National Fiddle Championship at Weiser, Idaho, in 1965; and appeared at the Newport Folk Festival with his dad, Lue, later that same year.[11]

Raised on a farm in Oklahoma, Byron says that one of his earliest memories is from when he was only three or four years old. Lue was playing the fiddle and Byron crawled beneath his dad's legs and grabbed the bow. His father put the fiddle up under his son's chin and placed the bow in his own hand, playing as if Byron was fiddling. By the age of five, Byron was playing for real, and he won his first fiddle contest at ten, beating his dad. Berline's style was developed from listening to Texas and Oklahoma contest fiddlers, characterized by playing the melodies in a straight and accurate manner plus adding ornamental notes to add flavor.[12]

During the break in one of the shows at the Ash Grove, Lamar Grier struck up a conversation: "Roland, what have you been doing?"

"Well, I've been playing electric bass in a dance band."

"You have? Well, listen. Bill's going to be needing a guitar player when we get back to Nashville, because Doug Green is going back to the University of Michigan. He took some time off to help Bill out."

"Oh, really?"

So Roland went to Bill later, saying, "Bill [Monroe had corrected him earlier when he addressed him as "Mr. Monroe," saying, "My name is Bill"], I hear you're going to be needing a guitar player when you get back to Nashville. You heard me; you know what I can do. I could get better at it if I was a Blue Grass Boy."

"Well," Bill said, "I tell you what. I'm not looking for a hotshot picker. I just want somebody who will try real hard and play good rhythm guitar—and doesn't drink."[13]

Everyone knew Bill Monroe didn't like to drink, and he didn't want the Blue Grass Boys to drink either. He especially hated beer, often ranting about those he called "beer hogs," saying, "I don't see how they can drink that old sloppy stuff!"[14] He did, however, occasionally talk of how he enjoyed the taste of good whiskey. Roland White told his friend Jim Renz, "Bill didn't like to drink, but he had a liking for Kentucky elderberry wine. He liked mead [a fermented drink made from water and honey]." Roland related how Monroe had tried some mead that a friend of White's had made. It was in a jar and Bill tried it and said, "That's some good stuff." Roland offered him a little bit more. Monroe seemed very happy that night.[15]

Drinking didn't appeal to Roland all that much, so Monroe didn't have anything to worry about on that score. Roland felt he could learn to play rhythm guitar the way Bill wanted it, so he told him, "Well, I'll try real hard. I can do all that."

"Let me talk to the boys about it."[16]

Roland never really believed that Bill had actually conferred with the Blue Grass Boys that night. Many years later, however, Berline told him that he had indeed talked to them. Byron and James had been sitting together at the Ash Grove when Bill came up to them and said, "I want to see you two on the bus, right now." They were a little worried. Was Bill going to fire them or what? When they got on the bus, Bill just gave them a little spending money (about twenty dollars each) and then asked them, "What do you think of that little White boy?"

"White boy?" Berline asked. "What are you talking about? What white boy?"

"You know—the one that plays the guitar."

They realized then that "White" referred to a name, not race. Yes, they said. Roland would indeed be good, both as a singer and guitar player.[17]

When the time came around to leave LA, Bill asked Roland, "Are you coming with us?"

Roland said, "Yeah, 'cause I talked to my wife."

"Go ahead and try it for four or five months, and if you like it, send for her."

They performed at a coffeehouse in San Bernardino the next day and then later traveled to Fort Worth to play another show. After that they had another gig in Hugo, Oklahoma, booked by Bill Grant (who two years later started a bluegrass festival in Salt Creek Park near Hugo). Next they went to Anniston, Alabama, to play at a former air base before going to Nashville.[18]

Bill had just composed a tune called "The Gold Rush," which Byron had a big hand in writing and had been working on in the dressing room at the Ash Grove. They played it with Roland on stage that first night, and later they practiced it on the bus for several days until they got back to Nashville. Bill was trying very hard to get Byron to use long bow strokes instead of short ones. He liked Byron's knowledge of how to play the old-time tunes, but he wasn't too crazy about hearing lots of notes with swinging rhythm, the way Byron had learned from contest fiddlers in the Southwest. Bill said, "I don't want that jerkin' the bow. I want that long bow 'cause that's why I hired you."[19]

Monroe had rigid guidelines for the role of the rhythm guitar as well. He actually sat Roland down to instruct him on how to make it sound, even picking up the guitar himself and strumming some rhythm.[20] They worked through several songs in that manner as Monroe attempted to demonstrate his concept of bluegrass timing, which had a forward "lean." I witnessed Monroe do this with several guitar players when I was in the band, but when I heard him play, I thought it sounded a little bit sloppy. The important thing was the timing, however.

Roland stayed at Lamar Grier's house in Nashville for a couple of weeks. That's where he first met David Grier,[21] Lamar's son, who was around five years old at the time. Roland helped him learn how to play the guitar, and David was also influenced by Clarence White, whom he heard on some Kentucky Colonels tapes that his father had.[22] Now recognized all over the world as a flat-picking guitarist extraordinaire, David is a three-time winner of the Best Guitar Player of the Year award from the International Bluegrass Music Association (IBMA).[23] Back then, Nashville wasn't a bit like it is today. Roland said in a 2017 IBMA interview, "Nashville was just a small community. There were people like Jimmy Martin, Bill Monroe, Flatt and Scruggs, the Osborne Brothers, Jim and Jesse—and that was about it. So I got to know all those people."[24]

After that, Roland moved in with Byron Berline, who had a little apartment on Dickerson Road (north of downtown Nashville). A couple of months later, when Lamar left the band and went back to his home in Laurel, Maryland, Roland rented the house that Grier had been living in. In Roland's recollection, the first *Grand Ole Opry* show he performed with Monroe took place in late May 1967. He rode down to the Ryman Auditorium with Lamar because he didn't have a car yet. Byron drove in from his apartment on Dickerson Road. James Monroe was there too. All the songs they performed were ones they had been doing on the road, so Roland was pretty familiar with everything. The first tune they played was "Watermelon Hangin' on the Vine" (Bill's theme song), which required an opening run on the guitar. Roland was nervous, hoping he wouldn't screw up. He pulled it off just fine, though. Then Bill said, "Howdy, howdy, folks!

We've got a new guitar player with us from the state of Maine. What's your name, boy?"

"Roland."

"Roland White, from the state of Maine!"

Roland wasn't looking at the audience at all. He was kind of scared, looking at Bill and the band, and at James Monroe, who was standing closest to him. Often the Blue Grass Boys didn't seem to smile much while performing. They were so focused on doing their jobs as musicians that relating to audiences took second place, which was unfortunate, especially for Roland, whose natural stage demeanor had been much more relaxed before taking the job as a Blue Grass Boy. (I can certainly relate to that myself!)

The second number they played on the Opry was "Muleskinner Blues," which begins with a mandolin kickoff, followed by a G-run on the guitar. Roland pulled that one off perfectly too. Later Lamar told Roland, "You got the job because you could do the damn G-run. He's tried other guitar players and they couldn't do it." Clarence had been right: if you can do the G-run, you've got the job.

It was very hot in the Ryman Auditorium that night. There was no air-conditioning. People were all using little fans on sticks to try to keep cool. It was only May, but it was already sweltering and humid. The Blue Grass Boys were wearing suits, ties, and hats, so they were almost suf-focating from the heat. Despite the heat, Roland handled his job like an old hand. He didn't have any stage fright at all once the show got under way. The next song they performed was "Footprints in the Snow." Byron kicked it off on the fiddle and Bill sang it. The announcer, Hal Durham, chimed in then, thanking Bill before going to a commercial. The sponsor was Goo Goo Cluster candy bars, and Durham said, "And now here's Mr. Monroe. What do you think about those Goo Goo Clusters, Bill?"

Bill said, "Go get a Goo Goo, it's good."[25]

Goo Goo was a longtime sponsor of the *Grand Ole Opry*, but most people don't know about the origins of the confection. (Kristie had never even heard of Goo Goo Clusters until her first trip to Nashville, but she's never forgotten what they taste like.) "All of the ingredients that go into a Goo Goo Cluster are foods your taste buds remember: luscious cara-mel, smooth creamy marshmallow nougat, and fresh roasted peanuts all covered with a thick coating of real milk chocolate."[26]

Here is the story of how Goo Goo Clusters got their name:

The most popular myth is due to Goo Goo's longtime partnership with the *Grand Ole Opry*. To this day, many people think the partnership was the basis for the candy's name (GOO = *Grand Ole Opry*). However, the Opry was formed in 1925, 13 years after the candy was introduced. The marketing campaign—"Go get a Goo Goo, it's good!"—was such a success that many still identify one with the other.

The true tale of how the candy got it's [*sic*] name is that Howell Campbell was riding the streetcar to work one day and told his fellow passengers about this new candy he'd made. He mentioned that he was struggling to find a name for it, and a few passengers made suggestions, but nothing excited him. Eventually conversation shifted, and a school teacher inquired about Campbell's young son. Campbell told her that he'd just said his first words: "goo goo." The teacher exclaimed, "That's what you should call your candy—Goo Goo!" From there the first slogan was born: "Goo Goo! It's so good, people will ask for it from birth."[27]

Early on Sunday June 25, Bill Monroe and the Blue Grass Boys took off for Bean Blossom, Indiana, the site of the Brown County Jamboree Park. Bill had purchased the fifty-one acres in 1951 from Francis Rund and family and had been putting on country music shows there for many years. The grounds included a show barn (built by Rund in 1942–1943) and three tourist cabins (also built by Rund).[28] Bill's first bluegrass festival was already in progress. It had started on Saturday and was to continue through Sunday. It had been advertised in the *Brown County Democrat* as the "Big Bluegrass Celebration."[29]

When they arrived, Denzel Ragsdale (the cowboy sound man Bill employed, also known as "Silver Spur") explained to Bill that they were expecting a big crowd. Not everybody was going to fit inside the barn, so he was going to place some additional speakers outside. That was exactly what happened. Bill had mentioned the celebration many times on the *Grand Ole Opry*, talking it up, and there had been posters printed at Hatch Show Print in Nashville and displayed all around the area, as far as Indianapolis (about thirty-five miles north).[30]

The advertising worked well and the barn was packed for the show. There were just as many folks standing outside. Bill's brother Birch collected money at the gate from every car that came in, and there were *lots* of cars.[31] The celebration was an unqualified success, and Bill did very well financially that weekend. Roland remembers going to the back of the bus and seeing grocery sacks full of cash lying around unattended (something I also witnessed when I was a Blue Grass Boy). Bluegrass bands went in there when the festival was over to get paid in cash from the bags.

Bill and the Blue Grass Boys stayed overnight in a little hotel down the road from Bean Blossom. The next morning Bill took the boys back to the park. He had something he wanted to show them in the woods at the north end. There was nothing but trees and bushes growing up everywhere. Bill said to them, "Now, if you look down there, there's a stage." Roland couldn't see anything but trees, so he walked over to where Bill was pointing. Sure enough, there was a stage, but it was in a severe state of disrepair. The wood was black and decaying, and it was falling in on itself. It was probably there when Monroe bought the park.[32]

"So we went back there and looked at it," said Roland in a 1999 interview. "You couldn't even step on it, it was just a pile of rotted wood. It was a very small stage, too. I don't think there was a cover on it. If it had, it had fallen down also. There were saplings growing through it and everything. It was just covered—you couldn't even walk through there."[33]

"We used to put on shows down there," said Bill. The last time the performance platform had been used was in 1959 or 1960 for a show by Johnny Cash.[34] "Next year we're gonna come up here and we're gonna clear all this underbrush out, and we're gonna cut down a bunch of trees, and we're gonna build a great big new stage."

"What do you mean 'we'?" asked Roland.

"We—the Blue Grass Boys."

"Really?"[35]

That gave Roland a huge clue about working for Bill Monroe. He was going to be very demanding, expecting a lot more than just music out of his Blue Grass Boys. Monroe's band was distinctly different from the Kentucky Colonels, which had been comprised of equal members. Nobody got top billing over anybody else. In addition, Roland's brothers had both been in the group, so they knew each other, were very close, and felt relaxed performing together. Being in the Blue Grass Boys was a completely different ball game; each member was there to support Bill, and Bill expected a lot from them. He had one of the strongest work ethics anyone had ever seen.

A few things worked in Roland's favor: his army experience; the fact that he had been the one who bore most of the responsibility in the Kentucky Colonels band; and, perhaps most important, his supreme passion for playing music. Since bluegrass was his first love, playing with the "Father of Bluegrass" was going to be sufficiently awe-inspiring to help him take on the difficult and taxing job. He wasn't even playing his main instrument, but he was able to be close to the "master" and hear sounds that influenced his own mandolin playing for the rest of his life. All in all, it was a substantially worthwhile experience for him.

Byron Berline got drafted and left the band in September 1967. He had been a Blue Grass Boy for approximately six months. Roland was fortunate to have participated on several important and significant recordings with Byron. The recordings took place on August 23, 1967, shortly before Berline left.[36] The three tunes were "The Gold Rush," "Sally Goodin" (released on the 1970 album, *Bill Monroe and His Blue Grass Boys: Kentucky Bluegrass*[37]), and "Virginia Darlin'." "Sally Goodin" was Bill's personal favorite of all fiddle tunes; he even waited until he had the perfect fiddler before he recorded it. "Virginia Darlin'," written by Bill and reminiscent of the traditional tune "Red Apple Rag," was named after Virginia Stauffer, a friend of Bill's.[38] "Sally Goodin" and "Virginia Darlin'" were released in 1968 on a 45 rpm single (Decca 32404).

Roland remembers that on many of the shows, they played the old-time fiddle tune "Dusty Miller" for an extended period of time. He just about wore out his right arm playing rhythm guitar behind it. Monroe and Byron Berline would swap leads back and forth again and again on the tune while the rest of the band hung on for dear life. Many fiddlers claim that Bill played "Dusty Miller" faster than it was supposed to go. He had a forward tempo on it that could only be called relentless. He really put his own stamp on it! "Rawhide" was another challenge for Roland. It was very fast and Bill always wanted to keep on the front edge of the beat, which was very taxing for the guitar player.

After Byron left, he was replaced by Benny Williams,[39] who played fiddle in the band until the middle of March 1968. On March 23 Bill brought in

Kenny Baker, who had worked for Monroe earlier, in 1957–1958 and in 1962–1963. On this, his third stint, he would remain for sixteen years.[40] A coal miner from Jenkins, Kentucky, Baker had started out as a young man by playing the guitar. He had a distinctive right-hand finger style on that instrument. Though Kenny appreciated the music of one local fiddler, Marion Sumner, he really liked jazz. Glenn Miller and Tommy Dorsey were high up on his list. He wasn't truly motivated to learn the fiddle until he started hearing the music of Bob Wills, Stéphane Grappelli, and Django Reinhardt during his time in New Guinea during World War II. During the postwar years he worked in country bands around Jenkins, and in the 1950s he worked for country singer Don Gibson.[41] My personal experiences playing and recording with Kenny Baker and the Blue Grass Boys were among the most memorable of my entire life. His bow arm was the most flexible I ever saw, and the tone he got from the fiddle was unsurpassed.

The Blue Grass Boys at that time consisted of Roland on guitar, Kenny on fiddle, James Monroe on bass, and Vic Jordan on banjo. Vic had previously worked with Jimmy Martin, the "King of Bluegrass," twice: November-December 1964 and for eleven months during 1966–1967, replacing Bill Emerson (1938–2021). Between those periods, he worked with *Grand Ole Opry* members Wilma Lee and Stoney Cooper. He had participated on one recording session with Jimmy Martin, supplying banjo on "Living Like a Fool," "Union County," and "Uptown Blues."[42]

In May 1968 Doug Green finished college and went back to Nashville. By then, Arline and Roline had joined Roland, and they were living together in a duplex on Hilltop Lane, in the Inglewood neighborhood. Doug told me a little bit about those days: "Roland and I had stayed in touch and he was renting a duplex. . . . He said, 'The other half is open,' and so I moved in next door for [at least] a year. It was one of the best years of my life 'cause we jammed almost every night. We just played and played, and his wife at the time, Arline, was just a delightful woman and we just bonded as people."[43]

Roline, who was a small child at the time, was a favorite of Doug's. He still has a chipped tooth from when he was bouncing her on his knee. Her head came up and hit his chin and broke a piece off of one of his lower teeth.

Both Doug and Roland were doing some house-painting jobs during the day. Roland had to keep bringing in money to support his family, because

L-R: Kenny Baker, Bill Monroe, Roland White, and Vic Jordan performing at Sunset Park, West Grove, Pennsylvania. Photo by Artie Rose.

Bean Blossom, Indiana, Brown County Jamboree, 1968. Bill Monroe and the Blue Grass Boys performing at the second Bean Blossom Festival on the stage they helped build. L-R: Kenny Baker, Bill Monroe, Roland White, Vic Jordan, James Monroe. Photo by Doc Hamilton.

being a Blue Grass Boy didn't always pay the bills. Other jobs Roland had in Nashville included cleaning carpets and working at a gas station/store. Arline had a job as well, working at a hospital as a nurse's aide.

Music occupied every spare moment. There was a steady succession of other musicians who came over to the duplex to pick: "Alan Munde," said Doug Green, "an Oklahoman who was living in Nashville and working as Jimmy Martin's banjo player, was in and out, and of course Clarence came by once in a while . . . and we sang trios all the time. Roland taught me so much. He was just a great friend and a great mentor to me." Doug was going to graduate school at Vanderbilt University, with a major in literature at that time. (Today he talks about that: "See, I'm using my degree: I write literate songs now.")[44]

While on the road with the Father of Bluegrass, Roland found out about one of Bill's other great loves: baseball. Back in the 1940s, Monroe had traveled around with his own tent show, putting on exhibitions that were like old-time minstrel shows, carnivals, and circuses all combined.[45] He would challenge local baseball teams to matches with the Blue Grass Boys as a way to drum up interest in the shows. Years later, he always carried baseball equipment on the bus.

Roland tells this story that took place after Byron had left the band:

On one of the trips we made, in the fall of 1967, we were going to play at a little schoolhouse in North Carolina. Bill said, "I want us to play ball." He had four or five gloves up there, two baseball bats, and several baseballs. Bill grabbed all the stuff and carried it out. James [Monroe] was pitching and Bill was hitting, and I'd go out and chase the ball.

After a while, Bill said, "Roland, you're up. You ever play baseball?"

I said, "Yeah, I did in school."

I hit a couple of really nice ones, and then he said, "Vic [Jordan], you want to get up here and hit some?" Vic did and then James got up. Benny Williams, who had not yet been replaced by Kenny Baker, took his turn at bat too. Anyhow, Bill got back up to bat and hit a fly ball. James was pitching, and it went way over his head. Vic said, "I got it, I got it," and it him right in the head, knocking him flat on his back. Bill ran up to him and said, "You all right, boy?" Vic said yes, but he had a goose egg and he was glad he could cover it up with his hat when he was on stage.[46]

During Roland's time as a Blue Grass Boy, something historically interesting happened in Nashville on March 15, 1968: the Byrds performed on the *Grand Ole Opry*. They were the first rock band ever to do so. The group had traveled to Music City to record part of their famous *Sweetheart of the Rodeo* album.[47] The Nashville *Sweetheart* recordings took place March 9–15 at the Columbia recording studio in Nashville. (The rest of the album was recorded later, April 4–May 27, 1968, at the Columbia recording studio in Hollywood, California. Clarence White contributed some guitar work on those later sessions, and shortly after that, he joined the group, replacing Gram Parsons.)

Needless to say, the Opry audience and staff weren't exactly cordial to the Byrds. They didn't like the idea of hippies performing on their radio show. The group was considered by some to be pretenders who were making fun of country music.[48] Chris Hillman, bass player for the group, had this to say: "To let you know how hostile the audience was, they were shouting things like 'Tweet tweet' and 'Cut your hair!'" Road manager and touring percussionist Jimmi Seiter recalled, "Roland White was backstage to support us, and Lloyd Green came to make sure the other musicians treated us decently.[49] Skeeter Davis also liked the Byrds. Roger McGuinn (guitar and banjo player for the Byrds) said, "Skeeter Davis took us under her wing, and she was very kind."[50]

The Byrds were scheduled to perform Merle Haggard's "Sing Me Back Home" and "Life in Prison." They did the first song to an unresponsive crowd and some booing was heard. When it was time for the second song, Gram Parsons broke the rules and did an original song, "Hickory Wind," saying, "This is for my grandma." The acting emcee, Tompall Glaser, exploded with fury. Seiter said, "You could see Glaser turn red from the neck up." (The Opry ran on a tight schedule, and each segment was timed to allow for commercials and other acts.) Ironically, according to author David Meyer, the Byrds' performance is now ranked at number thirty-three among "The Eighty Greatest Moments in Opry History."[51] I asked Roland if he remembered that performance. He did, and then he joked, "They're all hippies there now."

Roland told me another Opry story, about the song "Midnight on the Stormy Deep": "Bill told me to learn the song, so I did. We got on stage and I could not remember the words. It was on the Opry. It was terrible." Roland was supposed to be singing lead, with Bill singing tenor harmony.

When the second verse came up, Roland drew a blank. Bill just ended the song, going chop-chop-chop-chop-choppity-chop-chop on his mandolin. "Anyway, as we walked backstage, I said, 'Sorry, Bill, I learned the song but I just couldn't remember the words.' Bill said, 'Oh, you never learned it, you never learned it.' I studied up on it and practiced on it some more, and a couple of weeks later on the Opry I said, 'Well, I've got the song now, Bill.' He said, 'No, you don't; no, you don't.' So we never did sing it again."[52] No second chances for the Blue Grass Boys.

Roland has endless stories about traveling on the road with Monroe. One was about a time when the Bluegrass Special pulled into a truck stop. Roland, who was going to get some coffee, asked Bill if he would like some as well.

"No, I'll get it," said Bill.

So Roland left the bus, got his coffee, and then went into the restroom. There he saw Bill, lighting a cigarette, coughing a little bit as he took his first drag. Roland quickly turned around and shut the door, because Bill hadn't seen him. He was really surprised because everybody thought Bill didn't smoke. When Roland got back on the bus, he said to Virginia Stauffer, who was traveling with them, "Virginia, I saw Bill in the men's room smoking a cigarette."

She laughed. Roland asked, "Does he smoke?"

She said, "No, he doesn't, but once in a while I'll find a cigarette missing out of my pack. He says it calms his nerves."[53] Bill must have been one of the few people who could smoke an occasional cigarette and not become addicted.

Roland was not one of those people.[54] He had quit smoking many times only to start up again a few months later. He told me that first cigarette "just like made me numb all the way down my legs and hands and everything."

> It relaxes you. I remember the first time I ever lit a cigarette up in Maine. This friend of mine—he was about two years older than I was—I was fourteen. . . . We had these trees we used to climb and look out over the highway. . . . I had my favorite tree. Anyway, I came back down and he was there smoking a cigarette. He said, "Here, try some." So I did. I coughed. He said, "Try it again." I did, and I coughed it back out, and I got so numb I almost fell down.[55]

Good thing Roland wasn't sitting high up on a tree limb when he took his first drag.

Roland told me another funny story about Bill:

One day we stopped for breakfast. Bill ordered ham and biscuits. He had some left over, so he carried them out to the bus in a paper bag, placing them on a luggage rack. He was going to feed them to his dogs when he got home. A lady came on the bus. [Bill had lots of female admirers.] She smelled those biscuits, discovered the bags, and opened them. She asked Bill, "What are you doing with these ham and biscuits?"

"I'm gonna feed 'em to my dogs," he said.

"Well, they'll be spoiled by the time you get them home."

Bill said, "You can't hurt ham."[56]

Roland learned to drive Bill's bus. One night, after he had been behind the wheel for a while, he asked Bill, "Don't you ever get your mandolin out and play some?"

"Well, if you get it out for me," answered Bill.

"What do you mean? Pull the bus over and go under your bunk and get your mandolin for you?"

"Uh-huh."

So Roland pulled over and went to the rear of the bus, getting Bill's case out from under the bed. He brought it up front and set it on the seat behind him, next to Bill. Then he started driving again, and after a while he heard the click-click of Bill's mandolin case being opened. Bill started playing his mandolin very lightly.

That was the first of many times that Roland listened to Bill pick while they traveled down the road. He learned a lot from those sessions. Monroe would play tunes on the bus that he never did anywhere else. Old fiddle tunes and original compositions flowed from his fingers, and Roland soaked it all in, taking note of Bill's timing, phrasing, and dynamics. He would request a break to a song, such as "Live and Let Live," and Bill was happy to run through it for him several times, improvising and doing different things with the melody.

He would play a number that Roland had never heard and ask, "You know that tune, Roland?"

"No, I don't."

"I learned that from my uncle Pen." Bill Monroe's uncle was a good fiddler who knew lots of Kentucky tunes. Bill showed many of them to Kenny Baker, who later recorded several songs on Monroe's *Uncle Pen* album,[57] a wonderful classic that Roland later wished he could have been a part of.[58]

Another night while Roland was driving the bus, he was listening to Monroe working on a little variation of "Soldier's Joy," tinkering around with certain licks. Bill asked Roland what he thought it sounded like. Roland tried to figure out what Bill wanted him to say, so he tried things like "It sounds like 'Soldier's Joy' to me" and "It sounds like a fiddle tune." He couldn't seem to give Monroe the answer he was looking for. Finally Bill scowled and said, "It sounds like bagpipes." Then he put his mandolin away and wouldn't play anymore.[59]

Bill let Roland try his mandolin once in a while, but it was hard to play because the strings were so high up off the fingerboard. Later Roland talked Monroe into resetting the neck, which had pulled away from the body slightly, and it was much better after that. I tried my hand with that mandolin a little bit too in the mid-1970s when I was with Bill, and I thought the strings were way too high. Some folks might argue that the extreme height of the strings was the reason why the mandolin always sounded so good and had so much volume. That's disputable, but Bill was used to it. He had strong hands from doing lots of farmwork. He always fussed with the bridge too, trying to get it placed in just the right spot.

Monroe taught Roland how to hold the pick when playing the mandolin. "Monroe actually sat down with me and positioned my hand the right way." Roland totally rebuilt his right-hand technique after working with Bill Monroe. Early on, he anchored his fingers on the top of the mandolin. After working with Monroe, he taught himself to play with a free right hand. He was more self-confident about his mandolin playing after that.[60]

Bill's private nighttime concerts on the bus were some of the most memorable moments of Roland's days as a Blue Grass Boy. Even now, whenever Roland plays or records a Monroe tune, he'll emulate Bill's mandolin style very closely on at least part of it while adding his own interpretation to the rest of the piece. Sometimes he plays the "galloping horse" rhythm that Bill occasionally threw in. Roland learned those stylistic elements while he drove the bus, listening to the Master of Bluegrass playing just for him.

Roland participated on two other recording sessions with Bill. One had twin fiddles played by Benny Williams and Vassar Clements.[61] The session took place on November 9, 1967.[62] The selections were "Train 45 (Headin' South)," "Kentucky Mandolin," and "Is the Blue Moon Still Shining?" The third session, which took place on November 14, 1967,[63] had Kenny Baker on fiddle, and the numbers they recorded were "I Want to Go with You," "Walls of Time," and "Crossing the Cumberlands."

"Crossing the Cumberlands" was a slow, haunting banjo tune that Monroe composed for Lamar Grier. Unfortunately, by the time it was recorded, Lamar was no longer in the band and Vic Jordan played the banjo on it. Vic remembered hearing Lamar play the tune. It was tailored to Lamar's style and therefore sounded best when Lamar played it. (Vic did a great job too.) A groundbreaking tune, "Crossing the Cumberlands" didn't adhere to the common banjo stereotypes: it wasn't fast, it was in a minor key, and it had actual melody incorporated into it instead of just finger rolls over chords. Bill recalled how "Crossing the Cumberlands" came about: "We had broken down in our bus up there on the Cumberland mountains and while I was sitting there I could picture the pioneers heading west and how slow they was going and what kind of trouble they was having. 'Crossing The Cumberlands' has sort of a mournful touch to it—kind of Indian tones to it."[64] Roland's guitar backup on the recording was in keeping with the spare nature of the melody, and he put in several distinctive bass runs that conveyed a clear sense of where the chords were going, which were all-important to the atmosphere of the tune. His guitar was featured quite prominently in the final mix.

Roland and Vic truly enjoyed working together. Musically, they appreciated each other's playing styles, and a synergy developed between the two instrumentalists. Their friendship, however, was further cemented by countless other memorable experiences. Playing bluegrass music for real is an out-of-the ordinary lifestyle, to say the least, and a unique bond exists between those who have lived it.

Kristie and I caught a fascinating glimpse of that rare bond when we paid a visit with Roland to Vic Jordan's home in Nashville in March 2015. Vic and his wife, Jean, were down-to-earth, friendly, and hospitable. After they served us coffee, we settled down to a three-hour conversation about the old days, when Roland and Vic played together. I'm glad we had the chance to have that conversation, because Vic passed away a little over a year later (August 26, 2016). I'm told he had been seriously ill, but Kristie and I never noticed it, as he seemed quite energetic and talkative. He passed along some interesting historical information, not only about Roland and himself but also about banjo players he had known and admired.

As I sat on the couch in Vic's living room, listening to his recollections, I noticed a framed eight-by-ten glossy color print on the end table to my left: it was the cover photo for the album *Big and Country Instrumentals* by Jimmy Martin and the Sunny Mountain Boys. It showed the famous picture of Jimmy's band at the time (1967), standing behind a rail fence. In the foreground, their instruments were leaning up against an old-fashioned plow. The band members were wearing black pants and vests, with white shirts and yellow hats. On the left stood Vic Jordan next to Vernon Derrick, the mandolin and fiddle player. Next to Vernon stood the "King of Bluegrass," Jimmy Martin, and the bass player Bill Yates next to him. Jimmy was flamboyantly dressed, as always, in a richly decorated sports jacket and a hat ornamented with a brocade-like pattern. I was impressed because I had grown up staring at that album cover while listening to the music, trying to learn from it. I never dreamed I would one day be sitting and talking with one of Jimmy Martin's Sunny Mountain Boys.

The conversation between Vic and Roland started with their memories of a 1968 trip to the Brown County Jamboree with the Blue Grass Boys. It happened on April 23, Roland's birthday. They didn't go there to play music; Bill had other plans for the Blue Grass Boys. He had brought a truck up, and he had axes and a two-man crosscut saw. The Blue Grass Boys were going to be put to work clearing trees and helping to construct a stage for Bill's second bluegrass festival, which was to take place June 21–23, 1968.

"The first time we got up there, he broke out that crosscut saw," said Vic. "And he said 'Okay, who's gonna get on this with me now?' I felt young and about half scrappy, and I said, 'I'll get on there with you, boss.' He about pulled me out of my socks and shoes."[65]

Bill's intention was to use the crosscut saw and double-bitted axes for cutting trees to build the stage.[66] After a while they persuaded Bill to get a chainsaw. Kenny and James Monroe ran it; Bill wouldn't let Roland or Vic use it. The scene is further described in Tom Ewing's book *Bill Monroe: The Life and Music of the Bluegrass Man*:

"It took us forever to talk him [Monroe] into getting a chain saw," Jordan said. After they did, [Kenny] Baker "came close to taking a leg off with it, while up in a tree, trimming branches" (inflicting a nasty gash). Then the logs went to a local sawmill, to provide inexpensive lumber for the stage. As White recalled, "We loaded those trees onto this truck—I can't even remember how we did that. Bill had one truck, and I mean, those things weren't light. And we did it with ropes and all that kind of stuff, you know? There weren't any mules up there—we were the mules! And the hardest part was when you got back with the planks, inch thick planks, green, heavy stuff, and we had to load 'em on our shoulders, and they were every bit of ten feet long. And I remember . . . shouldering the first one off the truck, I almost fell to the ground. 'Well,' I told myself, 'I'm gonna do this!'"

The planks had to be carried about a quarter of a mile, across a steep dip in the path that's still there (then "a swamp," White said), to an area where a temporary stage had once stood and the new one was built. "Bill wanted it put back in the same place."

They built the new stage—thirty feet wide with two tune-up rooms behind it and covered with a tin roof about fifteen feet overhead—without a drawing or plan of any kind. "Bill never wrote anything down," according to White. "It was all in his head. Him and Kenny kind of worked that out—and what they told me to do, I did."[67]

One of the biggest trees had been made into a large beam to go across the top of the stage. It took everybody to get it off the truck. Bill, in a show of strength, grabbed it and put it over his shoulder, walking it to the front of the stage before throwing it to the ground. Roland could hardly believe it!

After they were there approximately one week, Bill and the Blue Grass Boys went up to Indianapolis to play at the Blue Flame Club on April 26 and 27.[68] Aside from that, plus one performance on the Opry in Nashville, they remained at the park, working every day.

The Blue Grass Boys fixed up the three run-down old cabins built in the 1940s by the park's original owner, Francis Rund, making them at least good enough to be able to sleep in. Bill purchased some old, used metal beds. Roland remembers them as being almost like army cots. "He must have got them from the Salvation Army," said Vic. "There was no bathroom. If you had to go, you just went out in the woods or one of the outhouses or something—or up to the barn." One of the cabins had ground squirrels living inside. Only one cabin had electricity and running water. That was where Bill and Virginia Stauffer stayed. (She traveled everywhere with the Blue Grass Boys while Roland was in the band.) That cabin also had a stove and refrigerator, and Virginia would fix them meals. Vic said, "She would make us breakfast in the morning, lunch at midday, and supper in the evening."[69]

Bill and Virginia's cabin was bigger than the others; it had a kitchen and an eating area. "We went in there to eat," said Roland. "There was a table set up. Virginia would fix potatoes, gravy, roast; sometimes we had pork chops."[70]

"We'd take showers up at the barn, remember that?" Vic asked Roland.

"Oh, yeah, man. I got so sick I thought I was gonna die. No hot water."

"Have you ever been in the old barn?" Vic asked me.

"Yes."

"All right, you know there was a concrete floor. Well, back by the concession stand the concrete sloped down, and there was a sliding door where they could back up a pickup truck and unload concessions and stuff."

"One hot dog at a time," joked Roland. He was referring to Birch Monroe's management of the food stand. Birch was Bill's brother, and his fame as a skinflint was well known—he was tight as the bark on a tree. He hated having to throw away leftover food after an event, so he bought only the bare minimum at any one time.

> We got a garden hose and strung it over a rafter right where that slope was so the water would run out. We found a wooden Coca-Cola crate that we could stand on while we were taking a shower. And we took turns laughing at each other, 'cause it got funny. I mean you'd duck under there and kind of get wet, then you'd stay out long enough to soap up, and then you'd jump back in there and try and rinse off as quick as you could. That was the only way we had to take a bath.

Vic also told a story about a dead tree on the grounds that had some honeybees in it. Bill and Kenny decided they wanted some of the honey, so they cut down the tree and ran away as fast as they could. After the bees had cleared out, they went back and collected the honey in some jars. It was so delicious, they had it practically every meal. They would pull the honeycomb out of the jars and let the honey drip on their bread. Nothing ever tasted better!

Roland went up to the barn one day to get something for Bill, and brother Birch came driving up in his car. Rolling down the window, Mr. Penny Pincher said, "Roland, come here."

"What do you want, Birch?"

"Just come here."

Roland walked over to the car and Birch got out and went around to the back to open up the trunk. Inside was a large wooden nail keg full of nails.

"Look what I've got here," said Birch.

"They look like nails." They were all sizes, rusty, and bent. Birch had been saving them up for a long time.

"I'm gonna take these out," Birch said, "and you get over there on that rock, and you straighten them out."

Roland said to him, "Hey, my dad was a carpenter, and nails like that—you know what he did with them? He just threw 'em away."

Bill came walking up at that point, and Roland turned to him, saying, "Bill, look here. He wants me to straighten out all these nails."

Bill said, "Birch, you go get rid of those things. Get out of here with that."

But Birch wasn't that easy to convince about recycling bent nails. Vic Jordan recalled Birch working on the new stage they were building, carrying a Maxwell House coffee can full of bent nails that he straightened out himself before using them to fasten boards in place.

One time brother Birch sent Roland out to distribute posters within about a thirty-mile radius. It took all day. Birch told Roland the names of certain stores whose managers would allow them to put up the posters, and he wrote them down on a list. Birch told him the posters were in his car, and he gave him the keys. Roland started it up and drove it to the park entrance. That was when he noticed that the gas tank was on empty. He drove the car back into the park and found Bill.

"Bill," said Roland, "this car is on empty and Birch wants me to go around and put up these posters."

Bill said, "Dammit. you know that man would drive to California and buy one gallon of gas at a time."

Birch liked ordering the Blue Grass Boys around. One time Roland was standing outside the barn when brother Birch came up to him and told him to whitewash it. Bill had already said they weren't going to paint it; they were going to leave it alone until the next year. Roland didn't know what to do, and Bill came running up to both of them, saying that the barn was just fine and didn't need whitewashing. Monroe started arguing with Birch, and for a few days afterward Birch didn't seem to like Roland very much.

As May passed and June arrived, they started wondering about whether they were going to get paid. "We asked Bill one time," said Vic, "Are we gonna get paid for this? We've got families.' His attitude was like 'Well, this is a labor of love—you're a Blue Grass Boy.' He didn't actually say that, but that's how he thought about it."

A bunch of posts were to be set into the ground in front of the stage to nail planks on for seating. As the festival date approached, Roland was still digging holes with a manual posthole digger. About ten rows were sunk into the ground, and Calvin Robins, a good friend of Bill's who was helping out around the grounds, told him, "Roland, I don't think you're gonna get this done in time."

"Well, if we had another posthole digger, someone else could help."

Roland ended up setting all the posts. He put the last one in on the first day of the festival, and the other band members were behind him, nailing planks in place. Festival attendees who had arrived early were watching them. It was probably entertaining to watch the Blue Grass Boys working so hard. It was all part of the show!

A square dance was held on the first night of the festival, with Monroe and the Blue Grass Boys providing the music. After a while Bill and Roland joined the dancers. "I could never square dance," said Roland in an interview. "They'd go left, I'd go right." He would go the wrong way and run into Bill, who would turn around and smack him on the rear end and get him going the right way.[71]

The festival was a success, and when it was over Bill called Roland to him and said, "Roland, I want to settle up with you." He paid Roland the whopping sum of $150 for working half of April, all of May, and most of June. Roland was stunned. He didn't know what the other guys got, but he didn't give a damn. He just told himself, "Well, it's time to look for another job." He would rather have stayed in Nashville and pumped gas than go through that again.[72]

Some people believe Monroe took advantage of the awe and respect musicians had for him. Most pickers never haggled over money; they just took what they were paid—and it wasn't much. Roland found out later that Bill wasn't above haggling over money when it came to how much *he* was getting, as we'll see.

In the fall of 1968, they traveled to Carlton Haney's bluegrass festival in Warrenton, Virginia, to perform. As they went up Highway 11 (Interstate 81 wasn't fully completed yet), Bill got out at truck stops every couple of hours or so to use a pay phone. Roland overheard the conversation one time as he walked by. Bill was talking to Carlton Haney, haggling with him, saying, "We ain't leavin' Nashville until you guarantee me more money." There was a moment of silence while Bill listened to Carlton on the other end of the line, and then he said, "No. No, I'm not comin'. I want more money. You'll have me playin' with everyone there at the festival. You'll work me to death. I'll spend hours and hours up there and all you're gonna pay me is five hundred dollars? I ain't a-gonna do it."

He made three or four of these calls as they drove up the highway, and finally Roland heard him talking on another pay phone at a truck stop restaurant, saying, "Okay, that'll be fine." The amount Bill received for playing the festival remains a mystery, but he obviously didn't have a contract, so haggling was his way of upping the price, even though they were already on their way to the festival. The festival was packed, and of course Bill Monroe was the main attraction, so he should have gotten much more than five hundred dollars. Things were cheaper back in those days—including diesel fuel—but that amount was ridiculous. (Carlton Haney did indeed work Monroe a lot at his festival. Monroe loved it, however. Roland said, "He enjoyed every bit of it—he was the center of attention.")[73]

During Roland's time with Monroe, he and the other Blue Grass Boys got paid twenty-five dollars a day on the days they actually performed and nothing on travel days. Monroe's money concerns were most likely the result of earlier years when he got paid hardly anything. My friend Mark Kuykendall, a veteran of both Bill Monroe's and Jimmy Martin's bands, has an old datebook of Monroe's from 1956 in which Bill recorded the amounts of money taken in at various shows. One entry lists three performances in a row in Maryland. The first day, they took in $49.00, the next day $189.00, and the third day $47.82. One string of shows in Florida netted $139.00, $46.15, $111.00, and $84.00. Often the band didn't get paid until later; Bill would make it up to them. The booking agent—listed only as "D. B." in the datebook—also got a percentage.

That fall, right after Thanksgiving, Roland went to WSM, located at Nob Hill, just southwest of the Nashville city limits on White Bridge Road. That was where Lester Flatt and Earl Scruggs were filming their TV shows. The half-hour program, sponsored by Martha White Foods, aired weekly and was syndicated to local stations across the South. They often taped a month's worth of shows on one day. Roland met Lester at WSM before their show early one morning, just about daylight.

Lester, getting out of his car, said, "What brings you out this early?"

"Well, I came to visit; is that okay? And I wanted to ask you something."

"Sure," said Lester, opening his car trunk and getting out his hat, clothes bag, and guitar.

"Let me carry something." Lester handed his guitar to Roland. They went inside to the dressing room. The coffee pot was already plugged in, so they poured themselves a cup each. Roland then said to Lester, "I've turned in my notice to Bill Monroe and I was wondering—would you and Earl ever consider using a mandolin player in your band again?" (Up until the early 1960s, Curly Seckler had been the mandolin player with Flatt and Scruggs's band. When Roland asked about the job in 1968, the Foggy Mountain Boys had been without a mandolin player for nearly six years.) Roland continued, "I'm going to stay with Monroe till the holidays unless he finds another guitar player."

Lester took a couple of sips of coffee and thought about it for a while. Then he replied, "Well, I don't know, Roland. I'm gonna tell you something, but you keep it up here [pointing to his head], and don't you tell anybody: after the first of the year, there's gonna be some big changes made in this band."

"Oh, really?"

"Yeah, and that's all I'm gonna tell ya."[74]

Roland doesn't know why Lester trusted him; perhaps it was because he liked him. At any rate, Roland stayed around and watched a taping of the Flatt and Scruggs *Martha White Biscuit Time* before leaving. Later he would be glad he had talked to Lester that day.

Shortly after Roland's encounter with Flatt, Bill and the Blue Grass Boys traveled to Watermelon Park in Berryville, Virginia, to play at Carlton Haney's fourth Labor Day weekend festival. In a motel room in Winchester, Virginia (near the festival), Roland and Vic helped Kenny Baker cut his first solo fiddle album, *Portrait of a Bluegrass Fiddler*.[75] Also present at the recording session were Del McCoury on guitar and Doug Green on bass.[76] "He'd been talking about some of the tunes he was going to do, and I'm sure I heard him playing them, but I don't remember getting together any time and rehearsing any of them," said Roland. "I might have backed some of the tunes up on guitar somewhere, sometime, so I knew the chords"[77] (which he played on the mandolin during the recording session). The project was completed in just a few hours, with the musicians running over each tune once or twice before recording it. It turned out to be an all-time classic. (I remember when that record came out. I obsessively worked on a banjo version of track number one, "First Day in Town," a powerful tune in G minor.)

Roland stayed on a few months longer as a Blue Grass Boy. The month of December 1968 was pretty slow for the group; they only played the Opry and didn't do much else. At one of those Opry shows, Bill said to Roland, "We're goin' to Europe in January. Can you stay on? I don't have time to train another guitar player."

Roland thought, *Train a guitar player?* He didn't train anybody. He recalled Clarence's words: 'All you need to know is the damn G-run.'

He said to Bill, "Really, you're sure? You can't find anybody?"

"I haven't been able to yet."

"Let me talk to Arline and see what she thinks."

Later, when Roland mentioned it to his wife, she told him, "Well, he's working." Roland called Bill's office and talked to Carolyn (who was Bill's secretary and first wife). He asked her, "Where are we going in Europe?"

"Well, you're going to Italy first, then Germany. Then you're coming back."

"We're not going to England?"

"No, not this time."

"Well, you tell Bill I'll be there. When do we leave?"

Carolyn gave him the particulars. When it came time to leave (February 1969), they climbed aboard the Bluegrass Special and took it up the East

Coast to Madison, New Jersey, to the home of Tex and Peggy Logan.[78] Tex and Bill were good friends. They spent the night there, and the next day Tex called up a couple of his friends, who brought over two station wagons and a car. They took them to the Boston airport, where they boarded a plane to Italy. They worried about their instruments the whole way, because the airline wouldn't let them carry them in the passenger cabin. They had packed underwear around the instruments inside the cases to help protect them. After landing in Rome, they retrieved their instruments and were thrilled to see they hadn't been damaged.

They went first to Naples, and the Blue Grass Boys (minus Bill) decided to rent a car. Vic drove because he was somewhat familiar with the town. When he was a child, his stepfather had been in the navy, and they had lived in Naples for a year and a half. He drove them past the house where he had lived. People drove very aggressively in Naples; they used their horns and their gas pedals but seldom their brakes. At intersections it was every driver for themself—no right-of-way.

They stopped at a restaurant not far from Vic's former home. Inside was a roving violinist serenading the customers. After the Blue Grass Boys were finished eating their spaghetti, the musician came by their table. The boys all pointed to Kenny Baker, saying, "He's a fiddler." So the violinist started playing to Kenny, and the rest of them got up from the table. Kenny, who was too polite to walk out on the musician, got stuck with leaving the tip.[79]

They returned to Rome to catch a flight to Germany. At the airport Bill was hungry. He said to Vic, "You used to live here. You can talk to these people."

Vic said, "Bill, I was only thirteen years old. I didn't learn that much Italian."

"Well, come on, you come with me now. You can tell 'em what I want."

So they went to the restaurant at the airport, and Vic read some of the menu items to Bill.

"Lasagna sounds good," said Bill.

When they brought out the lasagna, it was green pasta.

"Now, what is that now? I'm not gonna eat none of that, uh-uh," said Bill. "No, sir, I ain't eatin' that. You tell them to take that back and bring me somethin' I can eat."

So they sent it back and ordered spaghetti.[80]

They went on to Germany. They had a driver with a Mercedes-Benz, which Roland and Bill rode in, while the rest of the band rode in a van because they wanted to drink beer without Bill seeing them. At one point they passed by the post where Roland had been stationed in Mannheim. He really wanted to go in there and look around, but there wasn't time.

They stopped at a buffet on the autobahn. It had typical German food: sausage, sauerkraut, bratwurst, and other local dishes. Going through the line, Kenny Baker pointed out items that he wanted. At one point he said, in a big loud voice, "I believe I'll have some of that there kraut."

"Mr. Baker, Mr. Baker, please," said their driver, "it's *sauer*kraut—don't say 'kraut.'"[81]

One night they stayed at a little hotel, and Roland shared a room with Bill. In the morning, Bill asked Roland to fetch them both some coffee. Roland asked for some at the hotel desk, and the clerk said he would bring it up to their room. When he arrived with the coffee, it was in tiny cups and extremely strong—black as ink. Bill came out of the bathroom and asked, "Where's the coffee?"

"Right there," said Roland, pointing to the tray with the tiny cups.

"What? That ain't much coffee."

"Well, it's pretty strong, Bill."

Bill put a little sugar in the cup of coffee, and took a little sip. Then he said, "I can't drink that."

Since Roland had been stationed in Germany, he knew what to do. He went back to the hotel desk and asked, "Could I have a cup of American coffee?"

"Yes," said the clerk. He brought up a large mug. It was strong but not as strong as the coffee in the tiny cups.[82]

They played at military bases in Germany: officers clubs and enlisted personnel venues. The servicemen liked hearing the American music; bluegrass made them feel like they were back at home.

After they returned from their European tour, they went back to Tex Logan's house, where they spent the night once again. The next morning Roland asked Peggy Logan if he could use the phone to make a collect call home. She said, "Don't call collect."

"That's all right."

"No, don't you call collect—I'll know about it. Go upstairs in our bedroom, where it's quiet. There's a phone up there."

When Roland called home, Arline asked, "How was the trip?"

"Well, fine."

"Where are you?"

"I'm at Tex Logan's house. We just got back yesterday afternoon."

"Lester called," Arline said.

"Really? What's going on?"

"Lester and Earl broke up."

He dropped the phone in total surprise, thinking, 'There's been a Flatt and Scruggs my whole life—they can't do that!'[83]

"What?" he asked when he had picked up the phone again.

"Yeah, they broke up."

"Oh, that's not gonna last long.'

"Oh, yes, it is," she said. "Lester left the band. Don't call him now—he's not going to be doing anything for the next two or three months. When you get home, you call him."

Roland found out later from Lance LeRoy (a talent agent who managed the careers of many bluegrass artists), that Lester had left the band one night at the *Grand Ole Opry*, Saturday, February 22.[84] He had played the first show with the band and then informed the Opry management that he would not be doing the 10:30 show. The band had to perform without him.

The Blue Grass Boys went back to Nashville, stopping on the way to do appearances in Roanoke, Virginia, and Washington, D.C. When he got home, Roland called up Lester on the phone. Flatt was still up in Sparta, Tennessee, which was his hometown (he hadn't yet moved to Nashville).

Lester told him, "'Yeah, what I did was, I left the band, then I hired the boys back and they're gonna stay with me. Louise wants Earl to start a new band with his sons.'"[85]

Louise, Earl's wife, had been Flatt and Scruggs's business and booking manager since the mid-1950s. Earl's new band turned out to be the Earl Scruggs Revue, featuring Gary, Randy, and Steve Scruggs. Highly successful, the Earl Scruggs Revue incorporated rock influences with the bluegrass genre. In time they appeared with many of the top singing stars of the day, including Bob Dylan, the Byrds, and Linda Ronstadt. This later led to Earl's inclusion in the Nitty Gritty Dirt Band's groundbreaking album, *Will the Circle Be Unbroken* (on which he played nearly half of the tracks).[86]

"We're not gonna do anything for a couple of months, because there's a lot of legal stuff to go through," Lester told Roland. "We'll be gettin' together at Uncle Josh's house sometime—then we'll give you a call. If the old man's [Bill Monroe] got any work, just go ahead and do it. You gave your notice. He hasn't found anybody, has he?"

"No, he hasn't."

So Roland continued to be a Blue Grass Boy for a couple more months, and Bill never asked him what he was going to do. Roland kept quiet about his plans to join Lester Flatt.

In late February, Vic and Roland went up to Indiana with Bill to purchase another bus. They took Dan Long, a diesel mechanic, with them to help get it started, as the bus had to be pulled by a truck with a chain to pop the clutch in order to get it going. After they brought the bus back to Nashville, Roland got a call from Uncle Josh, who lived not too far from Roland's house in Madison, Tennessee. Josh told him, "We're getting together tomorrow at my house with Lester, Paul, Jake, and me. You want to come on by? We'll play a few tunes and see how it's gonna work out."

Fiddler Paul Warren (1918–1978) was influenced by fellow Tennessean Fiddlin' Arthur Smith. Warren had played with the famous country duo Johnny and Jack and appeared on several of Kitty Wells's major recordings, including "Release Me" and "It Wasn't God Who Made Honky Tonk Angels." He joined Flatt and Scruggs in 1954, replacing Benny Martin. He can be heard on all of the Flatt and Scruggs recordings from 1954 until 1969. After the breakup with Scruggs, Warren stayed with Lester Flatt until 1977.[87] He was inducted into the IBMA Hall of Fame in 2013.

Bass player English P. "Jake" Tullock (1922–1988) was a mainstay in Flatt and Scruggs's Foggy Mountain Boys group. He joined the band in 1954, left for a while, and rejoined permanently in 1958, staying with Lester after the breakup with Earl Scruggs until he retired in 1971. Besides playing bass, he sang harmony and was a comic. His stage nickname was "Cousin Jake."[88] Tullock was inducted into the IBMA Hall of Fame in 2018.

Roland agreed to meet Lester's band the next day. He didn't think to ask him who was going to play the banjo. He pulled up to Josh's house the next afternoon, and Vic Jordan pulled up behind him. Stepping out of his car, Roland said to Vic, "What're you doing here?"

"I think I've got a job. What're you doing here?"

"Well, I think I've got a job too."

Vic had kept his plans secret, just like Roland. Josh Graves had also called Vic, saying, "I told Lester about you and he wants to know if you'd like to come and audition."

On the way to the front door, Roland told Vic, "Boy, the old man's really gonna be mad at us! He won't speak to us. He'll treat us just like he does Lester." Roland was referring to the fact that Bill and Lester hadn't been on speaking terms for a long time—ever since Flatt had left the Blue Grass Boys in 1948, joining up with Earl Scruggs, who had also left Monroe. The two had formed their own band, the Foggy Mountain Boys. That band subsequently became very successful and more famous than Bill Monroe and the Blue Grass Boys. That was due mostly to the TV exposure they gained from the Martha White TV show, as well as the soundtrack they provided for *The Beverly Hillbillies* television sitcom (along with occasional appearances on the show). Large audiences would show up for Flatt and Scruggs performances. As a result, they commanded much higher fees than Bill Monroe was getting. This generated some ill feelings between Bill and Lester. For example, they would pass each other at the *Grand Ole Opry* and not even look at each other. Roland and Vic were right to think Bill might give them the cold shoulder too. They were about to commit the unpardonable sin of going with Lester Flatt. It was like defecting to the enemy.

They went into Josh's house and played several tunes with Lester and the others. The music felt right; the players worked together as a team, and their styles all fit well with Lester's traditional concept and approach. When the audition was finished, Lester didn't mince words. "Well, boys," he told Roland and Vic, "we're gonna be leavin' in a couple of weeks. I'll let you know the dates and stuff. You're hired."

Roland's bluegrass journey was about to take a new and exciting turn. He learned immediately that working for Lester Flatt had one distinct advantage over working for Bill Monroe: a steady paycheck. Lester put his band on salary right away. "That was the first time I ever had a guaranteed weekly income—with Lester Flatt," said Roland in a 2017 IBMA interview.[89] The money came in whether they worked or not. "But I tell you what, we *worked*."

6

The Nashville Grass

Lester Flatt's band got its name from a write-in "name-the-band" contest that was held at the *Grand Ole Opry*. The idea for the contest was announced in January 1970, and the winner would receive a prize of five hundred dollars.[1] People wrote in with their name suggestions. Lester received twenty thousand pieces of mail, according to *Billboard* magazine.[2] Judges included Martha White Foods' chairman of the board, Cohen T. Williams, *Grand Ole Opry* manager Bud Wendell, and singer Porter Wagoner.[3] When a decision was reached, the winning name, the Nashville Grass, was announced by Williams in April on the Porter Wagoner portion of the Opry.[4] Lester liked the name right away, so he was happy to use it. One person who might not have been too happy with the choice was Danny Davis, whose band name, the Nashville Brass, differed from Lester's new band name by only one letter.

Also, the word "grass" in the band name was an intentional nod to the growing audience of hippies who were really beginning to warm up to bluegrass music. Though Flatt was personally opposed to hippies, long hair, and marijuana, he liked the double meaning that could readily be recognized in the name Nashville Grass. He often joked about it onstage, telling audiences to "keep on supportin' that 'grass."[5] For a short while he had been using the name Lester Flatt and the Foggy Mountain Boys, but later, by reciprocal agreement between Lester and Earl, the name Foggy Mountain Boys could no longer be used.[6]

It was a while before Lester began working lots of road shows, at least until the summer bluegrass festival season got started. The boys in the Nashville Grass didn't mind, because Lester had put them on a decent salary. It all paid the same, whether they worked or not. They were painfully aware that steady salaries were unusual in the dicey business of bluegrass music, so they appreciated the position they were in. Though personal appearances were scarce at first, they kept busy playing the *Grand Ole Opry*, as well as the Martha White programs. The Opry, by the way, paid a union-scale fee for each band member per show, but Lester got that money, since his band was salaried.

They often recorded one or two weeks' worth of Martha White radio shows in one session at the WSM studio. If they were getting ready to go on the road, they would sometimes spend a couple of days recording up to a month of programs. Each program was thirty minutes, including commercials, which they didn't do, so they just "lined out" the show beforehand and started rolling.[7] Their collective musical experience enabled them to perform spontaneously, without much rehearsal, and WSM appreciated their not using lots of expensive studio time.[8]

In 1969 Lester published a souvenir booklet. In it were some songs, a few pictures of the house he had recently moved into on the banks of Old Hickory Lake (north of Nashville), two pages of beginning banjo and Dobro lessons, and pictures of his band members, along with their families. Roland was pictured with his wife, Arline, who was pregnant with their second child, Lawrence, at the time the photo was taken. Their daughter, Roline, was also in the picture. The souvenir book was published before the band-naming contest had taken place, so the group was presented in the brochure as the Lester Flatt Show.

One of the first things Lester wanted to do was make an album featuring his new band. This would give him something to promote as an example of his new sound in order to line up some show dates. The first album the Lester Flatt Show recorded was called *Flatt Out*.[9] It was recorded on four different days. The band members, though on salary, always got union-scale pay for album recording sessions. The record contained bluegrass instrumentation with the addition of electric bass and drums. There was an amusing photo on the back cover: Lester was pictured wearing a crash helmet and sitting in a Lotus racing car. He was

THE LESTER FLATT SHOW
P. O. Box 602
Madison, Tenn. 37115

THE
LESTER FLATT
SHOW

From the back cover of the 1969 Lester Flatt souvenir booklet (before the group was named Lester Flatt and the Nashville Grass). L-R: Jake Tullock, Roland White, Vic Jordan, Lester Flatt, Paul Warren, Josh Graves. From the White family collection.

surrounded by the members of his band, including Roland, who were wearing pit crew coveralls. It took Lester, who wasn't thin, some time to get into the seat of the car because it was such a tight fit! Unfortunately, Roland's mandolin playing was hardly featured at all; the only mandolin solo included was on the song "That Was Before I Met You."

For the rest of 1969 and up through April 1970, the Lester Flatt Show continued to be the name used. On July 26, 1969, the group appeared at the Mariposa Folk Festival in Ontario, Canada.[10] On September 27, 1969, Lester and his band performed at Shindig in the Barn, in Lancaster, Pennsylvania.[11] They played at the first annual Indian Summer Maryland State Bluegrass Festival at Take It Easy Ranch in Callaway, Maryland, on

From the 1969 Lester Flatt souvenir booklet. L-R: Arline White, Roline White, Roland White. Arline was pregnant with Lawrence at the time this photo was taken. From the White family collection.

October 4, 1969.[12] On November 16 Lester and his boys opened for Porter Wagoner at the Virginia Theatre in Alexandria, Virginia.[13]

Roland was very fortunate in one respect while working with the Nashville Grass. His playing was accepted for what it was, not compared and contrasted with another mandolin player. Vic, however, was not so lucky. In 1970 he played a show with Lester at a county fair in Pennsylvania. When they drove up to the entrance of the fairgrounds, they saw a sign that read "Lester Flatt, Vic Jordan, and The Nashville Grass." Vic wanted to slide under the seat. Lester wasn't too happy. As a sideman, Vic knew he shouldn't be getting top billing alongside Lester. Apparently, since the name of the band used to be Lester Flatt, Earl Scruggs, and the Foggy Mountain Boys, the promoters felt there should be another name after Lester's.[14]

By 1970 bluegrass festivals were really starting to take off all around the country. They quickly became primary performance venues for Lester Flatt and the Nashville Grass. One of the first summer festivals they played in 1970 took place on June 13 at Jim Clark's Bluegrass Weekend at the

Lester Flatt and the Nashville Grass. L-R: Vic Jordan, Josh Graves, Roland White, Lester Flatt. From the White family collection.

American Legion Park in Culpepper, Virginia.[15] In August they played the fifth annual Pennsylvania Bluegrass Festival at the Big Country Ranch Resort in West Finley, Pennsylvania.[16] Lester and the Grass performed at the Chautauqua Park Bluegrass Festival near Franklin, Ohio, in September.[17] In October they played the second annual Indian Summer Bluegrass Folk Music Festival at Lake Whippoorwill Park near Warrenton, Virginia.[18]

Lance LeRoy became Lester's booking agent. He had always been a self-described Flatt and Scruggs "groupie," and he had admired Louise Scruggs's business skill as booking agent for the Foggy Mountain Boys. Lance had studied accounting in college and had been doing Lester's taxes since 1966. When Lester and Earl dissolved their partnership, Lance was more than willing to take on the job of promoter and manager for the Nashville Grass.[19]

Lance traveled with the group on the road, often riding shotgun on the bus during the wee hours. Roland frequently drove that bus; one of the reasons Roland got the job with Lester Flatt was his ability to operate it. Lester had a General Motors PD-4104, built during the 1950s, that he and Earl Scruggs had been using, but he soon got rid of it after his new band formed. He got a Greyhound Scenicruiser, and he had a driver at first. Lester also let Jake Tullock share the driving duties, because he knew from prior experience that cousin Jake was up to the job. After he got to know Vic and Roland a little bit better, Lester also trusted them with handling the Greyhound. It was a first-rate bus that would really hold the road—much better than the old 4104. They steered it all over the country, racking up thousands of miles.

Vic told me a story about one time when Lance LeRoy was riding on the Scenicruiser with the band:

> We were in the bus one time, and I had a way of getting up in the top bunk. You could put your arms on the two top bunks across the aisle from each other, get your feet swingin', and roll yourself right up there.
>
> Lance said, "Vic, I declare, ole Lance would sure love to know how you do that there. Could you show me how you do that?"
>
> I said, "Sure, Lance, come on, I'll show you." We went [toward the] back in the bus—Roland was driving it down the highway—and I showed him [Lance] how, and then I did it again.
>
> "All right, let ole Lance try it."
>
> Well, he jumped straight up, and when he did, his head hit the ceiling of the bus, and its plastic liner popped—pow! There was a crack in the liner, but the funny part—it had his hair hanging down from it, a few strands of hair, and we all got so tickled.
>
> I declare, ole Lance's not sure he likes that now. I don't think I want to do that anymore.[20]

Jimmy Martin was peeved with Roland White for joining the Nashville Grass. Roland had met him before, while working as a Blue Grass Boy, and Jimmy had heard him playing the mandolin. He really liked his style, saying, "If you ever leave Bill Monroe, call me up. I want you to play for me." Later, when Jimmy Martin found out Roland had joined Lester Flatt, he phoned him, angrily saying, "You promised to join my band."

Roland said, "I never promised any such thing."

Martin then said, "Don't you ever call me again."

Roland replied, "I didn't call you; you called me."[21]

Some other dates they played in Pennsylvania were the fifth annual Pennsylvania Bluegrass Festival at Big Country Ranch Resort in West Finley and the second annual Gettysburg Bluegrass and Folk Music Festival at the Black Horse Tavern Campgrounds in Gettysburg, Pennsylvania.[22]

Vic sometimes felt uncomfortable playing with Lester, because he imagined the audience members were comparing his playing to that of Scruggs. "We'd be on stage," said Vic, "and I could see the old-timers out in the crowd looking at me like 'He's all right, but he ain't no Earl Scruggs.'" Vic had asked Lester at the audition, "Do you want me to play like Earl? 'Cause there's only one Earl Scruggs, and I don't think anybody can play like him." Lester told him, "Baby, just play it like you feel."

Flatt was quite satisfied with Vic's banjo style. It had much of the same drive and flavor of Earl's playing but was just a touch more progressive, though not overly so. The licks Vic played worked well with Roland's creative mandolin work. Occasional melodic touches and flourishes characterized Vic's approach, much of which he based on a style developed by one of his banjo heroes, Bobby Thompson.

Bobby Thompson (1937–2005) invented a melodic style of banjo playing that contrasted with Scruggs-style playing. The style is characterized by inclusion of many more melody notes than in Scruggs-style banjo playing. Bobby's style can be heard in its infant stages on early recordings by Jim and Jesse and the Virginia Boys; their "Dixie Hoedown" is a great example. In the late 1950s, Thompson's new style was largely unappreciated; people weren't ready for it yet. Now it is commonplace and greatly admired. Vic Jordan, who got to know Bobby Thompson, told me how Bobby got started playing in melodic style: "Before Bobby Thompson came to Nashville, he was playing with Carl Story.[23] They were riding somewhere in a car, and the fiddle player said, 'Why don't you banjo players play the damn melody?' And it made Bobby mad. He thought, 'I'll show you!' And he started learning that stuff."[24] Beginning in the late 1960s, Bobby started doing recording work, playing as many as fifteen sessions a week on guitar as well as banjo. He was a member of the staff band on the *Hee Haw* TV show, and in the early 1970s he helped create Area Code 615, a group that combined country, rock, and bluegrass.[25]

Flatt Out was the last album Lester did on the Columbia label. He signed with RCA Victor in November 1970, but in the interim he recorded a limited edition album for the Pickwick label. It was recorded in 1969 at Nugget Studios in Goodlettsville, Tennessee. Vic said, "We went into the studio out in Goodlettsville in the morning, and when we came out in the afternoon the album was finished. We had rehearsed all the material before the session, and the songs were mostly standards. It came out in 1970, and it was called *The One and Only Lester Flatt*.[26] Numbers on the Nugget album included "Drink That Mash and Talk That Trash," "Daddy Sang Bass," "Mocking Banjo," "Down the Road," "I'd Like to Have Papa Show Me Around," "The Sunny Side of the Mountain," "Roll in My Sweet Baby's Arms," "Flatland Two Step," "We'll Meet Again Sweetheart," "I'm Gonna Sleep with One Eye Open," and "Yonder Stands Little Maggie."

Vic Jordan had this to say about "Yonder Stands Little Maggie": "I had a little chromatic more than melodic break that I did on 'Little Maggie.'" (Chromatic style, by my definition, involves the use of ascending and descending scales, complete with sharps and flats. It is used to "dress up" a tune, whereas melodic style is used to reproduce the actual melody of the tune.) Vic continued:

> Any resemblance to "Little Maggie" was purely coincidental. It was the same chord progression . . . play it first as "Little Maggie" and play it the second time the way you think it should be. Lester would announce it on stage, or on the radio show or wherever we did it: "Now, Vic plays a different style than anybody else ever has on this tune here, and I want you to listen." Well, I'm not the first one that played like that. I might have been the first one to play "Little Maggie" like that. But to him, that was all new stuff, just something entirely new.

Roland did a fine job leading "Mockin' Banjo," a tune originally written by Arthur "Guitar Boogie" Smith, who called it "Feudin' Banjos." Smith recorded it in 1955 with Don Reno.[27] Roland had learned the tune from a Bobby Thompson recording with Carl Story.[28] (He still has the 45 rpm single.) The tune, under the title "Dueling Banjos," was made famous in 1972 by virtue of its inclusion in the movie *Deliverance*. Eric Weissberg (banjo) and Steve Mandell (guitar) adapted it for the film score.[29]

The Nashville Grass made quite a few albums, and Lester's fans were pleased to find that most of the records were in the traditional vein, free from the rock influences that had characterized some of the final Flatt and Scruggs albums. Two of the albums that come to mind are *Changin' Times* and *Nashville Airplane*.[30]

In November 1970 Lester Flatt and Mac Wiseman performed together with the Nashville Grass at the South Carolina State Bluegrass Festival at the Myrtle Beach Convention Center.[31] Mac and Lester had worked together years before, and they really hit it off musically. Later they would make several records together.

About that time Roland started jamming more with banjo player Alan Munde, who would later become an important friend and musical partner. In an interview, Alan told me:

> There was a joint in town called Bobby Green's Dusty Roads Tavern. They had a sort of a bluegrass jam night there and I would go, and Roland would be there and we played music together. Roland was real nice to me. At different jamming places around town I'd see Roland. He even invited me one time to Christmas dinner, I believe. Lester had given him a ham, and he invited me and Gloria Belle over. [Gloria Belle and Alan Munde were both members of Jimmy Martin's band at the time.]
>
> He gave me a ride home one time from Bobby Green's because my car had broken down. In the Old Hickory area, there's a place called Rayon City. I lived there and Roland said, "Well, here, I'll give you a ride home." I said, "Well, I'll just wait and get a ride with somebody that's going my way." He said, "You don't live on anybody's way home. You better take the ride."

Alan appreciated Roland going out of his way.[32]

The next album Roland participated on with Lester was *Flatt on Victor*, released in 1971.[33] That record came out during the height of the "flower children" movement, and there was an amusing song on the album about hippies with long hair called "I Can't Tell the Boys from the Girls." Roland always laughs when this song is mentioned. It's ironic to note that Roland's brother Clarence was playing lead guitar for the Byrds during this same time, performing for the same group of people that Lester Flatt was making fun of. A similar song, "The Good Old-Fashioned Way," was recorded on that session but released at a later date.[34] That song also referenced the long hair that was in style, with a line that went "We believed in barber shops and razor blades."

Vic Jordan wrote a great banjo instrumental for the *Flatt on Victor* album. The song was called "Pick Away," and Roland came up with the title. It was written back in their Blue Grass Boys days. Vic had been driving the Bluegrass Special and Roland was riding shotgun. They were going through West Virginia, traveling up a little winding road. Vic had just written the banjo tune, and he didn't have a name for it. In the headlights a little green sign showed up by the side of the road that said "Pickaway—unincorporated." Roland said, "That'd be a good name for your banjo tune." Pickaway was just a wide spot in the road, but it was a great title for Vic's tune. Not only did he record it with Lester Flatt, but later he also made a classic banjo album of his own using "Pick Away" as the title number.[35]

On the *Flatt on Victor* album, authorship of the tune was listed as Vic Jordan and Gladys Flatt. Lester listed his wife's name with the publishing company as coauthor so he could get part of the royalties. He and Earl had done that many times in the past, listing their wives' names on publishing forms in order to receive royalty payments. The other instrumental on *Flatt on Victor* was "Cedar Hill," which was written by Roland White and Vic Jordan but also included Gladys Flatt as a coauthor. That was Lester's policy with regard to recording songs written by his band members.

Lester and the Nashville Grass played at a number of drive-in movie theaters. They would set up on top of the concession stand, and people would honk their horns instead of clapping. The music was piped through the little speakers that hung on the car windows. They also had their own sound system for people who wanted to stand up close to the band and listen. As the moist night air started to fall, the instruments would start sounding muddy and dead. Several times the band members asked Lester if they could stay and watch the movie, and he would always say, "No, boys, we need to get moving." So they would always go back to their motel.[36]

As mentioned earlier, Lester had given Roland the nickname Chee Chee. This nickname was even printed on several of the album liner notes. Roland didn't like it then and he doesn't like it now, but he's letting me include it in this book because it's a part of bluegrass history—and you can't change the past. "I'll tell you how the nickname got started," said Roland. "We were doing the Lester Flatt show on television, and he wanted me to stand up a little taller, so they put a wooden Coca-Cola crate under me. I stepped up on it and played and sang a song, and when I was done, he said, 'Awww, that's my little Chee Chee.' Josh said, 'Well, Roland, there you go—he's gonna call you Chee Chee from now on.' I couldn't do anything about it. That's Lester Flatt—you don't tell him anything."[37] (Roland had to stand on a Coke crate once before, when he was a Blue

Grass Boy. While recording "Walls of Time" in 1968, Roland sang lead and had to share a microphone with Monroe, who was much taller.[38])

Even to this day, if you go out into some of the small towns outside of Nashville, people who recognize Roland remember him as Chee Chee. Lance LeRoy sometimes called him Cheech. One can only speculate about what was going through Lester's mind when he called Roland by that name. Dictionary definitions of the word Chee Chee are many and varied, and virtually all of them are negative. I can understand why Roland doesn't like it. Monroe called me the "Dark Cloud" and I didn't like that either, so I can identify. One thing is indisputable, however: anyone who calls Roland by the nickname Chee Chee today does it only out of respect and love for the man.

The band's driver Jake Tullock suffered a heart attack in May 1970, and one year later he retired from Lester's band. He was replaced by Howard (Johnny) Johnson, who had played for Flatt and Scruggs and Ernest Tubb in the 1960s and had worked for Bill Monroe in the 1970s.

Lester put forward the idea of recording an album with Mac Wiseman, who was also with RCA Victor. The two singers had worked together in the 1940s on a radio show called *Farm and Fun Time* in Bristol, on the state line between Virginia and Tennessee. Both singers had distinctive styles that complemented each other very nicely. The idea was accepted, and in March 1971 they got together in the RCA studio in Nashville to record, backed by the Nashville Grass. *Lester 'N' Mac* was the result, and it was recorded over a period of three days.[39] The two singers traded lead vocals on many of the songs, with Mac singing tenor parts as well. One of the album's many highlights was the twin fiddles of Howdy Forrester and Paul Warren on several songs.[40] "The Bluebirds Singing for Me," written by Mac Wiseman, was the centerpiece of the album. On the chorus Lester would sing in mid-range and Mac sang high, each of them taking alternate lines. The instruments echoed that arrangement when solos were played.

In July 1971 Lester and his boys performed at the first annual Tennessee Bluegrass Festival in Cosby, put on by James Monroe.[41] In October they appeared at the very first *Early Bird Bluegrass Show* in the Ryman Auditorium during the DJ Convention.[42] Also in 1971 Vic Jordan left the Nashville Grass. He went to work for Jim and Jesse in February 1972 and was replaced in Lester's band by Haskell McCormick (Lester sometimes called him "Hack"). Roland and Vic had enjoyed a good run playing music together for four years, a lifetime in the world of bluegrass.

One of Lester Flatt's biggest fans was Marty Stuart. In our 2016 interview, Marty said, "Flatt and Scruggs were kind of special. They were like family members at our house, though I never met them. When Lester and Earl broke up, that was big in my mind. And then Lester came back shortly thereafter with a television show. He carried on with the Martha White show. I was very interested in who he had in his band. Roland, who he called 'Chee Chee,' was an interesting-looking character, and I loved the way he played the mandolin. I just kind of put my eye on him in the band—he was really cool."

In 1971 Marty got a chance to meet Lester's band at Bill Monroe's fifth annual Bean Blossom, Indiana, festival. (That was the same festival where Monroe and Flatt resolved their differences, ending their long-standing feud.[43]) Twelve-year-old Marty had come to the Brown County Jamboree as a guest with Jim and Jesse and the Virginia Boys. Carl Jackson was their banjo player, and his parents were friends with Marty Stuart's parents, John and Hilda. Marty had talked his mom and dad into letting him go with Jim and Jesse on the road trip.

"That was the first time that I had ever been to a big bluegrass show," Marty recalled. (I was there too, and it was also my first bluegrass festival.) "And there they were in person, Lester and Uncle Josh, Johnny Johnson [bass, guitar], Paul Warren, and Roland White."

Roland came off the bus and Marty walked up to him, carrying a mandolin and saying, "Hi, I'm Marty Stuart."

"Hi, Marty," said Roland, shaking his hand.

"Can I get up there and meet Lester Flatt?"

"Well, he's in the back, taking a nap. But when he wakes up, I'll let you know."

"Roland was so friendly to me," said Marty in our interview. "He gave me a pick, he gave me one of his scarves, and took time to show me things on the mandolin. And he gave me his phone number and told me to call him. And so I felt like I had made a friend."

Later Marty returned to the bus and saw Roland sitting in the driver's seat. He knocked on the door and Roland opened it. Marty asked, "Is Lester up yet?"

Lester Flatt and the Nashville Grass. L-R: Haskell McCormick, Jack Martin, Paul Warren, Marty Stuart, Roland White, Lester Flatt (behind Roland White), Johnny Johnson (behind Lester Flatt). Photo by Artie Rose.

"He's back there in the restroom. He'll be out in a minute. Come on up."

When Lester came out to the front of the bus, Roland introduced Marty to him.

Marty said to Lester, "You know, I feel like I know you. We watch you every Saturday night on the Martha White show." It was true that Lester seemed almost like family to Marty, who grew up watching and listening to the Flatt and Scruggs programs.

Lester took a liking to the twelve-year-old prodigy. "What do you play?" he asked Marty.

"Well, I play guitar and mandolin."

Later Marty asked Roland, "Now that I know you, do you think I could take a trip on the road with you?"

"Well, I don't know. I'd have to speak with your folks about it to make sure it would be okay. Where do you live?"

"Philadelphia, Mississippi."

"Well, we'll talk about it."

They would soon run into each other again. Roland had been telling Lester all about Marty wanting to travel with them, and Lester said, "Well, if he comes along with us, you're gonna have to take care of him. He's just a little boy, and he could get killed stepping off the bus along a highway or something. You'll have to watch him like he was your own kid."

Marty called Roland in September 1972 and said, "I've got two more weeks before school starts. Can I come on the road with you?"

"Let me talk to your mother."

When Marty's mother, Hilda, came on the line, Roland spoke to her about Marty tagging along on a road trip with the Nashville Grass. She told Roland, "Well, I guess it's all right. We can send him on the bus up to Memphis, and we'll have some people meet him there and make sure he gets on the right bus to Nashville."

When Marty was on the way, his mother called Roland again, telling him what time Marty was going to arrive at the Greyhound bus station in Nashville. Roland thought to himself, *What have I gotten myself into?*

He went down and picked up Marty and brought him to the house. Roland and his family lived in the back of Red and Birdie Smith's house at the time.[44] Roland had told Arline about Marty coming there, but she didn't really know what to expect. When he got there, they put blankets on the couch for Marty to sleep under.

The Nashville Grass took a road trip to Delaware, and a place was found for Marty to sleep at the back of the bus. He and Roland played and sang most of the way up Interstate 40 on the way to the festival. When Lester came back to go to bed, he said, "Why don't you all do that on the show tomorrow?" That's exactly what happened. Roland and Marty sang "Love Come Home" on the show and played an instrumental called "Bill Cheatham." Lester was quite impressed with how well Marty fit in with the Grass. He especially liked Marty's baritone vocal part on "Cabin on the Hill." Marty was included on all four sets at the Delaware bluegrass show, and Lester offered him a job at the end of the weekend.

On the way back, they traveled through Virginia and Knoxville, Tennessee, bypassing Nashville and going on down to Mississippi, where they were going to perform at the Choctaw reservation, which was located near Philadelphia. Every year the Choctaws held one of their finest get-togethers. On Saturday night a one-hour country music show was featured. Roland called Marty's parents and told them they could pick up their son at the Choctaw Indian Fair.

On the way down, Lester said to Roland, "You know, Chee Chee, I really like that little boy. You think maybe he could join the band?"

"Lester," said Roland, "he's just a kid. He still goes to school."

"I could get him that mail-order school."

"I don't know."

"His folks are gonna meet us down there, right?"

"Yes, they live in Philadelphia, Mississippi."

"Well, maybe you could ask them."

Roland told Lester, "I'll introduce you to them and you can ask them."

When he introduced Hilda and John Stuart to Lester, Hilda said, "It's so good to finally meet you. We feel like we know you real well from watching the Martha White shows."

Marty asked his mother about joining Lester's band, and she asked Lester for some more details.

"Yeah," said Lester. "I would pay him a salary like everyone else, and I would buy him this mail-order school. He could study at home."

"Gosh," said Hilda. "We'll have to talk about it and let you know."

Later, after school had already started, Hilda called Roland, saying, "We're going to send Marty up there. We're going to talk to Lester and arrange it."

So Marty came back to Nashville and Roland picked him up again. He joined the Nashville Grass at the age of fourteen. One of the earliest festivals he played as a full-fledged member was on the third weekend of September 1972, when the group performed at the first annual Walnut Valley Festival in Winfield, Kansas. Other headliners on that festival included a mixture of progressive and traditional performers: Norman Blake, the Bluegrass Country Boys, Dan Crary, Doc and Merle Watson,

Jim and Jesse and the Virginia Boys, Country Gazette, and the New Grass Revival.[45] These days that festival has become kind of a folk and bluegrass Woodstock—it's a huge event now—but in those early years it was a nice, somewhat smaller festival.

Marty stayed with Roland and Arline's family for several months. Marty needed a mandolin and Roland knew of one for sale, so he called Hilda, who said, "Well, if it's a good one, yeah, we'll buy it for him." After he had the mandolin for a while, Marty started playing Roland's guitar. Later, Marty bought his own guitar, and Roland gave him some reel-to-reel tapes of his brother Clarence's playing, which Marty listened to and learned from. Those tapes turned Marty into a lifelong fan of Clarence White. (He later purchased the 1950s modified Telecaster electric guitar that Clarence had used with the Byrds. He's played it ever since.[46])

In our 2016 interview, Marty remembered the first time he played on the Opry with the Nashville Grass:

Toward the end of Lester's segment he put me and Roland on to sing "Love Come Home." At the end of the song, the audience just kept going and I didn't know what had happened. I was up on my tiptoes playing Roland's mandolin, and I looked at Lester and I said, "What do I do?" and he said, "Do it again." So we encored our song and really hoped that my mom and my dad and my sister were listening, which they were, down in Mississippi. That's the way I started in Nashville. None of that would have happened had it not been for Roland's kindness and treating me like family.

I told Marty that Lester wouldn't have put him out front if he hadn't thought there was anything to put out there. "I've often wondered," Marty replied. "It was like hiring a chimpanzee in the bus—to put me on the bus with all those old guys. But they treated me like I was one of them. I was expected to stand up and be a part of the team."

I told Marty that whenever I had seen him onstage with Lester, he seemed very intense and focused on his mandolin playing. I could always tell that he was extremely serious about it. "Well, I wanted to get it right," he told me.[47]

After Marty had been staying with Roland and Arline for around nine months, he moved into Lester's great big house on the banks of Old

Hickory Lake. Roland and Arline already had two kids of their own to care for: Lawrence, who was only a year old, and their daughter, Roline, who was six.

In 1972 *Kentucky Ridgerunner* was released.[48] One of the selections on the album was a truck-driving song, "Backing to Birmingham," which was reminiscent of the Willis Brothers' 1964 hit, "Give Me 40 Acres and I'll Turn This Rig Around." There was also a great blues tune by Josh Graves that had been recorded back in 1970, "Flatt Lonesome." A piano solo by Hargus "Pig" Robbins was included in that number. Though it sounded good, a bluesy mandolin solo by Roland White would have been better. A majority of the songs had been recorded when Vic Jordan was still in the band, and others included Haskell McCormick on banjo. Altogether, Roland's mandolin was underrepresented in this album. Lester seemed to defer to Josh Graves on most of the instrumental work. Roland did have a good mandolin break on one tune, "Cuttin' the Grass," the first part of which incorporated sets of two alternating notes descending in a "stair-step" pattern, followed by a flourish of melodic phrases on the second part.

On the Southbound was the second album Lester recorded with Mac Wiseman, and Roland's playing was much more present than it had been on *Kentucky Ridgerunner*.[49] Listeners could hear his tasteful accompaniment behind the relaxed songs that Lester and Mac chose to present. The title selection, "On the Southbound," was a hobo song, and one verse had a line that went "I could almost hear the crickets." Roland's mandolin can be heard in the background, playing high "chirping" notes that really fit the mood. "Salty Dog" was resurrected once again for the album,[50] and Roland's memorable instrumental solo took a unique path, with the first half containing double stops,[51] contrasted by a second half of nonstop melody notes—an unusual approach to a song with a ragtime flavor.

Roland sang an old-timey duet with Lester on the 1973 album *Country Boy*.[52] One of the numbers, "No Place to Pillow My Head," was originally a public domain song titled "No Home, No Place to Pillow My Head." It dated back to World War I. Bill Monroe had recorded it many years earlier with his brother Charlie. When Lester recorded it, he listed himself and Monroe as coauthors and shortened the title. Roland had sung lots of tenor parts with Lester, but his standout vocal performance could really be heard well on that particular song, since it was just him and Lester singing. The tempo was slower than the Monroe Brothers' version, and it was reminiscent of the song "Gone Home," with its use of call-and-response choruses.

During live performances, Lester sometimes joked about his musicians in seemingly disparaging ways. He was like Jimmy Martin in that respect. "You name it and I'll feed it" was one expression both bandleaders used when introducing certain members of their group. Lester also used other nicknames for Roland besides "Chee Chee," and they weren't always flattering. But that was just Lester's way of adding humor to the program. In reality he and Roland had a very amiable relationship. They sometimes went fishing together on Old Hickory Lake in Lester's boat, where Roland remembered him occasionally expressing his sorrow over the breakup with Earl.[53]

In 1973 Roland was ready to leave Lester's band. One of the biggest reasons was that the Byrds had recently disbanded.[54] Clarence White had been the lead guitarist for that group since 1968, and he still lived in California, doing session work. Roland had been talking with him on the phone about reviving their old brother act. One morning early in 1973, Roland and Marty were on their way to WSM to do the Martha White radio show. Roland was driving a 1965 Impala that he had bought from Josh Graves. It was raining real hard, and the car leaked on the front passenger side, so Marty was sitting in the backseat. They were late as usual for the radio station, and when Roland pulled out, they got in a wreck. It was only a fender bender, but Roland got out of the car, slammed his hands on the hood, and said, "I'm done." That was the incident that tipped the balance for Roland. He turned in his notice to Lester shortly after that, and Marty moved into the mandolin position with the Nashville Grass. (Stuart stayed with Lester Flatt and the Nashville Grass until Flatt's death in 1979.[55])

Roland had worked for Lester Flatt for four years. It was the last time he ever worked *for* someone else musically; after that, he always worked *with* other musicians. That was the way he had started out, and that was the way it was going to be from then on. Those who have never worked as a sideman will never know how arduous and demanding it can be.

Lester Flatt's traditional brand of bluegrass had been preserved and carried on by Roland in an important way. Roland, together with Vic Jordan, helped put a new and different stamp on Lester's music while still keeping within traditional confines. They didn't alienate any of Lester's loyal fans; they just carried the music onward in the classic style, adding their own contributions and making the listeners happy.

During the time he had spent working for Bill and Lester, Roland had seldom been able to keep in contact with his brother Clarence. The phone calls with Clarence had revived fond memories of growing up together and discovering bluegrass as youngsters. Their paths had diverged since the old days, but family ties are never really broken. A reunion was bound to happen. It looked like Roland's bluegrass dreams were about to turn in a new and exciting direction.

7

The New Kentucky Colonels

Eager to return to his acoustic music roots, Clarence White was enthusiastic about getting back together with his brother Roland to re-form the Kentucky Colonels. He had just finished recording an album with Muleskinner (recorded March 27–April 14, 1973), a brand-new bluegrass group that was an exciting assemblage of traditional, progressive, and rock innovators. The music they played was a celebration of newfound freedom for its members, who had bluegrass in their blood and a desire for wider boundaries. The record, titled *A Potpourri of Bluegrass Jam,* was historically significant because of its originality, intensity, and unmatched musicianship.[1] The band members included several Blue Grass Boys alumni who had ventured far astray and then returned to the acoustic fold with fresh ideas and newer, more imaginative approaches.

Clarence was seeing the light of a new dawn. Bluegrass was back, and it was no longer going to be confined to rigid stylistic concepts. The Kentucky Colonels could be presented to the world once again, with fresh new windows of opportunity that hadn't existed before. For Roland and Clarence, it would be a triumphant return to the idealistic musical optimism of their youth.

The idea of getting back together with Clarence was irresistibly appealing to Roland. Clarence told him what he had in mind: "I have a chance to go to Europe, and I'd like to know if you'd like to go."[2] Eddie Ticknor, who had managed the Byrds for a while, wanted to set up some tour dates in Europe as Clarence's manager, and some additional shows would be organized by Martin Smith, a Welshman who worked for United Artists Records. Brother Eric was already on board with the idea, because Clarence had talked to him. (Eric had played in the early '70s as a fill-in with Linda Ronstadt, Arlo Guthrie, and some others and also worked as a roadie.) A trip to Europe! The three White brothers together again! How could Roland refuse?

Roger Bush was unable to make the trip, and Billy Ray Latham said he wasn't interested, because he'd been playing mostly guitar in another band and would have to get his "chops" up—meaning he felt he'd gotten a little rusty on the five-string banjo. But Clarence said they could get a banjo player and maybe find a fiddler who could play the music. Clarence was still living in California, where bluegrass fiddlers were few and far between. In Nashville, where Roland lived, there were all kinds of them.

Roland turned in his notice to Lester and quickly flew out to California to get together with his brothers to organize some rehearsals and show dates. It was an exhilarating time for Roland, Clarence, and Eric. They were filled with eager enthusiasm—the old days were coming back. Their band was going to be called the New Kentucky Colonels, and the banjo player was to be Herb Pedersen, who had been recommended by Clarence as well as by the Byrds' record producer, Jim Dickson.[3]

Herb Pedersen was from Berkeley, California, and had experience playing bluegrass on the West Coast, working with the Pine Valley Boys and with Vern and Ray (Vern Williams and Ray Park). Herb was also a guitarist and songwriter. In 1968 he played banjo for the Dillards on their *Wheatstraw Suite* album and later their *Copperfields* album.[4] Also in 1968 he filled in for Earl Scruggs for a week while Earl was in the hospital for hip surgery.[5] (Later he performed with many major artists, including Emmylou Harris, Kris Kristofferson, Gram Parsons, and John Prine.[6] In 1986 he joined the Desert Rose Band, recording many hits with that country-rock group.) Herb was also a good singer with a high vocal range that fit in well with the harmony vocals that would comprise much of the New Kentucky Colonels' repertoire. As an added benefit, he was already familiar with many of the Colonels' songs.[7]

Before going on their European tour, the New Kentucky Colonels wanted to get some U.S. performances under their belts. They set up some appearances at various places on the West Coast and even took time to do a tour on the East Coast, honing their act all the while.[8]

Wim Bloemendaal, a Dutch radio and television personality, wanted someone who knew the New Kentucky Colonels to record an interview with the band for use in promoting their European tour. He also wanted a few song samples. Byron Berline was chosen to manage the recordings. The group got together at Byron's home in Sherman Oaks, California, to make the tapes, and Berline participated too. They recorded "John Henry," "Willow Garden," "Hard Hearted," "If You're Ever Gonna Love Me," "Wicked Path of Sin," "If I Be Lifted Up," and "Stoney Creek." Several other instrumental tunes were included as well.[9]

On April 7, while Roland was in Los Angeles, he appeared with Clarence on Bob Baxter's *Guitar Workshop* TV show. Other guests included Country Gazette members Byron Berline and Alan Munde (Sierra Records released a video of that performance in 1998). During the show, Roland and Clarence performed an instrumental version of "I Am a Pilgrim" as only a brother duo can: Clarence went pretty far out on a limb a few times with his guitar playing, and Roland, sensing where Clarence was going, was able to follow him without getting lost. Roland took several solos with lots of bluesy tremolos (fast up-and-down motions of the pick), and his second solo was highly reminiscent (to me) of Bill Monroe's mandolin version of "I Am a Pilgrim." When Alan and Byron joined the White brothers on "Soldier's Joy," the music coalesced into the Country Gazette sound. Roland's Monroe influence again made itself known, Byron's fiddle solo was irrepressibly melodic and exciting to listen to, and Alan's banjo solo was an intriguing combination of Scruggs style and melodic style blended together with a seamless unity. Roland's mandolin playing on this live performance was a foreshadowing of his future home with Country Gazette.

The New Kentucky Colonels played at the Ash Grove on April 22, 1973. They were joined again by Country Gazette members Munde, Berline, and Bush, along with many other special guests.[10] Charged up after the shows and rehearsals, Roland returned home to Nashville to get ready for the overseas tour, which would include Holland, Belgium, England, Wales, and Sweden.

The trip took place the next month. The group flew together out of Los Angeles. Their first stop was Holland. When they arrived in Amsterdam, they were picked up in a late 1960s Oldsmobile by Ted and Nikki Boddy (pronounced BO-dee), managers of a beautiful old-fashioned Dutch inn called Wiechmann on Prinsengracht. Ted Boddy was from Oklahoma originally, and during the Second World War, while in Holland, he had met Nikki. Her mother owned three hotels, one of which was the Wiechmann on Prinsengracht. Situated across the street from a beautiful canal, the inn was the New Kentucky Colonels' headquarters for the next week and a half. (That same hotel was later to serve as headquarters for several other traveling groups, including Country Gazette, and Nikki even booked some shows for many of those groups.)

During their glorious stay in Holland, the New Kentucky Colonels traveled to different towns every day. The first show they performed was in a small nightclub also owned by the Boddys, called Boddy's Music Inn, just a few blocks from the hotel where they were staying. They walked to the gig, noting that everyone else—old and young—either walked or rode bicycles.[11]

In the city of Breda the band performed a concert at Het Turfschip, a large concert hall, and a recording was made of the performance, which has been recently issued on CD: *The New Kentucky Colonels, Live in Holland*.[12] Recorded early in the tour (May 1973), the concert was a joyous return to what the three White brothers did while growing up: making bluegrass. Their happiness could be felt throughout the program. Their playing was close and energetic, just as though they had never been apart for all those many years.

The CD is a festive joy to listen to. One number, "Never Ending Song of Love," illustrates how easily different styles of music can be incorporated into the bluegrass idiom. That song is followed up with a traditional straight-ahead bluegrass song, the Stanley Brothers' "The Fields Have Turned Brown." Here Clarence is at his best, playing looping, intersecting melody lines behind the singing and ending the song with an understated flourish that provides the perfect punctuation. "Is This My Destiny?"— composed by Helen Carter of the Carter Family and recorded in 1958 by the Osborne Brothers and Red Allen—is a highlight of the album, with Herb Pedersen singing the high part. There is a nice vocal arrangement on the ending. Roland sings "I Know What It Means to Be Lonesome," which he had performed many times with Lester Flatt and the Nashville Grass, and that song includes a lazy, swinging guitar break by Clarence. Overall, the *Live in Holland* album is one of the best New Kentucky Colonels recordings—not only because it's a live recording with song introductions, audience applause, and so forth, but because the group plays with such evident enthusiasm and enjoyment as well. It's also a very pleasant merry-go-round ride of Clarence White's guitar playing.

While they were still in Holland, Herb Pedersen fulfilled a commitment to join rock 'n' roll singer Johnny Rivers,[13] who was in France at the time. That was an unexpected negative development for the boys, but Eddie Ticknor saved them: he hired Alan Munde to replace Pedersen. Alan flew over and played the rest of the European tour with the White brothers.

One of the performances that included Munde on banjo was recorded directly from the sound board and later released on LP in 1976 under the title *The White Brothers: Live in Sweden*.[14] Taped at the Mosebacke club in Stockholm, it included two nights' worth of music that was bright, spirited, and polished—a testament to the incredible musicianship of all the players. In general, live performance recordings in those days were notoriously difficult to pull off because the chances for studio "fixes" were severely limited compared to today. The upside was the chance to capture the excitement and spontaneity of the live performance, which can never be accurately recreated in a studio setting. The album has now been rereleased under the title *The New Kentucky Colonels: Live in Sweden 1973*, with nearly twice as many selections included.[15] So fans of Roland, Clarence, Eric, and Alan now have a new treat—absolutely essential listening for bluegrass lovers.

Roland has said that the shows in Stockholm were the most fun he ever had playing music. That's no surprise, as the White brothers were all together again, and they had already been playing shows in Holland, which had them limbered up and tuned in with one another. "In my opinion, this is the best playing of Clarence's on record," says Roland in the liner notes of the rerelease. "I know it was the best music I ever made."

Roland goes on to talk about the popularity of Clarence in Europe because of his prior association with the Byrds. Many folks came to the shows just to hear Clarence. He showed them his first love—bluegrass—and his joy caught on. He no doubt opened the door for many listeners, converting them to the music that the Whites had grown up with. Clarence's acoustic style was blossoming into something very special: joyful, inspired, creative, and filled with the promise of even better things to come.

Alan Munde spoke of his esteem for the New Kentucky Colonels: "They had that wonderful, too rare ability to make those around them not just

The New Kentucky Colonels in Sweden, 1973. L-R: Alan Munde, Roland White, Eric White, Clarence White. From the White family collection.

sound better, but maybe sound and play the best they ever had. I think that was the case for me."[16]

The reissue of *Live in Sweden* contains some heavily Monroe-influenced music. Such songs as "You Won't Be Satisfied That Way," "Good Woman's Love" (which Monroe didn't write but performed often), "I'm Blue, I'm Lonesome," and "Rawhide" make me realize that Clarence easily could have been a lead guitarist with the Blue Grass Boys. He didn't shy away from fast numbers. Roland has several solos on the album that are just as good as, if not better than, Monroe's versions. "Sally Goodin" is one tune I'm thinking of in particular. I've often heard Monroe play that, and I think Roland gets every one of the nuances of Monroe's style when he performs this dance tune, which includes many variations on a basic theme. I'm sure he listened to Monroe play that tune on the bus many times when he was a Blue Grass Boy.

"Fire on the Mountain" is the blazing kickoff tune for the album. Hot, intense—it's hard to play this tune fast; take my word for it! "Mocking Banjo" was very much inspired by the Dillards' earlier version, which they called "Duelin' Banjo," but the New Kentucky Colonels version raises the bar by including a guitar/mandolin part. "Blackberry Blossom," a very popular tune during that time, is included as a banjo piece. Altogether, it's a very satisfying album.

Roland is very proud of both the *Live in Holland* and *Live in Sweden* albums, gratified that the memory of Clarence's acoustic guitar genius is being preserved for future generations to listen to and study. The recordings also document the incredible musical synergy of two brothers who had been playing together since childhood.

When the European tour was over, the New Kentucky Colonels flew into Washington D.C., and their friend John Kaparakis (1937–2020) drove them to Indian Springs, Maryland.[17] There they played at a large bluegrass festival on June 2. It was the first and last bluegrass festival Clarence ever played.

John Kaparakis was a guitarist and singer from Arlington, Virginia, whom the Whites had known since their original Kentucky Colonels days. John played rhythm guitar with the band at the festival. Since Alan Munde had other commitments with Country Gazette, the Colonels needed to hire another banjo player. Clarence asked Roland about Jack Hicks,[18] who was performing there with Bill Monroe. Roland had no doubts, as Jack Hicks was among the best banjo players Monroe ever had, so he would be great. They approached Hicks, who was happy to sit in with them on the shows.

One of the songs the New Kentucky Colonels performed at the festival was "Take a Whiff on Me," a folk song about cocaine use that had been performed by many groups in many different ways. Clarence had done it with the Byrds. The Greenbriar Boys had recorded an up-tempo bluegrass version of it in 1964. Roland remembered a negative reaction to the song by some of the older members of the crowd at Indian Springs. "As soon as they realized what the song was about," said Roland, "you could hear the sound of many lawn chairs being folded as they got up to leave."[19] Roland had performed for a lot of those same people when he was with Lester Flatt, but changing times were catching up with those folks, and they weren't always open to the changes.

Later that month Roland, Clarence, and Eric played another tour in the Baltimore and Washington, D.C., area. Country Gazette was on those same shows, and their banjo player, Alan Munde, was once again included with the New Kentucky Colonels.

The New Kentucky Colonels performing at the bluegrass festival in Indian Springs, Maryland, June 2, 1973. L-R: Jack Hicks, Roland White, Eric White (on bass), Clarence White, John Kaparakis. From the White family collection.

On June 28 and 29, Roland and Clarence recorded four selections in Los Angeles. Warner Brothers wanted to produce an album featuring Clarence. The songs were "Never Ending Love," "Why You Been Gone So Long," "Alabama Jubilee," and "Last Thing on My Mind." The musicians included Byron Berline, fiddle; Roger Bush, bass; Herb Pedersen, rhythm guitar/vocals; Clarence White, guitar/vocals; and Roland White, mandolin/vocals. Additional pickers were Leland Sklar, electric bass; Ed Green, drums; and Ry Cooder, slide guitar. The recordings were produced by Jim Dickson.[20]

From June 30 to July 10 a country rock tour was conducted in Annapolis, Maryland, and Philadelphia, Pennsylvania. The New Kentucky Colonels were part of that tour, which also included Country Gazette, Gram Parsons, Emmylou Harris, former Byrds members, and former Flying Burrito Brothers. Each show lasted three hours and they were great fun for both audiences and musicians. There was a finale at the end of each performance in which all of the musicians returned to the stage. Pleased with the success of the concerts, Warner Brothers began planning another tour, which was to take place that fall.[21]

On Saturday, July 14, the White boys drove up to Lancaster, California, to visit their mother, Mildred. Their youngest sister, Rosemarie, was living with her at the time. That same night they drove to a bar in Palmdale called BJ's to play with Eric's country band. Mildred came with them, along with their uncle Johnny. Also performing with them that night was "Cajun" Gib Guilbeau, a singer of Cajun and country songs who played the fiddle and guitar.

In a March 18, 2015, interview, Roland gave the following account of what took place after the show was over:

> That night we were stepping out of the club and we were parked on the main highway—Sierra Highway. Clarence's car was in front of the club and our uncle John was parked across the street. We were going to my uncle Johnny's house and my aunt Jeanette, his wife, was going to cook us breakfast at two o'clock in the morning.
>
> I had my mandolin with me and Clarence opened up the trunk of his vehicle. The cars were just *flying* by, and he said, "Boy, this could be a dangerous place here." Then he told me, "I'll ride with Uncle Johnny and you drive my car."
>
> I said, "Okay." So I stepped around the front of the car, opening the driver's side. It was a two-door Pontiac. I looked around and I didn't see anything. Clarence said, "You'll need the key."
>
> "Oh, yeah." I turned around and reached out, and this car hit him, threw him into me, which threw him back on the car and sent him up the street; and I flipped over his car, and I was on my face on the sidewalk with a dislocated shoulder. And it stunned me.
>
> Eric came out and said, "What are you doing down there?"
>
> I just said, "Clarence! Where's Clarence? What happened? Where's Clarence?"
>
> I looked around, and my uncle Johnny was there. He had come back across the street to where Eric and I were. Right then this paramedic drove up—he happened to be off duty, or maybe he was on duty—I don't know for sure. He said, "Don't touch him." My uncle John said, "Clarence, are you okay?" Blood started coming out of his mouth, and his nose, and his ears.

The woman that was driving [drunk] had just kind of went up and turned, going across the street, and Clarence had fallen off of the car. He was lying there, with his boots off. It pulled his boots off.

They figured she was doing about forty miles an hour, which was the top limit on the highway. Anyway, they got the ambulance, and the paramedic said to me, "Are you hurt?"

I said, "Well, my shoulder feels funny." It was all out of joint, you know.

He said, "Well, you need to get in there with him." So I got in the ambulance too. Uncle Johnny took Gib Guilbeau and Mom, and we all went to the hospital. They tried to save Clarence, but they said that every bone in his body was broken, and if he survived this, they said, he would have been a vegetable—he was just broken all over—he was brain dead and then his heart stopped. So that was the end of that.[22]

The sudden, totally unexpected disaster was a tragedy of monumental proportions: Clarence White—one of the most brilliant musicians of his time—was gone. There are many published sources that talk about the music world's loss of Clarence. While true, the world's loss doesn't begin to compare with Roland's personal loss. For anyone who lives through a tragedy of this nature, the need to honor the memory of the lost loved one becomes a driving force. Roland—ever the responsible older brother—has taken on this duty with love and pride. His music career has become a living memorial to Clarence, inspiring countless other musicians.

Clarence White was about to take bluegrass and acoustic music to its highest level ever, breaking new ground with his guitar style, which has no equal to this day. Roland was part of this exciting new adventure, and his dream of bringing a reunited Kentucky Colonels band to new listeners—just when bluegrass music was enjoying its greatest upswing in popularity—was forever ended. The curtain was brought down on one of the most promising careers in music, and the momentous potential of a bluegrass band on the verge of unprecedented success and achievement was forever ended.

Marty Stuart, one of Clarence White's biggest fans ever, said in his foreword to the book *The Essential Clarence White*, "I wonder where he would have led us with his guitar by now? . . . Like Hank Williams and

Jimi Hendrix, Clarence also left us with an unfinished masterpiece of a life and its works."[23]

Clarence had been getting a good bit of session work in Nashville, and he knew a lot of producers there who would have set him up with plenty of work opportunities. He was going to move to Music City; that had been the plan. He had been talking to Roland about these plans on their way up to Lancaster, shortly before the tragedy occurred. Clarence and the New Kentucky Colonels had been scheduled to perform in September at the second annual Walnut Valley Festival in Winfield, Kansas. The festival promoters had planned to honor Clarence on Saturday night by including him in a four-guitar onstage jam session with Doc Watson, Norman Blake, and Dan Crary.[24] Those same three guitarists had performed on the jam session the previous year, and Clarence was to take a fourth chair in 1973. Winfield was always an important mecca for acoustic guitar enthusiasts from all over the world, and Clarence White was held in the highest regard among the followers of that event. Tony Rice (1951–2020) was brought in to replace Clarence for the onstage guitar jam at Winfield that year.[25]

Roland was still getting over another tragedy at the time of Clarence's death: Eric White Sr., Roland's father, had passed way in 1972, at the age of fifty-seven. Both together and individually Eric Sr. and Mildred had been a primary source of support and encouragement. They had instilled confidence in their boys, which was crucial to their later success. To lose that source of strength was hard enough to deal with, but losing Clarence was an additional burden that Roland had to shoulder. However, he wasn't ready to quit playing; his bluegrass dreams hadn't been given a knockout blow yet. Instead, they were redirected into a band setting that was in many ways a continuation of the Kentucky Colonels. That group was Country Gazette.

Country Gazette

Clarence's funeral took place on Thursday, July 19, 1973, at St. Mary's Catholic Church in Palmdale, California. There were over one hundred musicians in attendance, including Gene Parsons, Kris Kristofferson, Rita Coolidge, Bernie Leadon, Roger McGuinn, and Chris Hillman.[1] Many others wished they could have been there. Clarence was obviously loved and respected by his colleagues. The funeral mass was approximately one hour long, and for those who were not familiar with that type of traditional service, it was somewhat disappointing. "All these musicians in there and no music!" stated Byron Berline. "We hated that."[2] Those of the Catholic faith undoubtedly felt that a solemn service was the most appropriate way to honor the departed, but the rest of the funeral attendees were disillusioned. Byron added, "Everyone there expected and wanted more than that. . . . We wanted something that really honored Clarence."[3]

The interment took place at Joshua Memorial Park in Lancaster, where Clarence's father, Eric Sr., was also buried.[4] As they laid Clarence to rest, Gram Parsons started softly singing "Farther Along," a gospel song that Clarence had sung many times with the Byrds.[5] Bernie Leadon joined in, and moments later everyone else added their voices. It was a spontaneous outpouring of affection, and it filled the need for a more meaningful eulogy that had been missing earlier. Byron Berline was so moved he couldn't sing. "Everybody tried to sing with them, but when I tried to sing nothing would come out. I got so choked up. . . . I could not sing a lick.

They sounded great and I was so pleased they did that. It was something Clarence would have appreciated. . . . I know we did."[6]

The tragedy of Clarence's death only caused Roland to redouble his efforts, sharpening the focus of his musical journey. It was important for him to go on; Clarence would have wanted it that way. After Clarence's death, Roland became even more helpful in encouraging younger Nashville musicians. It was a good way to help him deal with the tragedy. He kept on playing at the Station Inn, where most bluegrass pickers congregated. Roland could be seen there often, and that's where I first got to know him and was honored to play with him a few times. Looking back on those days, I have great admiration and respect for him carrying on the way he did.

After Clarence's graveside service, Byron Berline asked Roger Bush, "What would you think about asking Roland to join the Gazette?" Roger jumped at the idea. Country Gazette was soaring in popularity, and having Roland in the band would make it a dream situation.

Country Gazette had already made quite a splash with two previous albums on the United Artists label: *Traitor in Our Midst* (1972), and *Don't Give Up Your Day Job* (1973).[7] Clarence White was a featured guest on *Don't Give Up Your Day Job*, playing lead guitar and Dobro. His solo on Berline's "Huckleberry Hornpipe" is a classic, and pickers still love to play that tune to this day. I remember being impressed with *Traitor in Our Midst* when it first came out, but I was positively bowled over when I first set down the stylus on *Don't Give Up Your Day Job*. It was a perfect album, in my opinion. (It also made me a little envious: I would have given anything to have been Alan Munde in that group!)

Country Gazette was started during the summer of 1971 by Roger Bush and Byron Berline. They had been playing some shows with Kay Starr (1922–2016) earlier that year as part of a group called the Dillard Expedition, featuring Doug Dillard, banjo; Byron Berline, fiddle; Roger Bush, bass/banjo; and Billy Ray Latham, guitar/banjo.[8] (Kay Starr had a big hit in 1950 with "Bonaparte's Retreat" and, two years later, with "Wheel of Fortune," which became her signature song. One trade paper called her a "deep-voiced brunette thrush."[9]) Doug Dillard was unable to complete all of the Kay Starr shows, but Roger and Byron decided to play the shows under a different name. Byron's wife, Bette, came up with "Country Gazette" from a crossword puzzle she'd been working on.[10]

Berline had enjoyed a lot of success as a fiddler besides having played with Bill Monroe's Blue Grass Boys in 1967. He was much in demand, having appeared on records with the Rolling Stones, the Byrds, and many others.

Byron asked Chris Hillman if he knew someone who could play guitar and sing tenor with their new group. Chris suggested Kenny Wertz,[11] who had been a member of the early '60s bluegrass group the Scottsville Squirrel Barkers. (Their album *Bluegrass Favorites* was one of the records I cut my teeth on when I was learning the five-string banjo.[12]) Byron and Roger tracked down Wertz, who had been working as a dishwasher at a hotel in Lake Tahoe. He was hired for the position, and Byron found Kenny a Martin D-18 guitar. Kenny started playing rhythm and singing a lot of lead, as well as high tenor.

The Gazette had originally hired Herb Pedersen to play the banjo, but before the first album was recorded, Pedersen dropped out. He was very busy singing with various groups, recording and playing guitar and banjo. To replace him, Byron brought in his old college buddy from Oklahoma University, Alan Munde. The group got a steady gig playing at Disneyland, which, while it lasted, was grueling—with many shows a day. The band quickly became tight because of their multiple daily performances at Disneyland. During that same time, the group went into the studio and cut their first album, *Traitor in Our Midst*. Herb Pedersen, though no longer a member of the group, contributed with some vocal and guitar parts.

United Artists had signed the Gazette with some initial reluctance, because they already had what they thought of as a bluegrass group, the Nitty Gritty Dirt Band. Later the Gazette found itself growing into a leading bluegrass band, opening for such influential artists as Crosby and Nash, the Steve Miller Band, and Don McLean. It was the start of a nearly two-decade run of Gazette music that left an enduring mark on the bluegrass world.

Kenny pulled out of the Gazette after they recorded *Don't Give Up Your Day Job*, so they began looking for a guitar player. Byron said, "Tony Rice had contacted us wanting to play with Country Gazette. Roger knew Tony and I knew of him. At the time, Tony was in Kentucky playing with J. D. Crowe. We flew Tony to Annapolis and when we began rehearsing, realized he could not sing tenor. That kind of disillusioned him and us. . . . It just did not work out. He could sing, just not tenor. Tony Rice went back to Kentucky and we continued looking for a guitar player and tenor singer."[13] They found who they were looking for in Roland White.

After the demise of the New Kentucky Colonels, Roland was eager to proceed with his career, and taking a position with Country Gazette seemed like a natural step. He didn't want to go back with Lester Flatt; he thought of that as taking a step backward. Besides, Marty Stuart was already playing mandolin with the Nashville Grass. Roger and Byron asked Roland if he could learn the guitar parts from the two albums they had already recorded, and Roland unhesitatingly said yes. He needed something to latch on to and occupy his thoughts—to keep his mind on music. Back in Nashville he went over the two albums, playing along with the recordings until he had the guitar parts down.

"It was great because I had played with Roland with Bill Monroe," Byron told me in an interview. "We needed a guitar player back then [in 1967], and he was interested so we picked him up with Bill. It was kind of neat because when we needed another guitar player with Country Gazette [in 1973], Roland was available."[14]

"He fit in real well [with the Blue Grass Boys] and we had a good time together. I really enjoyed Roland. We roomed together when we were playing with Bill Monroe, and we got to know each other pretty well. And of course he knew Roger Bush really well from the Kentucky Colonels, so it was kind of an easy fit. I thought we had a pretty good sound."[15] Roland's longtime acquaintance with Alan Munde was also a plus.

Roland White's entry into Country Gazette initiated a prolific series of recordings comprising a major body of work that is foundational to modern bluegrass. The albums flowed out in a steady progression over the next several years and did much to influence a younger generation of pickers. The amazing energy of Roland White and Country Gazette was captured for all time in these recordings. That energy affected me and my own playing in a most profound way.

The Gazette members were part of a larger circle of West Coast blue-grassers who often performed and recorded together. An ever-widening flood of musical crossbreeding took place. One fortunate recording event took place in 1974, when LeRoy McNees took part in an album with Ga-zette members Roland White, Byron Berline, and Roger Bush. The album was released on the Manna Records label, highlighting two brothers who sang gospel music: Dave and Steve Hatfield. The record was titled *Blue-*

Country Gazette, Kerrville, Texas, Bluegrass Festival, 1974. L-R: Alan Munde, Byron Berline, Roger Bush, Roland White. Photo by Rick Gardner.

grass Gospel According to Steve, LeRoy, and Brother Dave.[16] The reunion of Roland and LeRoy resulted in several later recordings that brought the two original Kentucky Colonels together.

Bluegrass fans were pleased when the third Country Gazette album came out in 1975. Because of their heavy touring schedule, the band didn't have time to go into a studio. As a result, a live album was made. *Country Gazette Live* was recorded over a two-day period at McCabe's Guitar Shop in Santa Monica, California, in 1974.[17] Instrumentally, the album was a showcase for Byron Berline and Alan Munde. In addition to playing the fiddle, Byron played some distinctively creative mandolin solos. His style was very "notey"—quite different from Roland's, which has always been about phrasing, timing, and creative improvisation without the steady streams of melody notes. Roland played some excellent lead guitar on the album, including a version of Jimmy Bryant's "Laughing Guitar," which Clarence had often played. He also did most of the lead singing, one of the highlights of which is the song "Will You Be Lonesome Too," which he had heard Lester Flatt perform many times.

The Gazette did two tours of Europe in 1975, performing in France, England, Holland, and Switzerland. Byron left the Gazette that same year, after having become disillusioned with the fact that everyone in the group lived so far apart: Roland was in Nashville, Alan was in Texas, and Roger had recently moved to Arizona. The only time they ever got together was on the road.[18]

Berline was eventually replaced by Dave Ferguson,[19] who played on the next Country Gazette album: *Out to Lunch*.[20] Ferguson was listed on the record as a contributing musician rather than a full-fledged band member. Pedal steel guitarist Al Perkins was also included. The album jacket featured a couple of great shots of the group sitting around at a hamburger stand near Alan's house in North Hollywood. The core group consisted of Roger Bush, Alan Munde, Roland White, and Kenny Wertz (who had rejoined the group). Roland again did most of the lead singing on the recording, and there are two songs that are a definite nod to the Bakersfield sound: "Down, Down, Down," written by Tommy Collins and previously recorded by Buck Owens and Rose Maddox, among many others, and "Sing a Sad Song," written by Wynn Stewart and previously recorded by Merle Haggard. "Sing a Sad Song" is performed as a straight-up country dance song, with steel guitar by Al Perkins. Perkins also played steel on "Last Thing on My Mind," which was included on the album as a tribute to Clarence. Roland's brother had wanted to add steel by Al Perkins to his 1973 recording of the song, but because of his untimely death it never happened.

Out to Lunch was released in the U.K. under the title, *Sunny Side of the Mountain*. The label, Transatlantic, changed the title because they already had a band called Out to Lunch. Beginning with a Gram Parsons song, "Still Feeling Blue," the album featured lots of the trademark Country Gazette harmony singing, which was often characterized by a high baritone part above the tenor. It was an unusual (though not totally original) vocal sound for the time—taking the high lonesome sound of bluegrass and kicking it up a notch. They also double-tracked some of the vocal parts—in other words, they overlaid two different tracks of the same vocal part to give it a different sound. It wasn't traditional, to say the least. "Jim Dickson [the Gazette's producer] had a real active ear—he wasn't a very knowledgeable bluegrass fan, but he liked the music and he could hear things in it that maybe if you were just a strictly bluegrass person you wouldn't hear. He would sort of bring those things out," Alan Munde told me.[21]

The title tune, "Out to Lunch," was a lightning-fast instrumental with some unusual chord changes. Another instrumental on the album was "Forked Deer," a traditional old-time tune played by Dave Ferguson on fiddle with rolling banjo backup. The sound was reminiscent of the 1965 recording *Pickin' and Fiddlin'* by the Dillards with Byron Berline.[22] Roland sang a high lead vocal on "Sunny Side of the Mountain," an old song that Jimmy Martin had recorded and often performed. As a former member of Jimmy's band, Alan was well acquainted with that one. Munde's "Uncle Clooney Played the Banjo (But Mostly Out of Time)" was another instrumental on that album. It has a pretty melody, and this recording featured a nice improvisational break by Roland that stood alone and didn't sound like an attempt to duplicate the banjo melody.

In a correspondence I had with Kenny Wertz, he told me a story about those days:

> I have nothing but good memories of working with Roland. He was always a professional with a focused attitude. He really loved playing good music but was very serious in his preparation. I remember back around 1975 we were playing the Oxford Hotel in Denver. It was winter time and very cold outside. Roland got the flu and had a temperature of 103 but he still went on and played all 3 sets that night. The next day we were invited to the home of Dick Brown [later the banjo player for Lost Highway] to have barbecued steaks. After Roland ate he curled up in a "papasan chair" and fell asleep. Roland was always a positive influence on my music endeavors and was never critical but always positive and helpful. Roland and I still keep in touch. He's a great guy and great musician.[23]

That group toured Europe again—playing in Holland, England, Wales, Switzerland, and other places. Several of the venues were the same ones that the New Kentucky Colonels had played in 1973. Additionally, they played at the Montreux Jazz Festival next to Lake Geneva.

Alan recorded a banjo album in Fort Worth during the summer of 1975, on Slim Richey's newly formed Ridge Runner label.[24] (My first solo album, *Ladies on the Steamboat,* came out on that same label.[25]) Mike "Slim" Richey, who was a jazz guitarist, produced many of the Gazette's solo albums. Alan's record *Banjo Sandwich* was the first recording made by Ridge Runner, and it featured Roland White as well as other Country Gazette members Dave Ferguson and Roger Bush.[26] My old friend Doc Hamilton played guitar on the recording.[27] It was essentially a Country Gazette album and has since become a classic—in many ways equal to Earl Scruggs's iconic *Foggy Mountain Banjo* album. Ridge Runner record number three, *Dave Ferguson: Somewhere over the Rainbow,* was also basically a Country Gazette album because it included Roland, Alan Munde, and Roger Bush—along with other musicians Joe Carr (guitar), Dan Huckabee (Dobro), Stephen Bruton (guitar), and Greg Ferguson (guitar).[28]

The same year, Roland recorded a solo album on the Ridge Runner label: *I Wasn't Born to Rock'n Roll.*[29] The record was a landmark in Roland's career and a much-sought-after classic for many years by bluegrass collectors. It was finally rereleased on CD in 2010 on Tompkins Square Records. This too, in many ways, was a Country Gazette album, since it included musicians Alan Munde, Kenny Wertz, Roger Bush, and Dave Ferguson. One of the tunes on *I Wasn't Born to Rock'n Roll* was "Kansas City Railroad Blues." It's an exciting tune that is credited by many to Fiddlin' Arthur Smith. I remember Bill Monroe playing it all the time, and he had a strikingly realistic "train shuffle" on part of it. You almost felt like you were riding on the train when he did that; his mandolin had such a deep, throaty tone. Roland, who remembers listening to Bill play that shuffle while riding down the highway on the bus late at night, did a great job of recreating the sound on this album. Roland sang a couple of lines on the song that I've never heard anyone else do:

> *I'm goin' to Kansas City, just to look around*
> *If I don't find the one I love, I'm Alabamy bound.*

When I asked him where he learned that short vocal interlude, he couldn't remember. It really fits in well, though, and I'm glad he included it.

There was quite a bit of Flatt and Scruggs influence on *I Wasn't Born to Rock'n Roll* too. "I'm Head Over Heels in Love with You" was pure Lester Flatt, with the exception of the high baritone on the vocal choruses, which brought a Country Gazette flavor to the song. "Texas Gales," credited on the album to Molly O'Day, is a tune that was popular among pickers around Nashville at the time. I've heard other musicians call it "Texas Gals." Roland and Alan Munde made it into a mandolin-banjo duet on this album. "Powder Creek" was an original instrumental written by Clarence and Roland in the 1960s. Roland told me the story behind it: The two brothers were riding in a car with the Kentucky Colonels going down the New Jersey Turnpike in 1963, and Roland was picking the mandolin. He was creating a tune from scratch (much like Bill Monroe used to do). They stopped at a rest area and set up a reel-to-reel tape recorder in the restroom, recording it before they forgot it. Later they named it "Powder Creek." It was recorded for the first time on *I Wasn't Born to Rock'n Roll*.

Dobro player Dan Huckabee's 1976 Ridge Runner album was also pretty much a Country Gazette record.[30] *Why Is This Man Smiling?* featured Gazette members Roland White (guitar/mandolin), Alan Munde, Roger Bush, and Dave Ferguson—along with Joe Carr (guitar/mandolin), Gerald Jones (banjo), Mike Richey (guitar), Marc Johnson (bass), and Gary Bergman (guitar).[31]

Roland was once again reunited with LeRoy McNees on *Life's Railway to Heaven*, with Steve and Dave Hatfield.[32] Additional musicians on that album included Byron Berline, Roger Bush, Al Perkins, and John Hickman (banjo).

Also in 1976 the Gazette did another European tour, which this time included the International Festival of Country Music at Wembley Arena in London. (Other acts at that festival included Tammy Wynette, Waylon Jennings, Dolly Parton, Carl Perkins, Connie Smith,[33] John Hartford, the Dillards, Red Sovine, Jim and Jesse, Wanda Jackson, the Ozark Mountain Daredevils, and many others.) In October of the same year, Country Gazette performed at the Atlanta-Fulton County Stadium.

Dave Ferguson and Roger Bush departed from the band shortly after that. That left only Roland and Alan. A tour of Japan was undertaken, with Roger Bush returning temporarily for that string of performances. Bill Bryson (who later became a member of the Desert Rose Band) played guitar in Japan with the Gazette.

The Country Gazette album *What a Way to Make a Living* was made in 1977 and included Roland, Byron Berline, Skip Conover (Dobro), Slim Richey (guitar), Richard Greene (fiddle), and Bill Bryson (bass).[34] The recording was in many ways a return to classic bluegrass style. Gone

Country Gazette at Telluride Bluegrass Festival, Telluride, Colorado, June 22, 1979. L-R: Alan Munde, Michael Anderson, Joe Carr, Roland White. Photo by Rick Gardner.

was the high baritone vocal harmony, replaced by traditional bluegrass harmony. Roland sang lots of powerful lead vocals on this one, and he pulled out many time-honored songs from the bluegrass genre. "Goodbye Mitchell Jayne" was actually an old traditional tune they renamed. The real name was "Goodbye Liza Jane." It was meant to be a tribute to Mitch Jayne, bass player and emcee for the Dillards. Mitch passed away in 2010, so today the tune has become a genuine tribute to an important figure in bluegrass history. Mitch would have liked it that way. Roland's playing on this tune reminds me a little bit of Buck White's mandolin style. "The Old, Old House" was a George Jones song (cowritten with Hal Bynum), but Bill Monroe did it a lot, so now it's a bluegrass song as well as a country song. (I had the honor of playing banjo on Bill's recording of that song.) Bill sang it solo, but the Gazette version had harmony all the way through.

The unusual story of an album that was lost for nearly four decades and then recovered began in 1979. Jim Lauderdale made his first record that year in Nashville,[35] in collaboration with Roland White, along with some of the greatest pickers in Music City. When I interviewed Lauderdale in October 2015, he had this to say about those days:

> In 1979 I came to Nashville and ended up staying about five months, and I had two goals. One was to hang out with and sing with George Jones, and the other was to meet and sing with Roland White. I did not achieve that goal with George Jones, but I met Roland [at the Station Inn] and told him what a huge fan I was. He invited me over to his house. He became a mentor to me, and I just could not believe that I had the good fortune of being in his presence—and then to get to sing with him! Hearing Roland with the Kentucky Colonels on record was as important to me as any influential musical experience I'd had. And that included anybody in bluegrass, anybody in rock, or anybody in any genre of music. I held Roland up in as high regard as anybody in music that I loved.[36]

Certain indefinable qualities of Roland's had attracted Jim Lauderdale. First—and probably foremost—Roland was approachable. You could talk to him (most bluegrass people are like that). And his music was rooted in bluegrass, as was Jim's. Roland had been one of the pioneers and Jim was steeped in admiration for him, because he understood the important contributions Roland had made. Bluegrass had developed a lot since its early days, and Roland was one of the leaders who had nurtured that development. "A mixture of the kind of voice he had, his playing, his taste—it was just everything," Jim said in admiration. "I was real pleased when I got the Kentucky Colonels' studio album—and then I was hungry to get anything I could find by Roland."[37]

Jim got his wish when the Kentucky Colonels live recordings came out. He listened intently to the live European recordings of the New Kentucky Colonels. He bought every Country Gazette album that Roland was on. "*I Wasn't Born to Rock'n Roll* was just a flawless record to me," he said. "When I'd go see him at the Station Inn, many times he'd let me get up and do a few songs—and that was just so thrilling for me. He was important to me, somebody who was trying to make me feel as though I was really on my way. I observed how much people loved Roland and respected him, other musicians as well as fans."[38]

Roland recognized Jim's talent, along with his drive and desire to succeed. They got to know each other better. One time Jim went to Roland's house for a visit and he heard a jazz recording being played. He asked Roland, "Who is that?" Roland told him it was Thelonious Monk. "I had kind of vaguely heard of Thelonious Monk," Jim said. "Roland really had a broad musical knowledge and he was listening to some really heavy stuff."

A landmark recording, lost for many years and then rediscovered, came out as a result of Jim Lauderdale's association with Roland White. Here's how Jim related that story to me: "I kind of timidly approached Roland and said, 'I wish we could do some recording.' He said, 'Let's do it.' So I was just over the moon. He recommended Steve Scruggs—Earl's son—who had a recording studio in Earl's basement. We did the record in a few days. At one point Earl came down to the basement and asked us if we wanted some coffee. We said 'sure' and he brought a silver tray with some very nice coffee cups, and he was wearing a white apron." Earl was the perfect host.

"I was a fairly new songwriter at that time, but we recorded a few songs I wrote, which was a big milestone for me." Personnel included Terry Smith (bass), Gene Wooten (Dobro),[39] Stan Brown (banjo), Johnny Warren (fiddle), and Marty Stuart and Jim Lauderdale (guitar).

> I sent the tapes out to all the bluegrass labels I knew, but because I was an unknown and wasn't on the bluegrass circuit, it was kind of a catch 22: I wasn't playing the circuit, because I didn't have a record out, and I couldn't get a record deal, because I wasn't on the circuit. So I got turned down by all the labels I approached. That was my first taste of music biz disappointment. . . . I thought at the time that was going to be my major break.
>
> And then the masters just got lost. I left them there at the studio, and we can't locate them. I hope someday they'll turn up. I'd really like for the record to see the light of day.[40]

At the time I talked to Jim (2015), the masters still hadn't turned up. And then, lo and behold, a reel-to-reel tape—probably a rough mix—was found in 2017 among some of Roland's recordings. It was not the master (which still has never been found).

Jim listened to the tape and decided that *Jim Lauderdale & Roland White* was good enough to put out.[41] Indeed, being mastered from an analog tape, it's better sounding than many digital files would be. Lots of people involved in recording swear that analog tape, which was used for this project, is better than digital recordings. True, all releases are digital nowadays, but they are born in the digital realm to begin with, not transferred from analog recording tape. To many people, tape has a warmer sound, but it's more difficult and time-consuming to work with. It has to be wound and rewound many times to make fixes on certain tracks, and studio time is so expensive now that most people use digital technology to begin with.

"Forgive and Forget" was a great kickoff song for the album. One of Jim Lauderdale's originals, it was about as traditional-sounding bluegrass as you could get. Jim's voice was great, but one of the first things I noticed was the wonderful Dobro playing of the late Gene Wooten. His Dobro tone was very similar to the gutsy sound of Josh Graves. Roland's mandolin solo on "Gold and Silver" was a rambling, joyful adventure. After listening to this song, I can see why Jim Lauderdale wanted to hang out with George Jones: his voice was similar to George's and had some of the same kinds of inflections. Roland's tenor harmony matched Jim's lead singing like an ornamental border. "(Stone Must Be the) Wall Around Your Heart" was originally a Don Reno and Red Smiley song, recorded in the 1950s. No banjo was used on Roland and Jim's version. It wasn't really necessary, and it left more room for Gene's tasteful backup on the Dobro. Roland's tenor singing sounded a lot like Don Reno's on this recording.

For me, the real highlight of "Six White Horses" was Marty Stuart's incredible lead guitar playing. He started out with fingerpicking backup, just like Earl did on the Flatt and Scruggs record, but with a bluesier attitude. As the song progressed, his guitar cut through the background, punctuating vocal lines—each time with a totally unexpected tonal variation. His solo brought together many of the most appealing aspects of country and blues guitar: single notes framed by occasional chords, along with lots of string choking. Marty was born to play music, and it's little wonder he was so eager to hit the bluegrass trail with Lester when he was just a teenager—nothing could stop him.

A Gordon Lightfoot song was also featured on the record: "That's What You Get for Loving Me." I always did think Gordon Lightfoot should have a bluegrass band behind him, and this recording proves it. There were a couple of Delmore Brothers songs at the end of the album, and Jim and Roland really adhered to the spirit of the Delmores. "I'm Gonna Lay Down My Old Guitar" (often sung by Doc Watson) and "Nashville Blues" found a perfect home on this record. "Nashville Blues" is a song every musician who's ever lived in Music City can identify with.

I'm so glad this album was rescued from oblivion, and I'm also glad that someone of Jim Lauderdale's stature in the music world can still take pride in this early bluegrass recording, which is second to none. Moreover, the presence of Roland White makes it a classic.

My conversation with Jim Lauderdale never strayed far from what a nice person Roland White has always been: "I still have that feeling around Roland. He's the most down-to-earth person, and so disarming, that I still look at him in the same light as I did the very first time I met him. He's still as important to me as he ever was."[42]

The mingling of old and new that characterized Jim Lauderdale's recording was also a prominent feature of Country Gazette's next album, *All This and Money Too*.[43] Made in Fort Worth, Texas, the project can best be described as free and unrestrained. In addition to Roland and Alan, the record featured Michael Anderson on bass and Joe Carr on guitar. Electric influence was once again present, with Slim Richey on jazz guitar, Tommy Spurlock on steel guitar, and Mike McCarty and Michael Dohony on drums. Dave Ferguson played fiddle on some cuts.

Slim Richey's presence can be felt in the overall sound of the album. Roland was obviously inspired by Slim's jazz guitar playing. One song, "The Tracker," was reminiscent of the 1977 Slim Richey project *Jazz Grass*, which included some of the greatest players of the period performing jazz-oriented material.[44] On *All This and Money Too* Roland sang lead on "Cotton Eyed Joe," an old fiddle tune the Gazette modernized somewhat with a few chord changes and switching of keys. As one listens to "Cotton Eyed Joe," it seems to get more traditional as it progresses, and its position in the lineup was likely determined by the song that followed it—the Beatles' "Eleanor Rigby"—in order to highlight the marked contrast between traditional and modern.

Alan Munde used a phase shifter on the song "Eleanor Rigby." A phase shifter is an electronic effects device that creates a "psychedelic banjo" sound. Basically, phase shifters give the impression that the banjo sound is moving away and coming back in, creating a swirling effect. Phase shifters were somewhat of a fad among banjoists in the late 1970s. Peter Wernick was one of the more well-known users of the device.[45]

The tone of the album switched immediately back to elemental bluegrass conservatism after "Eleanor Rigby" with the inclusion of Lester Flatt's "Why Don't You Tell Me So." The instrumental backup becomes swingy and exploratory as the song moves along, reminding one that the rhythm must be rock-solid for the melody instruments to be able to stray and float around so freely. Roland displayed his country roots once again by singing the Lefty Frizzell song "She's Gone, Gone, Gone" (written by Harlan Howard). Signature Gazette harmony worked really well on that one, and the mandolin break was pure Roland White—wandering around but connecting at critical points to let you know he wasn't getting lost, just exploring.

In 1980 Alan Munde recorded a couple of Ridge Runner albums, *Festival Favorites, Vols. 1 and 2*,[46] that featured Roland playing solos on a bunch of great old tunes like "Under the Double Eagle," "Wildwood Flower," and "Salt Creek." The band name was listed on both albums as the Texcohomanewmexiline Ramblers and included Robert Bowlin (fiddle), Joe Carr (guitar), and Mike Anderson (bass).

In 1981 Country Gazette released another album on the Flying Fish label, *American and Clean*.[47] That recording included the same personnel as 1979's *All This and Money Too*, along with guests Tommy Spurlock (steel guitar), Slim Richey (guitar), Dave Ferguson (fiddle), Mike McCarty (drums), and Dahrell Norris (drums). One of the standout selections was "Love Lost and Found," a plaintive song with an equally plaintive mandolin solo by Roland. Another album highlight, "The Great Joe Bob," contained a fascinating story about a football hero gone bad.

Toward the end of that year, Michael Anderson left the Gazette and was replaced by Greg Kennedy (who had been a Blue Grass Boy in 1973). A few months later, Greg also departed and was replaced by Bill Smith.

In 1982 another devastating stroke of misfortune brought sorrow to Roland and his family. Shortly before the World's Fair in Knoxville, Tennessee, a fatal tragedy befell Clarence's widow, Julia "Susie" LeBlanc, and their ten-year-old son, Bradley. Susie was driving back home to Eastern Kentucky—Elkhorn City, near Pikeville—after having made a trip to Nashville with Bradley and his sister, Michelle (age fifteen). Roland was out of town at the time, playing in Utah. The route took her up through Knoxville, Tennessee. Roland's son Lawrence (age twelve) was also in the car, riding in the back. He was planning on spending a week at his aunt Susie's, and Roland was going to join them when he returned. A lot of highway work was going on around the area in preparation for the World's Fair. There was some equipment in the road, which the car struck—killing Susie and Bradley. The boy had been sitting behind Susie in the left rear seat, and he saw the highway equipment in front of them as the car sped toward it. He jumped up behind her and yelled, at which point impact occurred, and both Susie and Bradley were killed. Michelle and Lawrence were on the right side of the car—one in front, one in back—and weren't seriously hurt—at least not physically.

"It was terrible," said Roland. "The only one in Clarence's family left was Michelle. She stayed up there with her aunt Dorothy for a while, and then moved to Nashville when she was still in high school. She's been here ever since. It's still heavy on Lawrence's mind as well."[48]

Once again Roland immersed himself in music to overcome his grief. *America's Bluegrass Band* by Country Gazette was recorded in November 1982.[49] Bill Smith supplied much of the lead singing on that album. One of the highlights was a Kentucky Colonels medley featuring "I Might Take You Back Again," "The Crawdad Song," "Black Mountain Rag," and "New River Train." As Roland sang the first song, you could feel his passion for the Kentucky Colonels, a group that was still first in his heart. "New River Train" takes me back to the Station Inn in Nashville in the mid-1970s, when I used to hear Roland sing that one almost every time he performed. "The Master's Bouquet" was from the timeless old-time gospel tradition, sung by Roland with quartet harmony on the choruses and featuring twin mandolins by him and Joe Carr. "Charlotte Breakdown" was a frantic, forward-rushing banjo instrumental written by Don Reno, originally released in 1957. Roland and Alan played together so well on it that they sounded like one person playing two instruments. "Sweet Allis Chalmers" was a song that Kristie has always loved, because she was raised on an Iowa farm (hers was a John Deere family, though).

"Molly and Tenbrooks" was familiar to Roland, being one of Bill Monroe's most popular songs. It dates back to 1878, when a race was held in Louisville, Kentucky, at what is now Churchill Downs. The horse race was between two thoroughbreds: Mollie McCarty (sometimes spelled

McCarthy), from California, and Ten Broeck, a bay horse from Kentucky. Ten Broeck had been breaking speed records, and Mollie, it was said, had won every race she'd entered. A rivalry thus developed between California and Kentucky, and thirty thousand spectators showed up to watch the competition. The winner would get ten thousand dollars. For 2⅜ miles of the first heat, Mollie was mostly in the lead, but then her muscles apparently cramped up due to the heat, humidity, and muddiness of the track. Ten Broeck won the race and a folk song developed from it, attributed to the black population of Louisville. Mollie was rumored to have died, but in fact she lived and continued racing for several more years. Bill Monroe learned the song as a child in Kentucky.[50]

In 1982 another Alan Munde Ridge Runner album, *Festival Favorites: Nashville Sessions*,[51] was recorded with Roland White and several other great musicians, many of whom were located in the Nashville area: Sam Bush (fiddle),[52] Jerry Douglas (Dobro), Marty Stuart (lead guitar), Joe Carr (rhythm guitar), Blaine Sprouse (fiddle),[53] Larry Wexer (harmonica), and Bob French (banjo).

Joe Carr was doing much of the emcee work on the Gazette's live shows, and he was very good at it. He had an offbeat sense of humor, and during a show at the Smithsonian Institution in April 1982, he introduced Roland to the audience like this:

> Roland's played with a lot of different groups: Bill Monroe's Blue Grass Boys, Lester Flatt's Nashville Grass, and in the early 1960s—in Southern California—a group called the Kentucky Colonels. That group traveled around and played music at a time when bluegrass was not like today, when any bluegrass group of any caliber can command whatever price they want, and perform anywhere they want and be assured of two, three hundred thousand people showing up for the concert. Not true years ago in Southern California. There were actually vigilante squads organized just looking for bluegrass musicians—a dangerous time—a lot of time spent underground in Southern California, but they came through it nonetheless. In late 1965 they did have to change their name to the "Kenturny Cuckles" and perform as a breakfast cereal for a couple of years. They actually did better—at least they weren't as hungry as they had been earlier.[54]

In 1983 a fourth Alan Munde *Festival Favorites* album was cut: *Festival Favorites: Southwest Sessions*.[55] The band was called the Southwest Society of String Sizzlers. Once again Roland White was featured, along with Jim "Texas Shorty" Chancellor (fiddle), Robert Bowlin (fiddle), Bob French (banjo), Mark Land (guitar), and Bob Clark (mandolin). An original tune from Alan's early career was included, "Molly Bloom." It was fashioned from a musical "overlapping" scale particularly suited to melodic-style banjo playing. The tune springs into life after its elegant underlayment is established, and decorative variations are then added. It was originally recorded in 1969 by Poor Richard's Almanac, which included Alan, Sam Bush, and Wayne Stewart.

In 1983 Roland did a little moonlighting of his own with a studio band called the Dreadful Snakes. The inspiration for the band name came from a Bill Monroe song titled "The Little Girl and the Dreadful Snake." Besides Roland, the aggregation included Béla Fleck (banjo), Blaine Sprouse (fiddle), Mark Hembree (bass), Jerry Douglas (Dobro), and Pat Enright (guitar). I think the group should have been named "Pat Enright and the Dreadful Snakes," because his singing was the powerful voice that tied the band together. On the group's one and only album, *The Dreadful Snakes: Snakes Alive*,[56] Pat's rendition of "Blue Yodel #4" was among the very best recordings I have ever heard of the song. "Cash on the Barrelhead" brought his singing up yet another notch, and he hit the ball out of the park with "In Despair" (another Monroe song.) Pat has a way of singing a song that makes you think, *This is the true version—the way it's supposed to go. Other renditions just don't cut it.*

Roland did an equally fine job of singing on the Dreadful Snakes album. "Linda Lou," another Monroe song, was a great example. Roland sang it with obvious admiration for the master, and Béla Fleck's banjo backup was tasteful and unobtrusive. (I remember lots of people requesting "Linda Lou" in Japan when I was there as a Blue Grass Boy in 1974.) "Brown County Breakdown" was also included on the album. The Snakes crawled a little bit astray on that one, though, playing a calypso beat behind the first part. The original Monroe recording had "stops" on every measure. Roland sounded a little uncomfortable with that arrangement when he played his mandolin solo. I would love to have heard this band stay together long enough to develop a better blend of talent and dynamics. However, the singing by Pat Enright alone is worth the price of the album.

It was at about this time that the Nashville Bluegrass Music Association (NBMA) was started by Roland White and Charmaine Lanham.[57] The two of them went to Bill Monroe and explained their idea for a membership-based organization to promote bluegrass, put on concerts, and publish a newsletter. They organized performances at the Tennessee Performing Arts Center; the Station Inn; Mother Maybelle Carter's home in Madison, Tennessee; and other places, including the Bucksnort Trout Ranch. (About an hour west of Nashville, Bucksnort Trout Ranch has been a popular destination for family trout fishing for over fifty years. Pure cold spring water provides a home for the trout.) Bill Monroe performed at several of the NBMA shows. The organization, which has since been dissolved, was influential in promoting bluegrass in Nashville. Some consider the Nashville Bluegrass Music Association to be one of the primary forerunners of the IBMA.

Joe Carr left Country Gazette in 1984 and was replaced by Gene Wooten on guitar and Dobro. Of Gene's singing, Roland said, "He sang his butt off—he could sing 'Montana Cowboy' better than anybody I know!" Roland remembered traveling in a full-size Dodge van to Washington, D.C., to play at a concert venue called the Birchmere. Gene Wooten played rhythm on the Dobro, which is no small feat. He even put in the G-runs that are so ubiquitous in bluegrass rhythm guitar. Later in the show Gene switched to a flat-top, and only then did the rest of the band become aware that he hadn't been playing guitar before!

Also in 1984, Billy Joe Foster joined the Gazette as a bass player. From Duncan, Oklahoma, Billy Joe (1961–2013) not only played bass but was also an accomplished fiddler, banjoist, mandolin player, and guitarist. He was a talented songwriter as well. (Later Billy Joe Foster was a multi-instrumentalist in Ricky Skaggs's band, Kentucky Thunder.) Another banjo album titled *Alan Munde: In the Tradition* featured Roland White on mandolin.[58] Other personnel included Billy Joe Foster (fiddle/bass/guitar), Bubba Ray Bodart (guitar), Joe Carr (guitar/mandolin), Gene Wooten (Dobro), Craig Fletcher (mandolin), and Bill Evans (banjo).

In September 1986 Arline and Roland were divorced. He didn't remarry until May 1989 when he wed Diane Bouska, whom he met while they worked together in the Nashville Bluegrass Music Association. (In 2000 Roland and Diane formed the Roland White Band, the subject of chapter 10.)

Bluegrass Tonight was the next album the Gazette recorded.[59] "Don't Let Nobody Tie You Down," sung by Billy Joe, had some good advice for people brave enough to take it. The lyrics are an accurate description of Roland's philosophy:

> *1: The boss-man says, "Get busy,"*
> *But he ain't busy, is he?*
> *Don't let nobody push you 'round.*
> *If he gets in your hair, there's other jobs elsewhere.*
> *Don't let nobody tie you down.*
>
> *Chorus: You won't be satisfied until*
> *You see what's over one more hill.*
> *So if your feet are free, boy,*
> *Take this advice from me, boy:*
> *Don't let nobody tie you down.*

"Kentucky Waltz," an early Monroe classic, was a song very familiar to Roland from his Blue Grass Boy days. He kicked it off with a sweet mandolin intro—almost like honey dripping—and he sang the wide-ranging vocal part so effortlessly that he was even able to put in a little falsetto toward the end.

That same year Roland participated in a tour of Africa for the United States Information Service (USIS). The band consisted of brothers Terry and Billy Smith, Blaine Sprouse, and Roland. Billy had known Roland for many years. He told me:

> I first saw Roland as a Bluegrass Boy in Bill Monroe's band. Then on to Lester's band. The first time I met Roland was in Nashville [around 1974] at a club called "Franks and Steins." He was a hero to me, and it was a thrill to meet him. He was so kind, and we became friends. He came regularly to sit in and pick with us. Our band's name was "Blue Haze" [and it consisted of] Ingrid Fowler,[60] Alan O'Byrant, and Terry and Billy Smith. I've the greatest respect and love for Roland White.[61]

The first leg of the 1986 Africa journey was to Paris, and from there they flew straight to the Congo. The group played in Zaire, Nigeria, Ivory Coast, Congo, and Liberia (just before that country's civil war). The performances were for locals as well as United States embassy people. It was the first bluegrass ever heard in that part of Africa, and standing ovations followed nearly every show.

Billy Smith told me an interesting story that took place while they were in the Congo. He said they were able to receive only two TV channels at their hotel—one from the Congo and the other from Zaire. The shows were very basic, much like public access TV. Local musicians were often featured, and the shows were rebroadcast over and over. Roland and the group asked their escort officer, Steve Belcher, if he could arrange for the local TV station in Brazzaville to videotape a telecast of the band. Their request was granted and three numbers were recorded. One of them was a fiddle tune they had composed called "Bluegrass on the Congo." It was amusing to Billy, Roland, and the others to think of the local residents having to watch those three numbers over and over again.[62]

The next year Roland recorded his final album with Country Gazette, *Strictly Instrumental*.[63] It was the first full album of instrumentals made by the Gazette, and the inclusion of guitarist David Grier was an especially fitting choice. After years of growing up studying Clarence White's guitar-picking style, David did a brilliant job of complementing Roland's playing on that recording. The first tune on the album, "John Henry," immediately conjured up *Appalachian Swing!* David stayed true to the feeling of Clarence's version, using certain double string harmony sliding positions that were an obvious nod to Clarence. In addition, Gene Wooten on Dobro added a Kentucky Colonels flavor to *Strictly Instrumental* with his traditional "hound dog" style, which was closer to Leroy McNees's approach than many of the more modern Dobro styles. Kathy Chiavola,[64] who played electric bass on the album, enhanced the ensemble with her considerable knowledge and familiarity with the music. (A very talented singer as well as instrumentalist, Kathy is another musician who Roland helped to find work and make connections upon first coming to Nashville.) *Strictly Instrumental* was a powerful confirmation of the direction the Kentucky Colonels had been attempting to take bluegrass in a much earlier time.

All of these albums, solo as well as Country Gazette projects, derived from the same cadre of Gazette personnel, with a few changes here and there. Roland White was on all of them, though, adding his individual stylistic approach to an abundance of great music. These recordings represent an entire subgenre of bluegrass. A lot went on during the Gazette years, with interplay among all manner of trend-setting musicians who combined their talents to form an enduring legacy of music. Interwoven throughout was the distinctive thread of Roland White's mandolin playing, always fresh and new, always tasteful and understated.

Country Gazette carved a place in bluegrass music history with a blend of influences not heard in earlier bluegrass from the southeastern part of the United States. The Texas style of music got cross-bred with California Bakersfield style within the framework of bluegrass. "All of those people in Bakersfield were Oklahoma/Texas people anyway," Alan Munde told me. "I grew up in Norman, Oklahoma. . . . There wasn't a lot of bluegrass, but it was all real good. Byron was there, Buck White was in the area, the Stone Mountain Boys, Eddie Shelton [one of Alan's major banjo influences]. There was some good bluegrass around, but it just wasn't real thick. I jammed a lot with people who played pianos and fiddles and sang 'Bubbles in My Beer' [a Bob Wills standard] and 'San Antonio Rose'—that whole sensibility."[65]

When Roland brought his talent and personality into Country Gazette, he added a fresh and unique dimension to the sound—spanning the gap between old and new, east and west, Nashville and Bakersfield, country and bluegrass, and city and hillbilly. Most importantly, the Gazette was an extension of the original Kentucky Colonels, and it had the good fortune of coming along at an opportune time, when bluegrass was really taking hold in the mainstream musical landscape. Fate had twice prevented the Colonels from reaching their full potential: first in the mid-1960s, when it became hard to find work playing acoustic music, causing the band to be snuffed out in its infancy, its splendid promise unrealized. Later in 1973 the re-formed band, the New Kentucky Colonels, was just beginning to hit its stride when high hopes were once again dashed by the tragedy of Clarence's death.

The success of Country Gazette and its many musical spinoffs owed everything to the trailblazing efforts of the Kentucky Colonels. With the inclusion of Roland White, as well as Roger Bush, the resulting Gazette sound was a direct descendant of the Colonels. Country Gazette took a path that made their music more relevant to baby boomers who had been listening to rock and country rock, thus drawing in a much larger audience for bluegrass than ever before. Their style was less restrained by tradition than bluegrass groups from the eastern part of the United States. It was a West Coast thing—less inhibited and more willing to bring other influences into the genre. And it led lots of people to eventually gain an enhanced appreciation of the traditional influences that lived on in the music of earlier pioneers like Bill Monroe.

The exuberant sound of Country Gazette was largely due to the energetic and precise banjo playing of Alan Munde, who incorporated newer banjo styles with time-honored Scruggs approaches. Munde's background spanned the entire spectrum of bluegrass, from his association with newgrass pioneer Sam Bush to performing with the flamboyant traditionalist Jimmy Martin. Roger Bush was also a big contributor to Country Gazette's success. His bass-playing style consisted of more than just the straight lub-dub notes in the background; it was aggressive and lively, including lots of slapping to give the overall sound more color.

Roland White, however, tied it all together with his wide-ranging experience in the bluegrass field, stemming from the breakthrough music of the Kentucky Colonels to the more conventional sounds of Bill Monroe and Lester Flatt. Both his playing and singing reflected a neck-deep immersion in bluegrass, bringing a special authenticity to an already unique and preeminent bluegrass band. Roland did some of the finest playing of his career with Country Gazette.

Alan Munde, in the liner notes to the compilation album *Hello Operator . . . This Is Country Gazette*, writes, "Long-time picking partner and friend Roland White was the mainstay of the group from 1973 until his departure in 1989. He was an incredible force in the band and in bluegrass and provided me with a great education in the music."[66]

When work started getting slower for the Gazette, Roland decided to leave the band. He needed a steadier income, and Alan Munde began teaching full time at South Plains College in Levelland, Texas, where they had a bluegrass and country music program. In early May of that year, as the Country Gazette disbanded, Roland offered to be Bill Monroe's bus driver. He had driven the Bluegrass Special for Bill when he was a Blue Grass Boy, and he had driven Lester Flatt's Scenicruiser from 1969 to 1973. Bill was glad to have Roland, because he worked cheaper than professional drivers. He drove the bus through mid-August.[67]

A foretaste of what Roland White and fiddler Stuart Duncan would be doing together later in the Nashville Bluegrass Band could be heard on David Grier's 1988 solo album, *David Grier: Freewheeling*.[68] Grier's smooth, amazingly fluid improvisations were presented in a many-sided display, ranging in style from old-time to modern, and somewhere in the middle was Roland. One of the tunes, "Bluegrass Itch," bridged the gap between old and new. Roland's solo was very notey, but he occasionally lingered unexpectedly on certain notes before charging forward again. "Alabama Jubilee" was one of Roland White's staples from the Kentucky Colonels days, and David took what Clarence did on that one and moved it up another notch. "Roanoke" (a Bill Monroe original based on the old tune "Turkey in the Straw") showed how closely Roland had listened to Monroe when he was a Blue Grass Boy. On that tune Stuart Duncan played twin fiddle to himself (through the use of overdubbing), making the recording highly reminiscent of the original 1954 Blue Grass Boys recording, which featured Charlie Cline and Bobby Hicks on twin fiddles.

Toward the end of the 1980s, Roland began performing a great deal with Dobro player Gene Wooten and banjo player Richard Bailey (who later became an important member of the Roland White Band). One of the places where they often performed was the Station Inn in Nashville. To augment his income during that period, Roland took another day job. "I got a cool little job at 'Bean Central,' roasting coffee," said Roland:

> They had a roasting company on Broadway, and they also had a store in the south part of Nashville, near the Green Hills area, called the Cook's Nook. I did a lot of the work in that store also, like stocking the shelves. Joe Dougherty was the owner. I worked for him and I could get off anytime I wanted. They sold kitchen equipment, like coffeepots and coffeemakers—wealthy people would come in there and buy that stuff—it was a very high-priced store. I got hooked on the coffee too."[69]

The Cook's Nook occasionally staged kitchen cooking demonstrations, often using expensive Le Creuset enameled-iron cookware. When the demonstrations were over, they'd let employees take the cookware home. Roland and Diane's kitchen benefited greatly.

Bean Central was Roland's place of employment until 1989, when he became a member of the Nashville Bluegrass Band. He was about to join a steadfast group of committed musicians who had bluegrass dreams that matched his own, and the resultant ensemble would raise bluegrass to its highest level ever.

9

The Nashville Bluegrass Band

Kristie, Roland, and I made a trip out to Alan O'Bryant's house in Pegram, Tennessee, on March 19, 2015. Alan had coffee and cinnamon rolls ready for us, and we talked about the old days and the history of the Nashville Bluegrass Band. We sat around the coffee table in Alan's living room as he was putting some new tuners on his banjo. They had really pretty amber-colored buttons. Some interesting ideas about bluegrass, and music in general, came up in our conversation. We focused on those concepts in addition to Roland's history with the Nashville Bluegrass Band.

Roland brought up the group's beginnings, before he became a member: "I always looked at Alan and Pat as the beginning of the Nashville Bluegrass Band. . . . I used to go see them at the Station Inn and thought 'God, what a band!'" Coming together in 1984, the original members of NBB included Alan O'Bryant on banjo, Pat Enright on guitar, Mike Compton on mandolin, and Mark Hembree on bass. Fiddler Stuart Duncan entered the group in the fall of 1985.

Alan O'Bryant came from a musical family in Reidsville, North Carolina, with uncles and cousins who played old-time music. While in his teens Alan played with Pat Smith, a cousin of his dad's. Smith's sons, Billy and Terry, were also aspiring musicians, and Alan often performed with them, eventually forming a band. All three moved to Nashville in 1974. Alan played with James Monroe for several years as a member of the Midnight Ramblers. Through that relationship, he became acquainted with Bill Monroe, playing with him occasionally and maintaining a friendship until Monroe's death in 1996. O'Bryant wrote "Those Memories of You" in 1979, which later became a top five *Billboard* pick after it was included on the Dolly Parton, Emmylou Harris, and Linda Ronstadt album *Trio*.[1] Alan has two sons who are also musicians.[2]

From Huntington, Indiana, Pat Enright was given a guitar by his parents when they recognized his love for singing country music. He joined the navy in 1965, during which time he developed a fondness for bluegrass. In 1969 Pat relocated to California, playing a lot around San Francisco with a friend named Paul King. In 1973 he joined the Phantoms of the Opry, a short-lived group that recorded one album before splitting up. They also won the band contest at Bill Monroe's seventh annual Bean Blossom Bluegrass Festival in June 1973. In 1974 Pat moved to Nashville to pursue his bluegrass dreams. There he met and played with many different musicians, including future bandmate Alan O'Bryant. In 1978 he joined a group called Tasty Licks, which included banjo great Béla Fleck, and recorded two albums with that band. Pat also appeared on Fleck's first solo album, *Crossing the Tracks*.[3] In 1983 he recorded the famous *Dreadful Snakes* album. A year later he formed the Nashville Bluegrass Band (NBB) with Alan O'Bryant.[4]

Mike Compton was born in 1956 in Meridian, Mississippi (Jimmie Rodgers's hometown). His family had been playing traditional music for generations, and his mother encouraged him to play as well. At the age of fifteen, his father gave him a mandolin and he began learning the music of Bill Monroe, Flatt and Scruggs, and the Stanley Brothers. He moved to Nashville at the age of twenty-one, playing for nearly four years with Hubert Davis and the Season Travelers. In 1984 Compton joined up with Alan O'Bryant and Pat Enright as an original member of the Nashville Bluegrass Band. In 1989 he left the band and moved to the Catskill Mountains. Before a year had passed, he returned to Nashville and started playing with David Grier, with whom he recorded and toured in the United States and Japan. He then became a sideman with John Hartford and performed with him until Hartford's passing in 2001. He rejoined the Nashville Bluegrass Band in 2001 after Roland White left.[5]

Born in 1954 in Wisconsin, Mark Hembree was a Blue Grass Boy for almost five years during the early 1980s. Prior to that he'd played bass with the Monroe Doctrine from Colorado and the Piper Road Spring Band from Wisconsin. He auditioned for Bill Monroe on June 24, 1979, at the Southeastern Wisconsin Bluegrass Festival, near Mukwonago and played bass on the classic Monroe recording *Master of Bluegrass.*[6] He was an original member of the Nashville Bluegrass Band and stayed in that group until 1988. Later he returned to Wisconsin, where he now resides, playing bluegrass and western swing.

The first album produced by the Nashville Bluegrass Band, *My Native Home,*[7] was released in 1985 and spotlighted an a cappella rendition of "Up Above My Head," written by gospel and jazz singer Sister Rosetta Tharpe (1915–1973). Black gospel and a cappella singing then became one of the Nashville Bluegrass Band's signature trademarks, enabling the group to perform at many more venues than the usual bluegrass circuit—eventually playing at the White House, Carnegie Hall, and around the world, including the People's Republic of China, Iraq, Bangladesh, and Bahrain.[8]

In 1985, after *My Native Home* was recorded, one of the finest fiddlers anywhere, Stuart Duncan, joined the NBB. Originally from Southern California, Stuart learned the fiddle mostly by listening to records. His influences included Kenny Baker, Chubby Wise, and Vassar Clements. Stuart played his first major bluegrass festival when he was just a kid, with a band called the Pendleton Pickers at Norco, California, in 1974. It was the Golden West Bluegrass Festival, and that was where he first met Pat Enright, who was on the show with his group, Phantoms of the Opry. (I was there too, playing with Bill Monroe.) Stuart attended South Plains College in Texas, where he enrolled in a bluegrass music program. He toured with Larry Sparks in 1984 and played some with Roland White at the Station Inn in 1985, joining the Nashville Bluegrass Band later that same year.[9] Since then, in addition to playing with NBB, Stuart has done much session work and touring with major country artists.[10]

In 1988 the Nashville Bluegrass Band had a bus accident near Roanoke, Virginia, on their way to the Winterhawk Bluegrass Festival.[11] The road was icy. Mark Hembree was driving and couldn't get the bus stopped in time to avoid hitting a semi. All of the band members were injured, some worse than others. Mark suffered multiple broken bones in his hand, and as a result the bass-playing duties were taken over by Gene Libbea. The bus accident really bothered Mike, and he ended up tendering his resignation.[12] (He quit the music business for a while, but later he returned to Nashville and got back into playing music.)

Gene Libbea, NBB's new bass player, had grown up in Southern California. In the early 1960s, he began playing piano with his older brother Steve in local rock 'n' roll and surf music bands. Later on in the 1960s, they began frequenting a folk club in Redondo Beach, where they saw bluegrass artists like Byron Berline and Richard Greene. Gene started playing bass in a folk and bluegrass group with his brother and a friend. In the early 1970s, he attended a public TV taping of a Bill Monroe concert. When he got there, it was announced that Monroe's bus had broken down (where have we heard that before?) and that the Muleskinner band, with Clarence White on guitar, was going to perform instead. That really opened Gene's eyes to the immense potential of bluegrass. During the '70s, Gene and Steve played together in various California acoustic bands. They went to Europe a few times and played one whole summer at Disney World in Florida. Gene met the Nashville Bluegrass Band through Stuart Duncan and officially joined the group in 1989.[13]

On the official Nashville Bluegrass Band website, Alan says, "Not knowing we had just hired Gene Libbea, Roland White called wondering if we still needed a bass player. This presented NBB with the opportunity to work with one of our formative heroes and perhaps the greatest single influence on Mike Compton's approach to the mandolin other than Bill Monroe. Roland White was already a seasoned veteran and a bluegrass legend."

"Roland was like a guru to all of us young bluegrassers in Nashville," said Alan in our interview.

> He had found his voice as a mandolin player. A lot of us were trying to play like somebody else, looking for somebody to emulate. I've taken up the mandolin in my old age—mostly old-time tunes—but Roland, to me, is a huge example of somebody who approaches music, *period*, through the mandolin. He grew up playing the instrument. His whole experience of playing music is through the mandolin [though he does play other instruments]. I grew up playing the banjo. I knew what the chord was in "Foggy Mountain Breakdown" before I knew it was called E minor. It seems like a lot of the stuff Roland does on the mandolin is like that: it comes from *him* and not something that came from any kind of formal study of music.

"Whenever I'm trying to learn a tune on the mandolin," said Alan, "I might listen to the way a fiddler plays it, or I might listen to the way a banjo player plays it, or I might remember the way Monroe played it. But I'd sooner play it the way Roland played it, because it has a whole different twist on it." Bill Monroe's style was fast, with lots of shuffling around, but with Roland you can hear his choice of melody much better. Both styles are unique and important, and both styles are part of the musician: each tune is a personal interpretation unlike anyone else's.

Alan brought up another aspect of mandolin playing, something most of the great bluegrass mandolinists share in common: their right hand moves the pick up and down pretty much continuously, and they choose to get their notes either on the upstroke or on the downstroke or both, depending on the type of rhythm and syncopation they wish to convey. "I kind of picked that up from Clarence's lead guitar playing," said Roland.

We talked about tremolo techniques. (Bill Monroe sometimes called it "trembling.") "I don't do a fast tremolo," Roland said. "When Bill Monroe aged, his tremolo slowed down a bit, but it was never that fast." I mentioned that Buzz Busby had one of the fastest tremolos I had ever heard. It seems like some people can just do that. Alan talked about a local firefighter from Pegram who was great at it. A good tremolo is essential when playing slow songs or waltzes, where long notes are desirable. Having spent some time around Monroe, Alan recalled how Bill would get up in the morning and just start slowly playing a tremolo, moving the fingers of his left hand up and down the strings over the neck until an original melody would evolve. It was a fascinating process.

Roland mentioned another technique, often used by Monroe, that consisted of playing every note with a downstroke of the pick, "like in the tune 'Bluegrass Stomp.' Mike Compton is really good at it, and I'm not," he said. "I've always tried to keep away from doing that. I didn't like it. I'll do it if it's not too fast." I've heard '50s rock 'n' roll guitar players using that technique. It can add sharp intensity to the tune. Banjo innovator Don Reno also emulated the technique by using downward thumb strokes across all or some of the strings. It was always a real crowd-pleaser for Bill Monroe. Roland and I also talked about "hotshot" pickers who blow the audience away with wild licks. Taste and technique have to be in balance with each other, and Roland addressed that fact, saying, "You have to say something to the people. Alan does that same thing on the banjo. Stuart Duncan and Byron Berline do it with the fiddle. Kenny Baker did it."

Alan has looked at how different people develop as musicians in relation to the instrument they start out on. Their first instrument defines how they approach music in general. He turned to Roland, saying:

> It's interesting to me the way you approach a melody. . . . I always have to wonder if it's got something to do with the fact that you've played mandolin for so many years that your whole approach to music is through the mandolin. It's kind of the same way Earl Scruggs was to the banjo. He wasn't trying to sound like "Earl Scruggs"; he was just playing the song. Lots of pickers try to sound like somebody else, or they try to put stuff together with licks that they've heard someone else play. You're beyond that whole thing—you're just trying to play the song—trying to communicate the emotion associated with that song. But being able to do that with a mandolin the way you do—it's not like note choices from a saxophone. It's not like note choices even from a banjo, although you might be influenced by all of those things.

I was in agreement with Alan's analysis. Roland's mandolin playing sounds like mandolin playing. Is that a goofy thing to say? What I mean is, you want your instrument to sound like the instrument that it is, not like some other instrument. That's where I may have gone wrong in trying to play fiddle tunes note-for-note like the fiddle back in the early days of my banjo playing. True, I may have successfully accomplished that goal in many cases, but it didn't have a natural banjo "feel." Again, Roland's mandolin playing sounds like mandolin playing; it doesn't sound like he's trying to play something on a mandolin that was originally meant for another instrument.

"Roland is one of the first people that I think of whenever I'm trying to think of how to play something on the mandolin," said Alan. "I think of how I've heard him turn phrases—phrases that were very 'mandolinesque.' A good instrument will suggest things to you. You hear sounds that instrument will make, and you incorporate those sounds in your playing."

"Here's one thing that Clarence told me years ago," said Roland.

He said, "You need to stop listening to Bill Monroe. Do your own thing. Your mandolin playing will change a whole lot." This was back in the '60s. When I joined Country Gazette, with Alan Munde's style of banjo playing—different fills that he did—I started picking up that kind of stuff on the mandolin. I also listened to Earl Scruggs. In fact I had a banjo I tried to play. When I came to the Nashville Bluegrass Band, I had picked up all this stuff, these things to do, and they were the first band where I could kind of "trip out" a little bit. And the timing was always there. I didn't have to worry about losing them or confusing them, because they were so good. I remember telling Pat [Enright] one time that we canceled each other out with the mandolin and the guitar. I couldn't hear him—we were so close together rhythmically. He's such a great guitar player. The whole band was great.

The Nashville Bluegrass Band brought two elements of Roland's past together in a magnificent way. He had played with both Bill Monroe and Lester Flatt, and the Nashville Bluegrass Band was probably influenced by those two musical pioneers more than anybody else. Alan O'Bryant used to study Lester Flatt; he even patterned much of his emcee work after Lester. "How could you help but do that?" joked Alan when I mentioned this to him. Lester had always been one of his biggest influences, along with Bill Monroe and Ralph Stanley.[14]

Lester Flatt also had a great deal to do with the rhythmic framework of the Nashville Bluegrass Band. Roland's background with Lester proved to be right in step with Alan's concept of timing. "The whole approach to rhythm in the Nashville Bluegrass Band was something that Roland was right at home with," said Alan in our conversation.

Another thing that helped to make the Nashville Bluegrass Band a perfect fit for Roland was the fact that Mike Compton had studied Roland's mandolin playing as well as Bill Monroe's. Aside from Monroe, Roland was probably Mike's biggest influence. Roland stepped into Mike's shoes with no trouble at all, because they were both coming from the same background source. "Roland just fit like a glove," said Alan.

"Sometimes I'd do some rhythmic things while someone was singing," Roland said.

And I'd think, "Oh, I gotta straighten up my act!" I really felt like I was going to knock everybody out of time. I had to be really careful about that. But I didn't have to worry, because they were really solid. Especially when I was playing breaks to songs. I like to experiment. When I came into this band I thought, "This is the time to do it. If they don't like it, they'll tell me so." . . . Like breaks to songs—I did some crazy stuff. A lot of the material was like early country music. It wasn't all fast. Like Johnny Cash's "Big River"—tunes like that, they worked out great. They were all my favorite songs.

The first music Roland had listened to had been country music. When he was a child in Maine, his mother had been playing 78 rpm discs of mostly country songs. For him it was like coming around in a full circle. He was free to channel his lifetime of musical roots into the group. "The Nashville Bluegrass Band was just like open ground for me," Roland said.

The band, in my opinion, became fully developed when Roland joined. Before that it was an exciting, sort of experimental group with great musicians, but its personality really solidified with Roland's presence. Alan O'Bryant disagrees with me a little bit on that: "It was always kind of experimental. We never tried to play anybody else's game. We weren't gonna sound like Jim and Jesse. We weren't gonna sound like the Osborne Brothers. I mean, I couldn't get a job with any of those guys, so I had to start my own band."

"But your band wasn't 'So-and-So and His Blue Grass Boys," chimed in Kristie. "It was the 'Nashville Bluegrass Band'—more of a democratic band. That was unusual for that time [especially around Nashville]."

"It felt like the right thing to do," said Alan, "although John Hartford told us, 'A benevolent dictatorship is really the way to have a band,' and it really is. A democratic band is like the Council of Churches."

One thing has to be mentioned about Alan's vocal style. He had a unique mannerism when singing onstage, which wasn't really a stunt or a trick, but it always made people wonder "What is he doing?" He would hold his banjo up close to his face and sing into it, taking advantage of the instrument's natural resonance. Anyone who's opened up a banjo case has noticed how much the instrument will echo the sounds taking place around it before it is picked up. When playing it, the right hand is usually touching the head, effectively canceling out these harmonic vibrations. But when placed close to the singer's voice, without touching the head, the resulting reverberations have a way of complementing and reinforcing the vocal sound.

"At some point I started picking the banjo up to get the weight of it off my diaphragm so I could have a little more [vocal] control to hit high notes," said Alan in an interview. Soon after he started doing that, Alan noticed the banjo strings rang in tune with his voice, helping him to stay on pitch. The technique was especially useful during a cappella songs.[15] "Actually, I just had the lyrics printed on the back of the banjo," joked Alan.[16]

The Nashville Bluegrass Band won two Grammy Awards, both while Roland was in the band. Alan took us upstairs and showed us a glass-fronted cabinet that contained the Grammys, along with a bunch of IBMA awards. He opened the door and handed me a Grammy trophy. It was quite heavy, being made of a custom metal alloy called grammium.[17] The gramophone cabinet and tone arm of the miniature were plated in twenty-four-carat gold. Alan said he brought one down to the grade school in Pegram one time to let all the kids hold it.

"What's that big tall thing in the center?" I asked, pointing to the cabinet.

"That's an Indy Record Label Award. Roland's got all the SPBGMA [Society for the Preservation of Blue Grass Music] awards. That thing over there that looks like a big fishing lure is a Dove Award. It's for a gospel record that I produced on Blue Highway. That's the only Dove Award I'll ever get. I don't know if we'll ever do another gospel record, since we've backslid so bad," Alan said with a laugh.

When NBB won their first Grammy in 1993, Roland was the only one who went to Radio City Music Hall in New York to pick it up. The rest of the band didn't think there was any way they could win, so they didn't go. Roland said, "I told Diane, 'We're going to the Grammys—get some plane tickets.'" Sure enough, they won!

After our visit, Alan took us all out to eat at a barbeque place in White Bluff called the Perfect Pig. The food was great, and on the way out I grabbed a bumper sticker they were giving away as souvenirs. I still have it stuck on one of my instrument cases. It says, "The Perfect Pig: where a waist is a terrible thing to mind."

The 1990s were a golden era for the Nashville Bluegrass Band. All the elements from each member's background seemed to come to fruition, and the mutual respect was overflowing. Gone were the days when the bandleader called all the shots, booked all the gigs, told the band members what to wear, when to show up, and how to play. Bill Monroe is an example of a bandleader who was of the old school: he knew exactly what he wanted from his musicians—precisely the sounds he desired to hear, right down to the attack of individual notes (but he often had trouble communicating those concepts verbally). Roland had experienced what it was like working as a replaceable unit in someone else's band when he worked for Bill Monroe and Lester Flatt. His devotion to the genre and respect for the bluegrass pioneers he was working for overcame any loss of individuality he may have experienced. Most of the other members of NBB knew about working for a bandleader as well.

The Nashville Bluegrass Band personified what pickers of my own generation wanted a bluegrass band to be like. Perhaps it was the rock 'n' roll influence that we had all experienced while growing up. It didn't matter whether we liked rock 'n' roll or not. It was just the concept of a group of musicians working together as equal partners that took root in our minds. It was often difficult to get earlier generations of bluegrassers to accept that concept. For me (and many might disagree), groups like the Kentucky Colonels, the Bluegrass Alliance, the New Deal String Band, and Country Gazette were sort of lead-ups to a final convergence of ideals in the Nashville Bluegrass Band. The respect for tradition was still ever-present, but the talents of all the pickers were allowed to be spotlighted. The banjo, mandolin, and fiddle were allowed more elbow room; vocal arrangements were more diverse; and song material was expanded. The result was a musical cross-fertilization that did not discard the older influences but rather celebrated them.

Roland considered the Nashville Bluegrass Band "the coolest thing since Monroe and Flatt and Scruggs played together." In one online interview, he spoke glowingly about the members of NBB. Of Pat Enright, he said, "He's a great rhythm guitar player. He's just wonderful, he never does anything that doesn't work. It's straightforward and simple and no one knows how to do it except for Pat. It's hard to do." Of fiddler Stuart Duncan, he said, "Every time we play, he will do something that will make me just want to drop my pick." Of Gene Libbea: "[He] is the kind of bass player that nobody has in bluegrass. He has played all kinds of music. I really like what he does; he's an eye opener and other people need to

The Nashville Bluegrass Band warming up at a bluegrass festival before going on stage. L-R: Alan O'Bryant, Stuart Duncan, Pat Enright, Gene Libbea, Roland White. Photo by John Orleman. From the collection of Alan O'Bryant.

listen to what he's doing." And of Alan O'Bryant: "[He] is a hellacious banjo picker and singer. . . . He sings the heck out of anything he does."[18]

Roland broadened his musical style considerably with the Nashville Bluegrass Band by experimenting with different improvisations during his mandolin breaks and finding newer, jazzier chords to dress up his accompaniment. Some of those chords were suggested to him by Jethro Burns. Jethro (1920–1989) was best known as the mandolin-playing member of the comedy music team Homer and Jethro (Henry D. "Homer" Haynes and Kenneth C. "Jethro" Burns). The duo won a Grammy in 1959. They didn't receive as much serious public acclaim as they should have, mostly due to the comic nature of their repertoire. In fact, both were excellent jazz musicians, as their 1962 and 1967 releases, *Playing It Straight* and *It Ain't Necessarily Square*, clearly demonstrate.[19] Their genius comedy persona was what listeners loved, and that's what made Homer and Jethro unforgettable as a duo. They were sometimes called "the Everly Brothers of the Stone Age." After getting a record contract with King Records, they were quoted as saying, "Our records were an instant hit in shooting galleries."[20]

Here's a story Roland told me about the first time he met Jethro Burns: During one of the many NBB visits to the *Prairie Home Companion* radio show in St. Paul, Roland went into the theater early, entering by a huge back door. As the door clanged shut behind him, he heard a voice call out, "Who's there?"

"Roland White . . . who's there?"

"Jethro Burns. Let's pick."

"Okay, let me put my clothes in the dressing room and I'll be right down." They sat around and played all afternoon.

The first album NBB recorded after Roland came into the band was *The Boys Are Back in Town*.[21] It had some of the musical style that Roland loved most, and you can tell that his newfound delight in playing with the group was infectious. Some of the best-feeling music recorded by NBB was included in this album. "Long Time Gone" had the country feel that Roland was deeply rooted in. "Big River" contained a bluesy mandolin break over a powerful, strong rhythm. Alan O'Bryant played a Scruggs-like banjo break that makes me think that Earl would have sounded great picking with Johnny Cash. (In fact, Earl did record with Johnny Cash on a 1976 album called *The Earl Scruggs Revue, Vol. II*.[22] The song was Cash's "I Still Miss Someone."[23]) "Diamonds and Pearls" started out with Roland and Pat playing a duet on mandolin and guitar and illustrates what Roland had been talking about when he said they canceled each other out: their rhythm and timing were as one. "The Ghost of Eli Renfro" was a song I can remember hearing Joe Stuart singing back in the 1970s at many festivals I played with Bill Monroe and Buck White and the Down Home Folks. I'm sure Alan, who sang it on this album, also remembered hearing Joe doing the song at many of those same festivals. "Big Cow in Carlisle" was a tune written by Alan and Stuart Duncan with a heavy Monroe influence. It gave all the instruments a chance to really show off. Roland put his own spin on it, treading a fine line between the Monroe influence and his own style, celebrating both in expert fashion.

Home of the Blues contained a real gem of a song by Roland—"I'll Just Keep on Lovin' You"—written by country singer Floyd Tillman (perhaps best known for "I Love You So Much It Hurts Me").[24] Roland's voice inflections on this song were highly reminiscent of Tillman, and for those of us who love old country music, this was a real treat. "The Biggest Liars in Town" had a mandolin break by Roland that ended with the Monroe-style downstrokes that we talked about at Alan's house. "I'll Be on That Good Road Someday"—a song recorded by Flatt and Scruggs in the 1960s—had a notey mandolin break. There was no mandolin on the original recording, so Roland wasn't restricted by previous mandolin interpretations. Alan once again revealed his Lester Flatt influence, but he added a little growl to his voice occasionally, like T. Texas Tyler used to do. "Mississippi River Blues" had an incredible mandolin break that almost sounded like a human voice singing. Roland sang bass on "The First Step to Heaven," a gospel song with a nice message about self-realization. He also sang bass on "Roll Jordan Roll," a vocal part he traded with Isaac Freeman from the Fairfield Four on the second half of the song. They had met the Fairfield Four in 1990 through the efforts of Keith Case, who represented both groups.

The Fairfield Four were organized in 1921 by Reverend J. R. Carrethers, assistant pastor of the Fairfield Baptist Church in Nashville. In the early 1940s, they had their own daily morning radio show on WLAC in Nashville, which was syndicated to major U.S. cities. They began calling themselves the "Southland's Famous Fairfield Four." In 1946 they began making records. Their a cappella spiritual music influenced many singers, including B. B. King, who tuned in to their radio show every morning while he was still living in his hometown of Indianola, Mississippi. The Fairfield Four ceased touring in 1950 but continued to perform locally with varying personnel. The year 1980 saw a reemergence of the group, and they had even greater success than before, appearing with such personalities as Lyle Lovett, Elvis Costello, and John Fogerty. In 1998 they won a Grammy for Best Traditional Soul Gospel Album, and in 2000 they appeared in the movie *O Brother, Where Art Thou?*[25]

Alan did most of the lead singing on *Waitin' for the Hard Times to Go.*[26] The first song on that album, "Backtrackin'," contained a bit of tremolo by Roland on his mandolin. When I first read the title of the song, I thought it was going to be a banjo tune written by Joe Stuart with the same title.

He had shown me that tune back in the 1970s, and I'm sure Alan O'Bryant heard him do it too. "Kansas City Railroad Blues" had been previously recorded by Roland in 1976 on his *I Wasn't Born to Rock'n Roll* album. Alan turned it into a banjo tune.

The Nashville Bluegrass Band played lots of music that wasn't really bluegrass at all. The instrumentation, of course, belonged to the bluegrass genre, but lots of country songs were included in the band's repertoire, and Roland was fine with that. In fact, during one interview he said, "The bluegrass songs have been written . . . by Bill Monroe, Lester Flatt and others. Those songs have been done, they're like the old jazz standards, and they're great and I still like to listen to them."[27]

Jody Stecher was present at many shows by the Nashville Bluegrass Band. Here's what he recalled about Roland's performing style with them as well as with Bill Monroe:

I saw some Bill Monroe shows where Roland was the guitarist. He was always lively on stage. Again he didn't speak but he conveyed a lot through body language. Some years later I saw a number of Nashville Bluegrass Band shows when Roland was the mandolinist. I was intrigued, even fascinated, by the various ways he played rhythm. It was not your standard bluegrass chop all the time. He played various patterns according to the nature of song or tune being played. And as it was with his mandolin solos back in the 1960s he did not call attention to the unusual and highly musical things he was doing. He just did them and if someone noticed, so much the better. I noticed![28]

In 1994 Roland recorded a solo album, *Trying to Get to You*,[29] with not only fellow NBB members but other cream-of-the-crop Nashville players as well: David Grier, Gene Wooten, and Richard Bailey. I didn't get to hear this album until 2015, and the best surprise for me was getting to hear Diane Bouska (future member of the Roland White Band) singing harmony with Roland. One of the songs really sparkled because of Diane: "Midnight," written by Boudleaux Bryant and recorded by many singers, including Red Foley, Don Gibson, Porter Wagoner, and Wanda Jackson. Diane's tenor singing was really super and matched Roland's voice superbly. "Talk to Your Heart," with harmony by Diane, had the same spare eloquence as the early Ray Price version, but the crowning jewel on the album (in my opinion) was a duet by Roland and Diane, "Only You Can Break My Heart." Diane's voice fit Roland's just like Don Rich's voice fit Buck Owens's. To use an old expression, Diane's voice was like "pouring water out of a jug."

Another great moment on Roland's solo album was the Red Foley song "I'll Hold You in My Heart ('til I Can Hold You in My Arms)," in which Roland returned once again to his early country roots. This version had the same feel as Eddy Arnold's recording, and Gene Wooten's Dobro solo was highly reminiscent of Little Roy Wiggins's playing, which was heard on so many of Eddy Arnold's songs. Roland turned it into more of a swing number during the second half, complete with a bass solo by Gene Libbea. "Crazy Blues" had a little bit of the same "feel" as "I Saw Your Face in the Moon," which Roland had also recorded in 1976 on his *I Wasn't Born to Rock'n Roll* album. He was very much at home with this type of song. Some of the same simple jazz chord progressions are used in many songs of this genre, and they work well on stage during live performances. They give the musicians a chance to "stretch out," and audiences love to hear that happen.

Roland was in fine voice for *Trying to Get to You*, most likely because all the singing he had been doing with NBB at the time had sharpened his vocal cords. Richard Bailey's banjo playing on the album made me jealous! The tone he got was nice and even, both high and low on the fingerboard, and his solos were exquisite. Alan O'Bryant didn't play banjo on the album, but he sang a vocal part on "Trying to Get to You." David Grier played every one of his improvisational guitar breaks with totally effortless creativity. I'm sure every take was completely different for him.

Diane was vetoed several times on the project. "I tried to have a significant input on the album, but I met a lot of resistance. It seemed like they didn't want the wife to be saying anything on that one. I had some flak from the producer—he didn't want my opinions."[30] Some things still haven't changed.

NBB's album *Unleashed* featured Roland singing "Standing on the Doorstep of Trouble," which was reminiscent of the earlier Kentucky Colonels' sound.[31] He played a powerful "train shuffle" during his hard-driving mandolin solo. Alan and Stuart composed an old timey-banjo/fiddle tune called "Dog Remembers Bacon" for the album. Smooth, flowing, and very listenable, the melody was set down faithfully on the man-

The Nashville Bluegrass Band at the *Grand Ole Opry* with TV weatherman Willard Scott. L-R: Roland White, Stuart Duncan, Gene Libbea (holding bass), Pat Enright, Willard Scott, Alan O'Bryant. From the collection of Stuart Duncan.

dolin by Roland, with a characteristic shift in emphasis toward the end of his solo by jumping to the higher reaches of his fingerboard.

In 1996 Roland was reunited yet again with his old picking buddy LeRoy McNees. *LeRoy Mack and Friends of the Kentucky Colonels* was the name of the project, which featured the Nashville Bluegrass Band.[32] Roland played on the following tracks: "If You're Ever Gonna Love Me," "Wabash Cannonball," "I've Got a Lot to Thank My Daddy For," "Pickin' in Holland," "I Might Take You Back," and "Ashokan Farewell." Billy Ray Latham was also included on that album, in addition to LeRoy's Dobro hero, Josh Graves.

NBB's *American Beauty* had a really great song called "All Alone," with an old-timey—yet bluesy—Monroe-style mandolin tremolo.[33] In fact, the song sounded similar to an older Monroe original, "I'm So Blue." "Livin' the Blues" (Bob Dylan) started out with another guitar-mandolin duet that once again showed how perfectly Roland's and Pat's styles fit together. Roland sang the song, and though the lyrics were melancholy, his interpretation retained a feeling that was somehow heartening—an achievement only he could bring off. "Holiday Pickin'" went back to the early years of the Stanley Brothers with this Ralph Stanley banjo instrumental from 1958. Roland gave Bill Napier's original mandolin solo a fresh twist while still keeping with the spirit of the first recording. The only thing missing was a guitar solo (Gene Meadows played lead guitar on the 1958 recording). Clarence White would have been superb on "Holiday Pickin'," and the Nashville Bluegrass Band would have been a perfect home for Clarence.

The Nashville Bluegrass Band has achieved a degree of success seldom equaled in the bluegrass field. Their performance tours have spanned the globe, including such countries as Japan, Canada, England, Italy, France, Germany, Ireland, Denmark, Turkey, Switzerland, and Brazil, to name but a few. They have played lots of shows with the Fairfield Four, including a sell-out concert at Carnegie Hall. They have performed on the *Grand Ole Opry*, the *Renfro Valley Barn Dance*, the Lincoln Center in New York City, the *Prairie Home Companion* radio show in St. Paul, the Smithsonian Institution in Washington, D.C., and all over the United States—in towns both large and small. The group has set new standards for modern bluegrass. Its fusion of old and new has brought many new fans into the fold, and the music transcends the talents of the individual musicians. Each of them brings a lifetime of determination and devotion to the art form to create one of the most memorable bands of all time.

The Roland White Band

Roland left the Nashville Bluegrass Band in 2000. He wanted to start his own band, sing more of his own songs, and play more of his own tunes. NBB was so loaded with talent that it was difficult for everyone to get in everything they wanted to do. Roland had lots of new ideas going through his head and he was ready to branch out.

"I was going to have mandolin solos transcribed from a couple of albums I was on with the Nashville Bluegrass Band," Roland told banjoist Richard Bailey, "but there weren't even enough solos to put a book out. I thought to myself, if I'm going to do anything, I need to do it now. Would you be interested in playing banjo?"

Richard replied, "Well, yeah, as long as it's a band thing."

Roland said, "It's a band thing. We're all equal."[1] So that's how it started.

Richard Bailey is perhaps best known for his work with the enormously successful SteelDrivers group, which made their debut in 2005. Their eponymous first album was made up entirely of original compositions and was released in 2008 on the Rounder label.[2] This was followed by a series of more recordings, one of which, *The Muscle Shoals Recordings*,[3] won a Grammy for Best Bluegrass Recording.

Diane Bouska, Roland, Richard, and Todd Cook (on bass) had been picking a lot at the Station Inn. These musicians eventually became the Roland White Band. Because personal career advancement always meant less to Roland than the music itself, it was difficult for him to put his name at the front of the Roland White Band. It seemed a little self-centered to him. (Being a Midwesterner, I can identify with that notion. We're all very humble out here in Iowa.) Diane helped him get over that. Roland was the draw, so why not put his name up front where it belonged? Diane has been Roland's biggest supporter and best friend. She is the cornerstone of the Roland White Band, and she deserves special acclaim from the bluegrass world for the immeasurable support she has given the uniquely gifted and influential Roland White. Diane has made it her priority to ensure that upcoming generations of bluegrass pickers are made aware of the leading contributions and stylistic approach that Roland White has brought to the music world.

The first CD by the Roland White Band, *Jelly on My Tofu*, was produced in 2002 by Roland, Diane, Richard, Todd, and Mark Howard.[4] When I asked Roland how the tune "Jelly on My Tofu" got its name, he said, "We have a great French bakery here called 'Provence Bakery.' I would go there and I would toast a piece of bread, and I would get some solid tofu, mash it up, and season it with different things, and spread it on there—and then put some jelly on it."

Choosing the name "Jelly on My Tofu" reflects Roland's awareness of the ever-increasing array of artistic influences in today's world. To an extent, musical crossbreeding is necessary for the survival and growth of the art form, but prudence is also advisable. Bill Monroe was once heard to say, "Let's advance bluegrass music just one year at a time." In the case of "Jelly on My Tofu," the music isn't radically different in style, but the unusual title puts it in a different and unexpected setting. The CD was nominated for a Grammy. Pretty good for a debut band album!

The title tune was restrained and easygoing, just like Roland. He wrote a couple of other tunes for the project: "Rose City Waltz" and "Roland's Rag." "Rose City Waltz" fits into a traditional, danceable waltz genre. Simple bass lines by Todd Cook gave the tune a strong and reliable foundation. In "Rose City Waltz," respect was placed on the melody, which seemed to play out organically, as if it had written itself. Many of Bill Monroe's tunes were like that. He always believed that tunes weren't actually "written"; they were just "discovered," pulled from the spirit realm where they had always existed since the beginning of time. In "Roland's Rag," Todd Cook's bass played a big part in energizing the performance without being overbearing. Richard Bailey played a number of jazzy progressions on the song, and there was a part where Cook traded licks with

Roland, making for an interesting juxtaposition of high and low voicings between the mandolin and the bass.

Diane became a soul singer on "Flesh, Blood, and Bone." That type of blues singing really appeals to her, and she inspires the pickers to great heights of improvisation. "Cabin on the Hill" was a little different from how Lester Flatt did it. Roland's version didn't have the constant call-and-response after every line by the band. I always thought that was a little over the top, but Roland's version had the call-and-response after only a few of the lines, which makes me want to learn the song after all these years of ignoring it. "Hoping That You're Hoping" was every bit as good as the 1956 Louvin Brothers' recording. Roland and Diane sounded like a brother and sister singing together, complete with matching vocal inflections and phrasings. Roland was always a big fan of Ira Louvin's mandolin playing, and a little bit of Ira can be heard here. The simple and restrained banjo playing by Richard Bailey didn't distract from the vintage feel.

The entire album, to me, had something in common with the Nashville Bluegrass Band's *The Boys Are Back in Town*, and that "something" is Roland's exuberance in finding a new home for his music. That frame of mind was perhaps best reflected in the songs "Sunday Sunrise" and "Satisfied Mind." The birth of the Roland White Band was a celebration of his newfound freedom and creativity in his musical approach. When music means as much to you as it does to Roland, freedom to play it in your own way is like taking "happy pills."

Indeed, "freedom to be free" has become a defining characteristic of Roland's playing, along with a singular tendency to make every performance an imaginative stroll through an ever-changing musical landscape. Mike Compton had this to say:

> The way he uses his hands is completely economical and in control. He floats. His left hand is ultimately economical. I heard a friend of mine say one time, "His left hand looks like a little varmint running up and down the fingerboard." His hand position is sort of like a ball—his fingers aren't flying out all over the place. He shifts from position to position sort of like Monroe, where he's using chords a lot in finding his notes. He looks like he's in control all the time and it always looks like it's completely effortless. . . .

Roland's playing always sounds like it's his fingerprints. You can tell easily who it is when he starts playing. You think, "Yeah, that's what he would play. He's got his fingerprints all over it."[5]

After the *Jelly on My Tofu* album came out, the Roland White Band went to Japan and played at a festival called Country Gold. Judy Seal, in charge of management and booking for the band, took them on a tour with another band called Exile. She previously had taken the Nashville Bluegrass Band on a tour of South America. Charlie Nagatani, a famous country singer in Japan, was another headliner on the show. "They had a giant stage right next to a volcano," Diane told us. "It was a beautiful location, and some young Japanese women spotted Roland and they started coming toward him. One of them was going 'Ahh-ahh!' It was like they were in the presence of Rock Hudson. . . . They're very hospitable people."[6] There has been a lively bluegrass scene in Japan since the 1960s, and the music is still quite popular there.

Diane recalled another memorable experience with the Roland White Band: "Gatemouth Brown came and played with us at the Station Inn one time."[7] From Texas, Gatemouth had played many kinds of music: country, jazz, Cajun, R&B, rock, folk, and blues. When he played with the Roland White Band, he was adding bluegrass to that list. (Richard Bailey, who was working on a TV show featuring Gatemouth, managed to corral him for the bluegrass show.) Diane told us, "Gatemouth played the guitar with his fingers [instead of using a pick]. He gave me an elastic capo afterwards because I had one of those metal screw-on types, and he said, 'What you need is this old elastic kind.'" (Guitar players never use that style of capo anymore, but nobody ever told Gate that.)

On November 5, 2011, Roland took a break from the Roland White Band to do the *Prairie Home Companion* (*PHC*) radio show, with Garrison Keillor. It was a celebration of what would have been Bill Monroe's one hundredth birthday. Roland was the organizer of that Monroe tribute and a few others during that same year. I was lucky enough to be included on the *PHC* program along with several other Blue Grass Boys, including Tom Ewing, Mark Hembree, Bobby Hicks, Peter Rowan, and Blake Williams. Stuart Duncan and Kathy Chiavola also participated. Stuart wasn't a Blue Grass Boy, but he had played at Bill's Nashville funeral. Kathy wasn't a Blue Grass Boy either, but Bill had asked her to be! The show took place in Murray, Kentucky, at the CFSB (Community Financial Services Bank) Center at Murray State University.

We played all of Bill's greatest hits, including "Lonesome Moonlight Waltz," "The Gold Rush," "On My Way Back to the Old Home," "When the Golden Leaves Begin to Fall," "Molly and Tenbrooks," "The Old Old House," "Panhandle Country," "Kentucky Waltz," "The Walls of Time," "Muleskinner Blues," and "Blue Moon of Kentucky." Roland did a great job playing Bill Monroe's mandolin parts. It had to be a tough job capturing the essence of Bill's style while still maintaining his own identity.

All of us Blue Grass Boys told Monroe stories during the program. I told about how I first heard of Bill Monroe from records I had bought at the Hinky Dinky grocery store in Des Moines when I was a teenager. Then I told the story about running out of gas one night after playing at a festival with Monroe. I stayed behind in Bill's station wagon while he and the rest of the Blue Grass Boys took off in another vehicle. About an hour later, Kenny Baker and Ralph Lewis came back with a coffee can full of gas they had gotten somewhere. Word got around, and back at the festival the next day, the emcee presented Monroe with a siphon hose on stage.[8]

Roland told this story: "One time we were playing up in the Baltimore-Washington area and Kenny Baker was on the fiddle, and there was another fiddler there that had played with Bill Monroe earlier on. When any fiddler came around that had worked for Bill, he would invite them up to play. . . . So one night after the show, I asked Bill, 'Did you ever consider carrying twin fiddles on the road?' He said, 'They don't get along.'"

I was happy to get a chance to do that show with Roland, as well as with all the other Blue Grass Boys who were present. We belong to an ever-shrinking group, blessed with fond memories of working for the Father of Bluegrass. We'll never forget those days.

On June 7, 2012, Roland's brother Eric passed away. After Clarence's death, Eric had played electric bass for local bands at venues in the Lancaster-Palmdale area, including BJ's (where Clarence was killed), the Rock Inn, VFWs, and lodges. Gib Guilbeau was often a bandmate. Around 2005 Eric moved to Bakersfield, California. He was unable to play after that because of ill health. After Eric was laid to rest, Roland was the only one left to carry on the legacy of the Three Little Country Boys.

In 2014 the Roland White Band released *Straight Ahead Bluegrass*.[9] On that CD Roland played "Pike County Breakdown" much like Bill Monroe, with exactly the right feel and drive. "Powder Creek," which Roland had originally recorded back in 1976 on his *I Wasn't Born to Rock'n Roll* album, firmly established this tune within the "straight ahead" bluegrass category. Like Monroe's "Jerusalem Ridge," which also seemed a bit progressive in its day, it's now a part of today's bluegrass tradition. "On My Way Back to the Old Home" was a song that Bill Monroe sang on many of his shows, usually as the opening number. On this song Roland went back to one of *his* old homes: the Blue Grass Boys.

Brian Christianson's fiddling reflects a rich background in traditional bluegrass, and he provides a solid and masterful foundation to the Roland White Band. Winner of the Grand Master Fiddler Traditional Championship, he has performed many times on the *Grand Ole Opry* with Mike Snider. A native of Minnesota, Brian started fiddling at the age of eight. After earning a diploma in violin repair at Minnesota State College Southeast in 2000, he moved to Nashville and eventually opened up a violin shop with his wife, Nicole. The Fiddle House is a place where musicians can get their violins and bows repaired, and it's also a wonderful place for jam sessions.[10] (I took part in one during our 2015 trip to Nashville.) Brian plays with a serious, respectful attitude and a high regard for the melody. He's not showy. He carries out his solos with assurance, and when he slides into a note, he always arrives right on the money, with no loss of tonality on the way.

The Roland White Band is hugely blessed with the presence of Richard Bailey on banjo. He has played with Roland White probably as long as, or longer than, any other picker. Richard told me how he came to meet Roland around 1980 through Slim Richey:

> I was such a huge Alan Munde fan. I was such a huge fan of yours, and Larry McNeely, and Carl Jackson, and Ben Eldridge—anything that was progressive back then.[11] We [the Tennessee Gentlemen] played the Tulsa Chili Festival and Slim was there, . . . and he said to me, "I'm gonna go out and eat dinner with Country Gazette [who were playing at the festival]. Would you like to go out and eat with us?" I was in my early twenties and I'm like, "Would I, would I!" That's where I officially met Roland.[12]

A few years later Richard and Roland ran into each other again in Nashville. Roland needed a banjo player for an upcoming gig, so he asked

The Roland White Band at the Joe Val Bluegrass Festival in Framingham, Massachusetts, February 2015. L-R: Brian Christianson, Roland White, Diane Bouska, Jon Weisberger, Richard Bailey. Photo by Dave Hollender.

Richard, "What are you doing January the seventh?" "We'd just been in Nashville three weeks or so," Richard told me in our interview, "and I said, 'I'm not doing anything.' I didn't know where he was going with it. Then he said, 'Well, I'm playing the Station Inn. Would you like to play?' I said, 'Yeah, I'd love to.'" So that was the first gig Richard played with Roland.

"Roland and Diane taped everything—every Station Inn gig—they have a whole wall of Station Inn tapes. I have some live tapes; Roland's got all that stuff on cassette. He would tape every night that we played at the Station Inn. He was adamant about it because he said, 'I should have done it all those years when Clarence and I were playing, and I didn't, and now it's gone forever.'"[13]

Richard told me that Roland never talked a lot about Clarence or the Kentucky Colonels around him, except when the two were playing pool at the Springwater in Nashville. That's when Roland's memories would flow out and he was most apt to reflect on the old days:

Roland's one of the few people—Vassar [Clements] was another—they were super nice and they were always trying to help whoever was moving to Nashville—and whoever they took a liking to—and they would try to get them out and get them around people. Roland did that for me, and Vassar was the same way.

The other thing I like about Roland is when I was playing solos on vocal material it would be different, and sometimes I'd take some chances and sometimes I'd "fall off the limb." It bummed me out so much, and I remember telling Roland more than a few times, "Man, I'm really sorry," and he always said, "No, that's why I want you playing with me. I do the same thing. I don't want to play with somebody that plays it the same way every time. I want to play with somebody that takes some chances—they might work, and they might not."[14]

Roland has always taken chances career-wise as well as musically. In his quiet way he has made momentous and consequential decisions that forever changed the course of his journey through music. Striking out into uncharted territory has been the hallmark of his career, beginning with the Three Little Country Boys and culminating in the Roland White Band.

Roland's latest band represents a lifetime of musical experience. His unique frame of reference is drawn from the entire scope of bluegrass—roots to branches—with a personal stamp on all of it. Roland now brings his mastery of an art form unlike any other to his band, and the members respect his concepts and approaches while feeling free to make their own contributions. Roland wants it that way.

11

Roland's Family Ties

Much of the success and popularity of today's bluegrass music is directly attributable to the White family. Eric Sr. and Mildred both loved music, and they passed that along to their children. Without their parents' support and encouragement, Roland, Clarence, and Eric would never have pursued their musical ambitions. Their sister JoAnne also contributed her wonderful singing voice in the early years. The far-reaching influence of the Kentucky Colonels forever changed the landscape of bluegrass, opening many doors for those who came later.

Roland's first wife, Arline, loved and supported her husband's career. She sang as well and worked at many jobs to provide a stable base for Roland's music to flourish. Their children, Lawrence and Roline, are extremely proud of the musical heritage in their family, and Lawrence has been singing and performing since a very early age. Roland's youngest sister, Rosemarie, is positively bursting with pride at the musical accomplishments of Roland and Clarence, and it shows every time she speaks of them.

Today Roland is married to a lady who also takes music very seriously. Diane Bouska is now a member of the White family, combining her considerable talent with that of her husband. She's been around music all of her life too, just like Roland. It's a common bond between them.

Rosemarie

Rosemarie, Roland's youngest sister, has an entire wall in her home covered with framed photos of her older brother Clarence, and she's working on another wall with pictures of Roland. In a 2019 correspondence, she told me she was crying while she wrote about Roland. Living in California, she doesn't get to see him often enough and she misses him. "I was raised in a house of music . . . bluegrass music of course," Rosemarie told me. Born in 1955, she was close to seventeen years younger than Roland. The boys played for her a lot. "I would be awakened when the guys came home from a show, . . . and I always loved to hear them practicing as Billy Ray and LeRoy lived with us, since they were traveling a lot."[1] Rosemarie hadn't even started school yet when Bill Monroe came to the house, bringing along his Blue Grass Boys for dinner. She remembers them playing music together afterward, until the sun came up.

When Rosemarie was in junior high, she often went to the Ash Grove to hear the Country Boys. That was her introduction to live onstage bluegrass performances, and to this day she still thinks of the music of the Country Boys as being "true bluegrass." "I love Roland's music and only Roland can sing and play true bluegrass. . . . I'm very proud of his accomplishments, his recognitions and inductions. [One of the primary recognitions she spoke of was Roland's induction into the IBMA Bluegrass Hall of Fame in 2017.] Roland had a vision in his music at an early age, of what he loved, and he has stayed true to what he loved for all these years."[2]

She remembers as a child hearing the brothers speaking in French a lot, "especially if it was something they didn't want me to understand or hear." She never learned to play, most likely because her brothers and sister were so much older than she was, and they were so busy with their own playing and singing by that time. "I sang in church choir, but that doesn't count." (Of course, I would disagree with Rosemarie on that; many singers have carved out careers that began with singing in church. I haven't heard Rosemarie sing, but I'm sure she can do it very well, not only because of her choir background but also because of the music genes in her family.)

Rosemarie's parents would occasionally take her to Clarence's place, and when they got there, she'd be told to stay in the kitchen while numerous musicians and singers arrived. Those visitors often included people like Mama Cass Elliot; Gram Parsons; and Crosby, Stills, and Nash.[3] Eric

Sr. passed away when Rosemarie was seventeen, and Clarence passed away barely a year later. She has fond memories of her father sitting in the garage playing his fiddle and harmonica when she was in grade school. Her mother, Mildred, for some reason, was shy about singing in front of Rosemarie.

Rosemarie has attended lots of Roland's musical performances through the years. She heard the original Kentucky Colonels at the Ash Grove, Country Gazette at McCabe's in Santa Monica, and the Nashville Bluegrass Band in many different places. One experience she looks back on with happy memories is the 2016 Huck Finn Jubilee in Ontario, California. Roland was visiting Rosemarie at the time, and they attended the festival together. Some of the biggest names in bluegrass were performing there.[4] "Roland roamed around back stage as the bands played and I watched him go up to everyone, musicians, and talk to them. . . . [It's] amazing how he knows so many and so many love him." David Grisman called Roland up on stage with him, along with Peter Rowan. It was an exciting moment and people rushed the stage. "And if someone came to where we were sitting in the shade he was always generous in taking time to tell stories and answer questions. I hear Clarence was the same to anyone that came to him."[5]

Rosemarie gets emotional whenever she thinks about Clarence and Roland. "There's not many like Roland. . . . He's a gem, . . . always was and always will be remembered as a kind hearted soul."[6]

Arline

Roland's first wife, Arline Melanson, grew up in Beverly, Massachusetts, just outside of Boston in an Irish neighborhood. Her mother was Irish and her father was French Canadian. All of her siblings were nearly grown when she came along. Her mother was diabetic and passed away when Arline was only nineteen. Roland and Arline's children, Roline and Lawrence, shared memories of their mom in a March 2019 interview: "Her dad kicked her out then [when her mother died]," Roline told me. Arline then moved to California to stay with her sister Pauline. That's where she met Roland.

Roline talked about what a beautiful singing voice her mother had. Sometimes when Roland was performing at the Station Inn, he would get his wife up to sing. Arline loved and supported Roland all the way. It was a hard life for her because whenever Roland was away, she had to be both mother and father to Roline and Lawrence. This was especially true during the Country Gazette years. The band did a huge amount of traveling, as well as their own booking and managing. Even when Roland was home, he had to be on the phone a lot. Arline sometimes had to work two or three jobs. As a result, Roline babysat Lawrence many times, starting when she was nine years old. She cooked dinner for the two of them, and she put him to bed.

Arline worked as a nurse's aide at the "TB hospital" on Ben Allen Road in East Nashville. The hospital was closed in 1976 after the cure for tuberculosis came into its own. The building became a state office property, and Arline continued to work there as a security guard. Later, in 1978, she went to work at the Gibson Guitar factory, where she stayed for thirty-one years. (Production of Gibson guitars had been moved from Kalamazoo, Michigan, to Nashville by that time.) The company was bought by Henry E. Juszkiewicz, David H. Berryman, and Gary A. Zebrowski in January 1986.

Arline worked at several different jobs at the Gibson plant. She started off on the fingerboard line, mostly doing inlays, working on staining and quality control. She was employed in the custom shop for a while, doing veneer and inlay work. Eventually Arline was laid off and given a severance package that was supposed to consist of a week of pay for every year she had been employed, but that arrangement applied to just the first eighteen years, so she got only eighteen weeks of severance pay.[7]

"There was one time when everyone walked out of Gibson," Roline told me. "They wanted a union . . . because Gibson didn't pay them well, and they worked a lot of hours. Mom didn't join the picket line because she needed the money. Henry [Juszkiewicz] came through and fired everybody right there on the spot." Approximately half the plant had been on the picket line and consequently got fired. "Henry's belief was: 'anybody can be replaced,'" Roline told me. (By that time, both Roline and her husband had been working at Gibson too, and they each got laid off.)

Arline was a bartender and waitress at the Station Inn for many years. She tended the door there too. Lawrence joked that she was also the bouncer. "We weren't allowed up front where the music was," Roline said in our interview:

Top: Roland and his youngest sister, Rosemarie, March 2016. From the collection of Rosemarie Johnson. Bottom: Roland's daughter, Roline Hodge, at the Station Inn; Roland's son, Lawrence LeBlanc, 2017. From the White family collection.

They had a back room where there was a table. We weren't allowed up front, because they served alcohol, or bring-your-own-bottle. When they decided to find another place [they had to leave that location because it was too small], they wanted to make it more family-friendly. When they first moved out to where it's located now, we still could not be out front. After about a year or two, they decided "We want people to be able to bring their kids," so they quit serving hard liquor. They just served beer and food, and that's when we started being able to come out into the actual front and sit with the adults and listen to all the music.[8]

Arline had other jobs at the same time she was employed at the Station Inn. She would get up very early for her day job, come home for a while afterward, then go to the Station Inn and work until 3:00 a.m. On weekend days she would do other things to make money as well. She slept very little, and on Sundays she would try to catch up on her sleep.

She didn't have a lot of education. "She quit in fifth grade," said Roline. "She got mad at the nuns. They threatened to spank her and she told them, 'If you touch me I will leave, and I won't be back.' They tried to spank her, so she turned around and walked out and never went back."[9]

Roline and Lawrence

Roline told me this wonderful childhood story: "There was a song when I was little that my mom told me my dad used to play and sing for me. He'd pick me up when I was a baby and he would sing 'Baby Girl'":

> *Little girl (little girl) baby girl*
> *She's my darling little precious baby girl.*
> *Like an angel to me and I know that He*
> *Sent from Heaven my little baby girl.*
>
> *She's as sweet as the flowers in springtime,*
> *Her blue eyes, they sparkle so bright.*
> *Just a touch of her little baby hand*
> *Seems to guide my weary footsteps day and night.*
>
> *How those two little arms try to hold me.*
> *Her little heart's a blessing to our home.*
> *And at night when I'm far, far away*
> *As I dream of her, I'm never all alone.*

Roland had learned the song from a 1956 Stanley Brothers Mercury recording.

Roline's mother told her another baby story about potluck get-togethers at their home in Nashville. People would bring their instruments along and play and sing until two or three in the morning. "Mom would stick me in a box in the middle of the room, and I would sleep while everyone played. She'd put some blankets in there, and I would sit and listen to everyone until I fell asleep."

Roline grew up hearing music of all types from her mother's record collection—everything from the Isley Brothers to Conway Twitty. She wasn't a big fan of the traditional-style bluegrass music Roland played with Bill Monroe or Lester Flatt. She didn't hate it, but she hadn't yet acquired the taste for it. That came later. Her exposure to diverse musical influences gave Roline an appreciation of much of what Roland did with Country Gazette. She really liked their version of the Beatles' "Eleanor Rigby," for example. She loved Roland's work with the Nashville Bluegrass Band as well, because they put a different spin on traditional music. She also appreciated their a cappella singing, which was unmatched.

The song "Last Thing on My Mind" is very special to Roline: "My uncle Clarence, who I was very close to, sang that song, so it's always been one of my favorites, and it brings back a lot of good memories I have with him. He knew me from the time I was a baby. Mom has pictures of him carrying me around on his shoulders."

By the time Roline entered grade school, music was a big part of her life: "I used to sit on the side at the Ryman [Auditorium] on a little bench, in a little German dress that my dad bought me." He had purchased it for her when he was in Germany with Bill Monroe. "That was my favorite dress. I felt like I was Heidi in the Shirley Temple movie."

Roline's brother, Lawrence, came along in 1969. He took his first steps at Bill Monroe's farm in Goodlettsville; the White family had remained good friends with Monroe even after Roland had left the Blue Grass Boys, and they spent a lot of time at Monroe's place. Roline has pictures of herself eating candy with Bill at his house—boxes of chocolates with different fillings. (Bill always had a sweet tooth.) Lawrence began playing music when he was three. By the time he was six, Roland bought him a cello because he had started slapping on an old guitar they had, pretending it was an upright bass. The cello was about the right height for Lawrence.

Sometimes when Roland was on the road with Country Gazette, Marty Stuart would come and get Lawrence on the weekends. He would bring Lawrence along when he played with Lester Flatt on the *Grand Ole Opry*. In 1976, when Lawrence was six years old, they brought the cello along and he debuted with Lester. Flatt introduced him and he went to the front of the stage to play. He was wearing a hat, which he tipped to the audience. Then he placed his hat on top of the cello and started to slap it like a bass, to the tune of "Salty Dog Blues." He was a big hit with the audience, and there was a write-up about it in the *Nashville Banner*.

Lawrence still plays lots of music, of many different genres. Some of his past groups have included blues, rock 'n' roll, jazz, funk, and fusion. In our 2019 interview he told me, "Right now I play in the 'powwow circuit.' I sing on the drum with a lot of Native Americans." (Native American powwows include people who sing as they beat in unison on a large drum or drums. Several types of songs—with corresponding rhythms—are represented. Singing and drum styles vary from region to region.)

Lawrence and Roline both spent time at Lester's house on Old Hickory Lake. Lawrence told me, "His [Lester's] daughter, Brenda, used to watch us, and we'd play with his granddaughter Tammy a lot. We'd go fishing in the lake." "I had my first bicycle accident riding Tammy's bike," said Roline. (She cut her arm and still has the scar.) "It was a great place to ride bikes. . . . We could run down Lester's driveway and go down the street [to the dead end] and come back."

Occasionally Roland's family would travel to California, where Mildred and Eric Sr. still lived. Roline remembers her grandparents very well. "They were loud and stern," she told me. Lawrence doesn't have as many memories of his grandparents, but he does recall Mildred speaking with a heavy French accent. "I remember one time she got very irritated with us kids because we were in her way in the kitchen," Lawrence recalled. "She cussed us out, I do believe. She got on our case. She was pulling me toward the back door to get me out in the yard, but she spoke in French."

Every summer, when school was out, Lawrence got to take trips with Country Gazette. He did that from the age of seven till he was fifteen: "We went everywhere; from Vancouver to North Carolina, New York, Maine, Texas. I crossed the country with those guys a lot."

Lawrence told me that they bought a Hertz truck and had it fixed up with cabinets and shelving; they added two extra coach seats in the back and blocked it all off so the instruments could go through the back door. Above that they put a mattress that would sleep two people. In front of that was a bench that would sleep another person. The bench flipped open and they could put additional gear inside. Up above the cab they had more storage space. "It was the best damn little traveling van they ever had!" Lawrence said.

Roline didn't get to take her first trip with the Gazette until after she graduated, in 1982, because it was hard for a girl to travel with a bunch of men at such an early age. (Alan Munde had a daughter who couldn't go because of the same situation.) Roline said:

When I graduated from high school, Dad let me travel with Country Gazette in that vehicle. We went from here [Nashville] to Norman, Oklahoma, to pick up Alan [Munde]; then we went down to Texas and did a show in Amarillo; then we went to Denver, Colorado, and stayed with some friends they knew while they played their shows down there. Then we went to Grass Valley, California, and played the festival out there.

We went through Utah, stopped in Reno; I got to see the Hoover Dam. I remember when we were in Reno, Dad went and played the slots all night. He came in the next morning around six o'clock and I was out in the van because it was cool enough to sleep in that vehicle. He came in, the sun was shining, and I said, "Where have you been?" He said, "I won a hundred dollars, but I lost all of it. I've got a few dollars left and I want you to go back with me." I couldn't play, because I wasn't of legal age, but he did let me pull the handle on the slot machine.

We stopped back in Nashville, and I had the opportunity to go up to Pennsylvania with them and then come back, but I was tired. That was two weeks of traveling for me, and I realized then that I liked my own bed a lot better.[10]

Roline and Lawrence are as mutually supportive as siblings can get. "We've always been very close and been each other's rock and will continue to till the day we die," said Roline.

At its heart, music has always been a family enterprise with Roland. His lifeblood is infused with the power and strength of family ties.

A Visit with Roland and Diane

When Kristie and I visited Roland and Diane at their home in Nashville, she told us a little bit about her musical background. Diane was born in 1955 and grew up in Overland Park, Kansas (near Kansas City). Her dad, a lawyer, became good friends with Kansas City bandleader and jazz pianist Jay McShann. Diane remembers Jay visiting the family home and playing her mother's piano. She has a photograph of him sitting at the keyboard, and her baby picture can also be seen in the photo. Today she has it sitting on her own piano.

Her father was always listening to jazz. He was on the board of the Kansas City Jazz Festival for a few years. He attended lots of shows in clubs and concerts, and he often took Diane and her older brother along. The kids drank Shirley Temples and Cokes.

Diane's exposure to music also came from her father's large record collection. She started playing the flute in seventh grade and tried to copy jazz flute solos. In her early teens Diane got interested in Johnny Cash and Flatt and Scruggs. She enjoyed Doug Kershaw and Cajun music in general. The 1972 album *Will the Circle Be Unbroken* introduced her to many bluegrass and country greats such as Merle Travis, Pete "Bashful Brother Oswald" Kirby, Mother Maybelle Carter, Earl Scruggs, Doc Watson, Jimmy Martin, and Roy Acuff.[1]

Occasionally Diane could pull in the WSM *Grand Ole Opry* on her radio, and she became aware of many more country and bluegrass performers while tuning in to that broadcast. While she was a student at

Tulane University, in New Orleans, she started taking banjo lessons from a teacher living nearby. He sold her a Harmony five-string and the Flatt and Scruggs classic album *Foggy Mountain Banjo*. During that time, she saw me performing with Bill Monroe and the Blue Grass Boys at a festival just north of New Orleans. "I learned really fast and picked up the basics," Diane told us. "And then I did nothing but practice in my own house for the next twenty-five years, because I was too shy to go out and play. But in the last few years I've been out to play [banjo] more."[2] She is now very happy with her playing. (I've heard her—she's quite good!)

Diane moved to Nashville in 1978 and worked in the field of archaeology for five years. Then she went back to school, majoring in computer science. She was a computer programmer/analyst for many years. She also gave banjo lessons. Being a bluegrass lover, she spent many evenings at the Station Inn getting to know most of the same people Roland knew.

It is a fortunate circumstance that Roland met Diane. They shared many of the same musical tastes, and their personalities were harmonious as well. Her own musical background complemented Roland's. Their uncanny harmony singing illustrates their musical compatibility, and their life relationship is exactly that same way: mutually supportive, complementary, and magical.

Part of our conversation centered on their life together before forming the Roland White Band. In the 1990s they created a music publishing business.[3] They presented songs to producers and artists who might record them. "We got one major label cut," said Diane, "on George Jones's and Tammy Wynette's last duet album, entitled *George and Tammy: One*."[4] The song that got published was "It's an Old Love Thing" by Kenny Cornell.

Also in the 1990s Roland and Diane branched out from the music field: they made salsa (their own secret recipe). "We packaged it in twelve-ounce plastic containers," Diane told us. "A few local stores sold it. The Station Inn purchased it by the gallon. It was really good! People occasionally ask us if we still make it." (Unfortunately they don't.)

Our conversation turned back to the subject of music. Diane pointed out that bluegrass isn't their only interest:

We also play some swing stuff together, but we haven't taken it out much. I wish that we could record some swing music, because no one else can play those tunes the way Roland can—tunes like "Lady

Be Good" and "Old-Fashioned Love in My Heart." I've studied some jazz guitar and I have a bunch of chords that I can play along with it.

Roland plays jazz very interestingly and intelligently. You can really make sense out of it. He really has soul—he really says something. He doesn't just noodle around. [Performers like the Modern Jazz Quartet, Freddie Green, and Herb Ellis can be found in Roland's music collection.]

The most wonderful thing about Roland's playing is he really expresses his personality through his music. It's him. There's a lot of nuance and subtlety in his playing. He's got a bigger and more sensitive musical vocabulary than the average person.

She pointed out an interesting concept about Roland and his musical development: "His students will sometimes ask, 'Can you show me some scales?' Well, Roland learned what the scales were *after* he learned to play—and *after* he learned 'where the thought is on my mandolin.' When you're a kid, your parents don't sit you down and teach you the rules of grammar so that you can learn to speak. You learn by imitating and picking up the meaning and the structure with it."

I asked Roland to tell me more about his teaching. "My favorite teaching level is beginner to intermediate, but separately," Roland said. "And sometimes people think they're intermediate when they're really just a beginner. I teach out of my [first] book a lot [*Roland White's Approach to Bluegrass Mandolin*]."[5]

"He starts with technique, and how to touch the mandolin," added Diane. "How to hold it . . . how to hold the pick . . . how to make the right kind of sound with it." Needless to say, Diane really admires Roland's playing:

There's a lot of blues in his playing, and his backup is incredible, and I'm trying to put together a video to teach his backup. Most mandolin players just go "oomp-chuck, oomp-chuck, oomp-chuck" . . . not even knowing what chords actually work well together. They just know this one, and then that one, the same basic shape, which they just move wherever they have to on the neck. Roland has shapes that are close and move so that you just have a couple of notes that are different, and they're easier to make. There are interesting phrases and backup accompaniment rather than just strumming a chord along with it.

"I started doing more of that in Country Gazette," said Roland, "because Alan Munde has such great stuff to play behind. When I went with Nashville Bluegrass Band, I started trying to work in even more backup stuff. They were just my thoughts, and if it didn't seem to go with the lead singer or the fiddle or the banjo, I would just not do that again."

Like all musicians of Roland's caliber, the music develops through trial and error over a period of many years. It's never a completed process. Often, easier methods of getting the same sound are discovered after many years of doing it a harder way. When people say, "He makes it look so easy," that's because it *is* easy for that musician. After many years of practice, he or she has discovered the simplest and most economical moves required in producing the sounds they want.

Diane pointed out that Roland wasn't restricted in his musical experimentations with NBB. They never "vetoed" him. Roland told us, "Yeah, right, nobody said, 'You can't do that.'" "I'll bet it was kind of nice to be in a band where you felt free to do that," said Kristie. "Oh, that band was great." I could sense the admiration in Roland's voice.

In my opinion, one of the most positive developments in modern-day bluegrass music is the freedom to be creative. For too many years, musicians were required to play the way "the boss" wanted them to play, often leading them to lose whatever individual creative spark they may once have had. The Nashville Bluegrass Band was a showcase for original styles, and given the license to be creative, the musicians also made a special effort to acknowledge the pioneering approaches made by previous pioneers of the genre.

Originality as an outgrowth of earlier musical influences has always been a fundamental feature of Roland's playing. New music still springs from his brain, unrestrained and fancy-free, filled with the best of what he has absorbed during a lifetime of playing. "He has a bunch of original tunes that we have not recorded," said Diane. "He's got a great Spanish-sounding thing." (It hadn't been named yet at that time.) She was cutting up some vegetables to make us a salad.

Kristie and I needed to leave pretty soon, as it was over eleven hours driving time back to our place in North English, Iowa. As we ate, Diane told us more about Roland's teaching and mentoring of young musicians: "He seeks out and encourages musicians and makes it a point to get them up on stage and play and give them experience. And he'll sit and pick with people and talk and encourage them—aside from just giving lessons."

Workshops are something that Roland loves to do. He teaches at various learning camps around the country, sometimes eight or nine a year (at the time this interview took place). In fact, Roland had just received a call about teaching at an instructional camp in Ohio. The following month he would be at Mandolin Camp North in Massachusetts. Other teaching camps he has taken part in are Camp Bluegrass, in Levelland, Texas; Puget Sound Guitar Workshop; the Alaska Guitar Camp; Nash Camp, in Nashville; California Bluegrass Association Winter Camp; Northern Circle, in Canada; and FiddleStar Camp, in Lynchburg, Tennessee, for which people have to wait in line to sign up. "The teaching camps really took off for me after Diane and I put out my first mandolin instruction book," Roland told us. "Laurie Lewis called me about doing her 'Bluegrass at the Beach' up in Oregon.[6] That isn't going anymore, but it was a real nice camp. I did four or five of those."

Roland and Diane have both taught in Kansas City, at the Folk Alliance International Winter Music Camp. Diane gives guitar workshops around the country. She has also transcribed a lot of Roland's music and teaches it through the instructional books they have released. She produced the newly released CDs of the New Kentucky Colonels, projects that involved collecting the cuts, deciding what needed to be fixed, choosing artists and artwork, and manufacturing and sales.

I asked Roland about the mandolin he plays today (as of this writing). "I have a Gibson F-5 that was built for me in 2005. . . . The signature inside the mandolin is Danny Roberts." Roland gets a really deep tone out of the instrument, much like Monroe, but he doesn't have the strings set high above the fret board like Bill did. He has played the tone into the instrument by using it a lot, so string height isn't necessarily the only determining factor in musical tone. The player has a lot to do with it too.

Diane and Roland have shared many interesting experiences. They told us about the time they went to Mayberry Days in Mount Airy, North Carolina, in 2013. The event draws thirty to forty thousand people each year. Mount Airy was Andy Griffith's hometown. Diane and Roland were in a parade at the event, waving at the crowd from a car. People loved it! "People were crazy about anybody who had anything to do with the *Andy Griffith Show*," said Diane. "Actors come there year after year who were in only one episode. People dress up as some of the characters on the show. Guys have squad cars that are the same year as Andy's."

LeRoy McNees has been quite involved in the Mayberry event for many years. He had been talking to Roland and Diane for a long time about going there, and when they finally did, they got to play some music together. The band consisted of a local group of musicians who have backed up LeRoy every time he attends the celebration.

Very few of the original cast members are still around, but one of them (at the time of our interview) is Betty Lynn (1926–2021), the actress who portrayed Deputy Barney Fife's love interest, Thelma Lou. She lives right there in Mount Airy. One of the best-loved TV programs of all time, the *Andy Griffith Show* has been in syndication for nearly sixty years and has never been off the air. The Country Boys episodes can still be seen, and they'll never get old.

It was fun talking about the old days, as well as the not-so-old days, with Roland and Diane, but it was time for Kristie and me to head home. We really hated to say good-bye. Diane gave us a bag of pistachios to munch on during the trip back up to Iowa. When we got back home, I began working on this book.

13

Back to Where It All Started

Roland White and the Bluegrass Hall of Fame

"Roland White deserves a place in the Bluegrass Hall of Honor," Marty Stuart told me in our 2015 interview.

There was a time, in the late '70s and early '80s, when you could barely make a living [in bluegrass] . . . unless you had a job with the Osborne Brothers, or Ralph Stanley, or Monroe. Roland had to go find other work. He worked as a cook; he worked at a service station for a while—just to be able to play bluegrass music. He never complained, but he did it because he loved bluegrass. And you could always find him at the Station Inn, or you could find him teaching a kid how to play. He deserves to be honored for that.

People take it [bluegrass] for granted now, because it's everywhere. It's global. There's twenty-four-hour satellite radio. You can go almost anywhere in the world and hear banjos and fiddles and mandolins and people singing bluegrass music. There was a time, as you well know, that it was not the case. Roland was one of those people that helped promote it, invent it, and keep it alive.[1]

Two years after that interview, Roland was inducted into the International Bluegrass Music Hall of Fame.[2] Previous awards received by Roland White include induction into the SPBGMA Preservation Hall of Greats in 2010, the Distinguished Achievement Award from the IBMA in 2011,

Roland White with his IBMA Bluegrass Hall of Fame plaque, 2017.
Photo by Dave Brainard.

the twenty-first annual Mayberry Days key to Mayberry in 2013, and the Boston Bluegrass Union Heritage Award (along with brothers Clarence and Eric) in 2015.

Induction into the Bluegrass Music Hall of Fame was probably the most distinguished award Roland ever received. He joined his brother Clarence in that select group of pioneers who brought the music out and contributed to its wide acceptance today. Clarence had become a Hall of Famer in 2016, and both belong there together, to be remembered by future generations of listeners to one of America's fastest-growing genres of music: bluegrass. Players and fans alike rejoiced when Roland was chosen for the honor, for they all knew there was never a more deserving person to receive it.[3]

The award was presented at the IBMA convention in Raleigh, North Carolina, by Roland's old friend Jim Lauderdale. The plaque is at the Bluegrass Hall of Fame and Museum in Owensboro, Kentucky, on the banks of the Ohio River. The hall and museum are in a new building now, completed in 2018. Roland and Diane attended the grand opening in October of that year. The location is very fitting—just a forty-five-minute drive from Bill Monroe's birthplace in Rosine.

Roland is in some pretty tall company at the Hall of Fame, but in truth he would be the first to say that his real friends are the multitudes of fans who genuinely love him. He has stayed true to those people down through the years, never straying far from bluegrass, the first love of his musical life. He has been an inspiration for all of us, young and old, beginners and veterans, and friends and strangers who are connected to one another by the mutual bond of bluegrass.

I know lots of family bands who play bluegrass together, children and parents alike, and in each show they perform as a family unit—in the most literal sense. Rehearsals are a great way for them to share ideas and support one another. That's one of the best legacies left to us by Roland White. Coming from a musical family himself, including Eric Sr., Clarence, Eric Jr., and numerous uncles who played and sang, Roland has helped to nurture that family music legacy. More and more children are attending bluegrass teaching camps, and that's a great thing to see. As we have noted, Roland has taught at a lot of these camps, passing on his years of experience to help students learn the ins and outs of the art of acoustic music "straight from the shoulder."

Roland's induction into the Bluegrass Hall of Fame is a culmination of his dream of playing bluegrass as a career. Nothing better symbolizes his boundless faith in the significance of bluegrass as an art form and his willingness to make sacrifices to that end. He'll now be deservedly remembered as one of the true pioneers.

Roland White and Friends

Roland's most recent project, *Roland White and Friends: A Tribute to the Kentucky Colonels*, is appropriately titled, as two dozen different musicians contributed to the album, featuring a gathering of some of the finest performers to be found anywhere.[4] A lot of phenomenal players now hang out in Nashville, and Roland is doing his part to spotlight their talents. If he could make an album with a thousand different pickers, Roland would probably do it, and they would all be lining up to be included. He's a unifying force among the Nashville community of musicians, and the lucky ones chosen to be a part of the album are justifiably proud of their contributions.

Stellar guitar players were recruited to fill Clarence's shoes. In listening to the album, I am reminded again of the early classic *Appalachian Swing!* The picking is innovative and improvisational. One of the best examples is "Nine Pound Hammer," with Clarence-style guitar playing by Billy Strings.[5] "I Am a Pilgrim" is another example, and Molly Tuttle takes over the flat-picking duties.[6] Toward the end of the number, Roland plays a long solo that seems to reach for new, unexplored musical vistas. Molly takes that as a challenge, closing out the tune in the spirit of Clarence by reminding us that it's not the destination that matters—it's the journey.

"Listen to the Mockingbird" is a tune that I always enjoyed hearing Clarence and Roland play. Two guitarists were used on this selection: Jon Stickley and Josh Haddix. It is evident that they have listened to Clarence's various recordings of the tune, and they have accurately captured his approach. One can almost envision Clarence's fingers dancing around over the strings. "Listen to the Mockingbird" was written in 1855, and the mournful lyrics tell of a mockingbird singing over a lost loved one's grave. The melody is attributed to a black street whistler/guitarist named Richard Milburn, and the words are attributed to Alice Hawthorne, the pseudonym of songwriter Septimus Winner.[7] The chorus goes:

> *Listen to the mockingbird, listen to the mockingbird,*
> *Oh the mockingbird is singing o'er her grave.*
> *Listen to the mockingbird, listen to the mockingbird*
> *Still singing where the weeping willows wave.*

Scotty Stoneman turned this song into a slapstick comedy by playing amazing birdcalls with his fiddle. These can be heard on the 1965 *Live in L.A. with the Kentucky Colonels* album recorded at the Ash Grove.[8] "The Ash Grove," by the way, is an old Welsh folk song to which many different lyrics have been set. Most versions, however, tell a story similar to the one related in "Listen to the Mockingbird": the sorrow felt by the loss of a loved one. A portion of it goes as follows:

> 'Twas there while the black bird was cheerfully singing
> I first met that dear one, the joy of my heart.
> Around us for gladness the blue bells were ringing,
> But then little thought I how soon we should part.

"Roll in My Sweet Baby's Arms" is straight ahead but not ridiculously fast as it is sometimes performed. The guitar solo played by Brittany Haas evokes Clarence's style combined with the driving fluidity of Doc Watson.[9] "Soldier's Joy/Ragtime Annie" includes distinctive banjo breaks by Justin Hiltner,[10] who performs the tunes in D with the fourth string being played a lot. Molly Tuttle sounds much like Clarence on the first part of her solo on the medley and then adds some special touches of her own toward the end.

Roland resurrects "Little White Washed Chimney," and I'm so glad he keeps these types of songs in his repertoire. Some of the old stuff can't be beat. The fiddling on this number by Jeremy Garrett is edgy and seems to invigorate the melody, nudging it along with a forward lean. Bill Monroe would approve. The Mickey Newbury song "Why You Been Gone So Long" was a Kentucky Colonels staple. I always loved the verse about drinking a fifth of Thunderbird! "Alabama Jubilee" is a tune I love to play myself. I've done it with Roland, probably more times than he can remember. David Grier returns to play with Roland on "I Might Take You Back," adding his creative, improvisational flat-picking guitar style, perfected over many years. There is a simple, tasteful mandolin break that is pure Roland White. Kristin Scott Benson nails a Scruggs-style rendition of "Farewell Blues" on the banjo, using the C-tuning to get an ample, gutsy tone.[11] Roland lets everybody shine on that tune, saving his mandolin solo till almost last.

Jon Weisberger, who's been playing bass in the Roland White Band since 2003, coproduced the album and said this about Roland and the album:

The emphasis was on using younger musicians . . . a new generation of bluegrass pickers, because one of the things people love about Roland is he is so amazingly encouraging to younger musicians. We kind of wanted to honor that with the album project.

Roland's a joy to play with. The way that I feel about it is this: there are a lot of crabby people around bluegrass sometimes who have a lot of ideas about—this is the right way to play it, that's not the right way, it's not like it used to be—and yet I've never heard Roland do that. Instead, he is so welcoming and supportive of other musicians, and he really wants to hear their musical voice. [During] virtually every show we play at the Station Inn, he has one or two or sometimes more young musicians—teenagers and even preteens sometimes—getting up to play with us. He's so encouraging.

And the other thing is: he is such a unique stylist—it never takes more than a few notes to recognize who it is when he's playing. He has this wonderful combination of deep-rooted traditional approach with something really unique and creative and almost jazz-like in spontaneity and improvisational ability. . . . He's not afraid to leave space in his music. . . . It's been a wonderful experience to work with him.[12]

David Grier sent me these thoughts about Roland, which fit in nicely at this point:

The Kentucky Colonels were *the* band around our house. The comedy, the arrangements, the daring solos, the unique phrasing, the singing (brother harmonies), the command of their instruments, the wide groove, and the choice of songs all combined to make their sound unlike any other. It was (and still is) modern, but firmly rooted somehow.

Dad's Big 3 were Bill Monroe, Earl Scruggs, and Clarence White.[13] So I was hearing live tapes of these giants in the womb. I felt so in awe when I met Roland and couldn't believe he would pick with me when I was a child beginning to play the guitar. I would look forward to him playing with Country Gazette on the East Coast to see if he might be playing anywhere near where we lived! It was a highlight in my early development as a musician. He was funny, and cool. Always treated me like I was a person, not a child. I'm sure that was part of the reason I wanted to be a musician too: the fun hang!

I told Roland one day that I thought since he was the oldest, Clarence must have gotten a lot musically from him. But he told me that was all Clarence. I still don't know if I believe him completely.

One thing Roland told me years ago (and I'm starting to realize what he meant) was that it took a long while to learn how to play with Bill Monroe: how to find the right feel and fit in correctly. About the time he started to get it to his satisfaction he changed bands. Playing with Lester Flatt began again the quest of finding the right feel for that band. He knew each were different, and knew why. Of course that was back when bands didn't all try to sound alike!![14]

The influence of Roland White and the Kentucky Colonels is going to be preserved in the *Roland White and Friends* album. The Colonels were a formative band for Roland, and it's obvious that the group still occupies a fond and significant place in his heart. Our early successes in life drive us forward, seeking to regain what has been lost. In Roland's case, the loss was tragic. But maybe there's a good side: losing his brother was perhaps a primary motivator in Roland's career. Seeking to honor Clarence's memory has made him the persevering artist that we all admire. He'll never quit till he and Clarence are together again.

The Kentucky Colonels and the Bluegrass Hall of Fame

In 2019 the International Bluegrass Music Association inducted the Kentucky Colonels into their Hall of Fame. It was a fitting tribute to the group that started much of the modern bluegrass movement—a cadre of musicians who pooled their talents to create an enduring and vital force in the music world. Most of all, it's a tribute to the man who spearheaded that effort: Roland White. Without him, the group would not have made the inroads into the music world that they did, against tremendous odds.

A highlight of the Kentucky Colonels induction was a concert featuring surviving members of the original Kentucky Colonels band: LeRoy McNees, Roger Bush, and Roland. They were joined by Patrick Sauber (guitar), and Jeremy Stevens (banjo). As the group performed, a giant projected image of the original Kentucky Colonels appeared on the stage backdrop.

Kentucky Colonels performance at the 2019 IBMA Hall of Fame induction ceremony. L-R: Original Kentucky Colonel LeRoy McNees; original Kentucky Colonel Roger Bush; original Kentucky Colonel Roland White; Patrick Sauber; and Jeremy Stevens. Behind: Projected image of the 1960s full Kentucky Colonels band. L-R: Roland White, LeRoy McNees, Roger Bush, Clarence White, Billy Ray Latham. Photo: Willa Stein Photography.

Roland's musical roots have carried him far, to places even he could probably never have imagined. The music of the Kentucky Colonels is a fundamental part of those early musical influences, which were bequeathed to Roland by his parents, grandparents, aunts, and uncles. Roland has pioneered and shepherded the evolution of that music into what it is today. In that regard, he has had every bit as much influence as Bill Monroe. I consider myself honored to have known and played with both men.

Bluegrass music has evolved a great deal since the early days when the Kentucky Colonels were trying to make a go of it. Today's approach to bluegrass—with its characteristic freedom and individualistic interpretation—owes much of its existence to the struggle and hard work of people like Bill Monroe and Roland White. Both of them are noted for their encouragement of musicians from many different backgrounds, giving those players the confidence and inspiration to make their own contributions to the genre.

The Kentucky Colonels' Hall of Fame award is an affirmation of the best qualities of bluegrass: uniqueness, individuality, determination, and holding to dreams. Standing firm against tragedy and setback is one of Roland White's signature qualities. It has made him a hero in the world of bluegrass, a music that is already deeply rooted in the experiences of early American pioneers who made the perilous journey to the new world from other countries, working fiercely to overcome hardships and realize their dreams.

A Dream Fulfilled

Roland's time spent working for Bill Monroe at low pay and long hours playing guitar (not even his primary instrument) was like serving an apprenticeship. The Nashville Grass was a continuation of that. Those two jobs provided a springboard for Roland to achieve his full personal potential as a musician with his own creative independence. Country Gazette and the Nashville Bluegrass Band were platforms for him to display those gifts, no longer restrained by orthodox interpretations. The Roland White Band is the culmination of his lifetime of personal musical experience, and his bandmates have the good fortune to be beneficiaries of his hard-won expertise. The tragic irony in Roland's life is the fact that his first and most formative band, the Kentucky Colonels—the group he most wanted to succeed and flourish—was the one that was brought to a sudden and terrible end with Clarence's death.

Yet it has still been a rewarding life for Roland. He has never avoided the work required to achieve his dreams. First he learned to play the music, which is difficult in itself, requiring diligence and perseverance. Then he mastered the language of bluegrass, communicating a wide range of personal feelings and emotions through its vocabulary. Then he presented his music to the world, often through difficult channels. The bluegrass life of Roland White is distinguished and enviable—the gold standard of success stories.

Afterword

As Roland's earliest musical partner, Clarence White will always live on in everything Roland does. The two brothers represent one of the most desirable qualities in music: a completely organic symbiosis, influenced by elements they both grew up with and supported by a loving family. Usually musical partnerships are formed out of necessity—someone needs a certain type of musician to fill a vacancy in their band, and they get whoever is available. That person usually relies on "generic" musical phrases to fill in the gaps until a more solid musical vocabulary develops with the other band members. Unfortunately most bands don't stay together long enough for that rapport to develop. Roland and Clarence grew up together, learned to play together, performed on stage together, and recorded together. It doesn't get any better than that.

The early Kentucky Colonels' album *Appalachian Swing!* has all the elements of the brothers' mutual love for playing with each other. Whenever I think of Roland and Clarence picking together, I think of that album. There are six tunes on the album that feature mandolin and guitar solos only (with the rest of the Kentucky Colonels providing backup): "Nine Pound Hammer," "Listen to the Mockingbird," "Billy in the Lowground," "I Am a Pilgrim," "Sally Goodin," and "John Henry." The tune that contains the most back-and-forth solos between Roland and Clarence is "Nine Pound Hammer," and that's the one that always sticks in my mind. It seems like an endless jam between the two, and the album captures only a segment somewhere in the middle. Each solo is totally improvisational, a stream-of-consciousness experience as they play off of one another. It stops too soon when it seems like it should go on forever. The other mandolin-guitar duets are similar, but the one that is most moving to me is "Listen to the Mockingbird." It's the 1855 song about a mocking-bird singing over a lost loved one's grave. After learning about the song's history, I am struck by how much it fits Roland and Clarence: it's a duet between two loving brothers, one who has passed away and the other who still grieves. Their music will always be out there, transcending the boundary between this world and the other side.

I'll end this book with something David Grier told me: "Roland White has always been a role model, not only for me, but for many. Ask around, you'll see. He's been there, done that several times. There'll never be another like him: Roland White."[1]

People, Bands, and Venues

Additional information about some of the people, bands, and venues mentioned in this book.

Kenny Baker

Born in Kentucky, Kenny Baker (1926–2011) was perhaps Bill Monroe's best-known fiddler. He spent many years as a Blue Grass Boy, and Bill always introduced him as "the greatest fiddler in bluegrass." He had a masterful bowing technique, and he played old-time tunes galore, in addition to bluegrass. He made lots of solo fiddle albums—I was fortunate enough to be on five of them. Monroe liked Baker's fiddling so much that he used him on his 1972 recording *Bill Monroe's Uncle Pen*, an album he had been waiting a long time for just the right fiddler before making.[1]

Banjoy

Formed in 2002, Banjoy consists of Kristie Black, guitar/vocals; Bob Black, banjo/vocals; Paul Roberts, bass/vocals; Mark Wilson, guitar/vocals; and Joy Ward, fiddle/vocals. Kristie has been writing, performing, and recording music for over twenty years, participating in bluegrass and gospel groups. Paul Roberts is a banjo player, singer-songwriter, bass player, and guitar player. In addition to playing with Banjoy, Paul performs with the Great Bluegrass Herons, the McPunk Brothers, Goin' Up

Caney, and the Sharon Praise Band. He is a beloved and influential figure in the Midwestern bluegrass scene, and his unique approach combines old-fashioned Iowa humility with a wacky sense of humor, making him a favorite with audiences everywhere. Mark Wilson is an Iowa singer-songwriter and lead and rhythm guitarist, who is also a member of the Great Bluegrass Herons, the Burlington Street Bluegrass Band, and the McPunk Brothers. A world-class guitar flat-picker, Mark Wilson is unpretentious in his approach to music. He also performs as a solo act, performing a wide range of material that includes bluegrass, folk, country, and originals. Joy Ward sings and plays the fiddle with Banjoy and has appeared on eighteen different albums ranging from Celtic and folk to cowboy and bluegrass. She also performs with her husband, Mark Clark, in the group Castle Ridge.

Kristin Scott Benson

Born in South Carolina, Kristin came from a musical family. Picking up the banjo at age thirteen, she soon started playing in a band. After graduating high school, she moved to Nashville. Since then she has accumulated many awards, including four International Bluegrass Music Association's Banjo Player of the Year Awards (2009, 2010, 2011, 2019) and the Steve Martin Prize for Excellence in Banjo and Bluegrass (2018). She has been featured on many albums by the two-time IBMA Entertainers of the Year band the Grascals.[2]

Norman Blake

Born in 1938, Norman Blake grew up in Sulphur Springs, Alabama. Influenced by the Carter Family, the Skillet Lickers, and the Monroe Brothers (Charlie and Bill), he began playing guitar as a child and went on to mandolin, Dobro, and fiddle while a teenager. In the early '60s he began touring and recording with Johnny Cash. Later he was a member of the staff band on ABC television's *Johnny Cash Show*. He played on Bob Dylan's famous *Nashville Skyline* album. In 1971 he became a member of Aereo-Plain, John Hartford's group, which performed at Bill Monroe's Bean Blossom Bluegrass Festival in 1971.[3] He played for twenty years with his wife, Nancy. One of the many well-known songs he has written is "Ginseng Sullivan."

Gatemouth Brown

Clarence "Gatemouth" Brown (1924–2005) was considered by many to be primarily a bluesman, but he actually crossed over into many different styles, including nearly every form of roots music. His father played country, Cajun, and bluegrass. He was given the nickname "Gatemouth" by a teacher who told him he had a "voice like a gate."[4] He recorded an album with Roy Clark in 1979 and later appeared on the *Hee Haw* TV show.

Sam Bush

From Bowling Green, Kentucky, fiddler and mandolin player Sam Bush has been an innovator from the start. In his playing he has incorporated bluegrass with elements of rock, jazz, and reggae. He founded the New Grass Revival in 1972 after being inspired by an earlier newgrass band called the New Deal String Band. The New Grass Revival lasted for seventeen years and recorded many albums. Since then Bush has been a highly sought-after session musician, sideman, and soloist in his own right, playing with Emmylou Harris's Nash Ramblers, Béla Fleck and the Flecktones, Garth Brooks's backup band, and many more. The Kentucky state legislature passed a resolution in 2010 naming Sam Bush's hometown of Bowling Green as "the Birthplace of Newgrass."[5]

Kathy Chiavola

Kathy grew up in Kansas City, Missouri, playing guitar and singing folk, blues, and rock. Awarded a scholarship to the Oberlin Conservatory of Music, she earned her bachelor's and master's degrees in voice and studied in a doctoral program at Indiana University with Metropolitan Opera star Eileen Farrell. She moved to Nashville in 1980 and has worked with Mark O'Connor, Edgar Meyer, Jerry Douglas, Vassar Clements, the Doug Dillard Band, and Country Gazette. In 1995 she was voted Outstanding Background Vocalist in the Nashville Music Awards. She has sung on recordings with Vince Gill, Tammy Wynette, Kathy Mattea, Garth Brooks, Emmylou Harris, and Bill Monroe.[6] She recorded duet versions of "Stay Away from Me" and "The Old Old House" with Monroe in the living room of his cabin in 1994.[7]

Vassar Clements

Vassar Clements (1928–2005) was from Florida and joined Bill Monroe in 1949. His later fiddle career spanned the entire musical spectrum, as he played with the likes of Jim and Jesse, Faron Young, John Hartford, the Earl Scruggs Revue, the Grateful Dead, Dicky Betts, Jerry Garcia, the Allman Brothers, Linda Ronstadt, the Nitty Gritty Dirt Band, David Grisman, Paul McCartney, and many others. One of Vassar's signature compositions was "Lonesome Fiddle Blues," which bluegrass players became infatuated with back in the 1970s.

County Barn Dance Jubilee

Originally a radio program, Foreman Phillips's *County Barn Dance Jubilee* moved into a television format in 1954. The name was later changed to the *County Barn Dance*. It was televised every Saturday night from 7:00 to 8:00 p.m. After the TV broadcast, a dance would take place until 1:00 a.m. In addition to the Three Little Country Boys, the cast included the Three Little Country Girls, Red Murrell and His Ozark Playboys, Eddie Downs, Glen and Gary, Shirley Bates, Frank Simons, and Tex Atchison.[8]

Dan Crary

Born in 1939 in Kansas City, Kansas, Dan Crary is a highly renowned guitarist who has been one of the pioneers of the lead flat-picking style of melody playing. In the late 1960s, he played and sang with the Bluegrass Alliance, a groundbreaking newgrass band. With a long performing and recording career, Crary is part of a group of all-time guitar greats that includes Doc Watson, Tony Rice, Norman Blake, and Beppe Gambetta.

Dave Ferguson

Dave Ferguson began playing the fiddle at age ten. From 1973 through 1975 he played with the Southwestern bluegrass band the Stone Mountain Boys. Later he replaced Byron Berline in Country Gazette, appearing on several of that group's albums.[9]

Howdy Forrester

Fiddler Howard Wilson Forrester (1922–1987) was born in Vernon, Tennessee. His father, grandfather, and uncle all played the fiddle. In the 1930s he played for local square dances with his brothers. After moving to Nashville, he was given the nickname "Big Howdy." For a while he and his wife, Sally Forrester, who played accordion, played with Bill Monroe. He also recorded in the early 1950s with Flatt and Scruggs. He got a job playing on the *Grand Ole Opry* with Cowboy Copas, after which he joined Roy Acuff and the Smoky Mountain Boys. He stayed with Roy Acuff until he died. In 2015 he was inducted into the National Fiddler Hall of Fame. Bill Monroe said of Howdy, "He's the first man to play with me that played double-stop [two strings played together, creating a harmony], and [he] knows that neck all the way, and he knows how to get that tone out [to] give the fiddle a chance."[10]

Ingrid Fowler

Fiddler Ingrid Fowler (1941–1998) was the daughter of the famous bandleader Woody Herman. During the early 1970s, she and her husband, Bob Fowler, moved to Nashville from California's Bay Area, where they had performed in a bluegrass band named Styx River Ferry. After arriving in Nashville, Bob became a Blue Grass Boy, and Ingrid took a job playing with a band at the newly opened Opryland theme park.[11] Ingrid had been educated in classical music at the Juilliard School of Music. On one occasion, her father, Woody, who was on tour, brought his entire band into the Station Inn and played a concert. The band was so large it nearly filled the small club and listeners had to stand outside the door. Ingrid was very much like Roland White in that she was quite supportive of newcomers, providing much encouragement. Her fiddling was "sweet, and lilting with a subtle hint of classical."[12]

Josh Graves

Dobro player Burkett Howard Graves (1927–2006) was also known by the nicknames "Buck" and "Uncle Josh." He performed with the Pierce Brothers, Esco Hankins, and Wilma Lee and Stoney Cooper before joining

Lester Flatt and Earl Scruggs in 1955. After the breakup with Earl Scruggs, he stayed with Lester until 1971. Then he joined the Earl Scruggs Revue, playing in that band until 1974. He played as a featured soloist after that. From 1984 through 2006, he played and recorded with Kenny Baker, Jesse McReynolds, and Eddie Adcock. Graves fingerpicked in the Scruggs style for fast numbers and Hawaiian steel guitar style for slower songs.[13] He was inducted into the International Bluegrass Music Association Hall of Honor in 1997.

Doug Green

Country music historian Doug Green has written several books on cowboy and country music as well as a rhythm guitar instruction book. The group that he started in 1977, Riders in the Sky, performs regularly on the *Grand Ole Opry*. Doug sings, yodels, plays guitar, writes songs, and even does some acting with the group. Specializing in cowboy singing and comedy, Riders in the Sky appeared on the PBS show *Austin City Limits* and had a Saturday morning network television series in 1991 and 1992. Doug has also written liner notes for many recordings.

Lloyd Green

Born in Mississippi in 1937, Lloyd Green worked as a steel guitarist for Ferlin Husky and Faron Young but later on did mostly session work. He appeared on recordings with people like George Jones, Paul McCartney, and Ringo Starr. One of the most famous recordings he appeared on was the Byrds' *Sweetheart of the Rodeo*. Green, along with other trend-setting steel guitarists, such as Pete Drake, Speedy West, Buddy Emmons, Curly Chalker, and Ralph Mooney, helped to restore the popularity of the steel guitar, which had all but disappeared from country music before the 1970s.[14]

David Grier

Recognized by *Acoustic Guitar* magazine in 2000 as one of the Artists of the Decade, David Grier and his guitar style have been influenced by Tony Rice and Doc Watson as well as by Clarence White. He has played with many of the headliners in bluegrass, including Country Gazette,

Doug Dillard, Andrea Zonn, Tony Trischka, and many others. In 1996 Grier teamed up with Darol Anger, Mike Marshall, and Todd Phillips to create a modern bluegrass band called Psychograss. His most recent bluegrass ensemble, the Helen Highwater String Band, includes Mike Compton, Shad Cobb, and Missy Raines.

David Grisman

Grisman is a leading figure in the bluegrass, folk, and jazz world. In 1963 he joined the Even Dozen Jug Band with Maria Muldaur and John Sebastian. He also played with the bluegrass band Red Allen and the Kentuckians. After moving to San Francisco, he met Jerry Garcia and appeared on a Grateful Dead album titled *American Beauty*. "Ripple" and "Friend of the Devil" were the selections Grisman performed on.[15] In 1973–1974 he was in Garcia's bluegrass band Old and In the Way, and in 1975 he started his own group—the David Grisman Quintet—performing what is now called "Dawg" music.

Brittany Haas

Native Californian Brittany Haas's unique fiddle style was influenced by Bruce Molsky and Darol Anger. She has been featured as a member of Steve Martin's bluegrass band and has performed with Béla Fleck, the Yonder Mountain String Band, Tony Trischka, and Abigail Washburn. She is also a member of the group Crooked Still.[16]

Carlton Haney

Carlton Haney (1928–2016) produced the first weekend-long bluegrass festival at Cantrell's Horse Farm in Fincastle, Virginia, in 1965. Other festivals he put on took place in Camp Springs, North Carolina, and Berryville, Virginia. Two distinct elements pioneered by Haney at his first festival included Sunday morning gospel performances and a Sunday afternoon presentation that he called "The Story of Bluegrass." This involved former members of Bill Monroe's band recreating songs they had recorded with the Father of Bluegrass and discussing his influence on their own music.[17] Carlton Haney was inducted into the International Bluegrass Music Association's Bluegrass Hall of Fame in 1998.

Jack Hicks

From Ashland, Kentucky, Jack Hicks played in Bill Monroe's Blue Grass Boys from 1971 to 1973, entering the band while he was still a teenager. He did some recording with Monroe and had been one of the first banjo players Bill had allowed to use a little of the newer "melodic" style that had been growing in popularity around that time.[18] A striking example of Jack's melodic playing can be heard on "The Walls of Time," one of the numbers included on Bill and James Monroe's *Father and Son* album.[19] Later on he became a "Twitty Bird," joining Conway Twitty as a steel guitarist and banjo player.

Justin Hiltner

From Newark, Ohio, singer-songwriter and banjo player Justin Hiltner performs everything from bluegrass and newgrass to folk, country, and Celtic. He began playing at the age of seven when his parents bought him a banjo, and he and his brothers later formed a band. In 2019 he was nominated for the International Bluegrass Music Association's Collaborative Recording of the Year for his performance on Roland White's *Tribute to the Kentucky Colonels* album.[20]

IBMA (International Bluegrass Music Association)

Started in 1985, the IBMA is a trade organization for promoting bluegrass music. "The World of Bluegrass" was established in 1990 by the IBMA, featuring an annual trade show, concert, and awards presentation. In 1991 the IBMA's International Bluegrass Music Museum created a Hall of Honor (now called Hall of Fame) in Owensboro, Kentucky.

John Kaparakis

John Kaparakis (1937–2020) grew up in Arlington, Virginia. He was a firefighter by occupation and a devoted bluegrass musician since the 1950s. He was an important contributor to *Bluegrass Unlimited* magazine since its founding in the 1960s. John was a member of the Lonesome River Boys (along with Rick Churchill, banjo; Dick Stowe, bass; James

Buchanan, fiddle; and Jack Tottle, mandolin). They recorded a 1961 album, *Raise a Ruckus*,[21] which was issued by Riverside Records. He became good friends with Clarence and Roland White and wrote the extensive liner notes for the 1975 Kentucky Colonels' album, *Livin' in the Past*.[22]

Bill Keith

Bill Bradford Keith (1939–2015) made a huge impact on the banjo music scene with his stylistic approach that incorporated the use of melodic fingerpicking in addition to the more common Scruggs-style approach. Some have called him the "Father of Modern Bluegrass" for his trailblazing approach. It could be argued that he would have to share this title with Bobby Thompson. Keith also played steel guitar and was the inventor of a specialty type of tuner for the banjo. He also transcribed a large volume of Earl Scruggs's classic banjo breaks, which later became a major part of Earl's instruction book, *Earl Scruggs and the 5-String Banjo*.[23]

Charmaine Lanham

Charmaine Lanham was one of the original founders of the Station Inn, along with her husband, Marty; Red and Birdie Smith; Jim Bornstein; and Bob Fowler. The Station Inn opened in 1974, and Roland White was part of the original Station Inn "family." Charmaine is now a prominent Nashville-based photojournalist.[24]

Jim Lauderdale

Born in North Carolina, Jim Lauderdale has had bluegrass music cooking inside him from day one. In 1999 and 2002 he recorded albums with the late Ralph Stanley and the Clinch Mountain Boys. The two albums were *Jim Lauderdale and Ralph Stanley and the Clinch Mountain Boys: I Feel Like Singing Today* and *Jim Lauderdale and Ralph Stanley: Lost in the Lonesome Pines*.[25] Jim is a prominent singer-songwriter whose songs have been recorded by the likes of Vince Gill, Patty Loveless, George Strait, Blake Shelton, the Dixie Chicks, and many more.

Lance LeRoy

A key figure in bluegrass, Lance LeRoy (1930–2015) was born in Tignall, Georgia, and moved to Nashville in 1966. He played fiddle as a youth, playing occasionally for square dances. He became Lester Flatt's personal manager and agent in 1969 after the break with Earl Scruggs, and he stayed in that position until 1979, when Flatt passed away. He helped to found the International Bluegrass Music Association and was a 2000 Hall of Honor inductee.[26]

Laurie Lewis

Grammy-winning singer, songwriter, producer, bandleader, educator, and fiddler, Laurie Lewis was a founding member of the bands the Good Ole' Persons and the Grant Street String Band. Her earliest childhood inspiration came from many of the folk, blues, and bluegrass groups that she heard at the Berkeley Folk Festival in the 1960s. She was awarded the 2011 Performer Award from the Folk Alliance FAR-West.[27]

Tex Logan

Tex Logan (1927–2015) learned the fiddle during his childhood in Texas. He wrote a wonderful tune called "Big Spring," which Bill Monroe played occasionally. He worked briefly as a full-time musician in Wheeling, West Virginia. He was also a songwriter, and his best-known song was "Christmas Time's A-Comin'," which was recorded by Monroe and is played by nearly every bluegrass band today. Tex held parties at his home for Monroe and his band from 1965 through 1974 (sometimes twice a year), which included a big supper and all-night music.[28]

Maddox Brothers and Rose

Roselea Arbana "Rose" Maddox was born in 1925. Her brothers were Clifton R. E. (b. 1912), John Calvin (b. 1915), Fred Roscoe (b. 1919), Kenneth Galmer "Don" (b. 1922), and Henry Ford (b. 1928). After migrating to California in 1933, Rose, her brothers, and her parents found farm work at first, becoming "fruit tramps." Settling in Modesto, one of the things they did for money was collect whiskey bottles and redeem them at one cent apiece. When they found that music paid better than any of the other occupations they had tried, they began performing on radio station KTRB and many other places. During World War II, while some of her brothers were serving in the military, Rose performed sporadically with other bands. After the war, the group re-formed.[29] Rose Maddox was one of a select few early female country singers that included Molly O'Day, Cousin Emmy, Jenny Lou Carson, Cindy Walker, and Rosalie Allen. Of these, only Rose Maddox continued to be active and popular through the 1950s and early 1960s.[30]

Del McCoury

Born in 1939, Del McCoury is a banjo and guitar player who was part of Bill Monroe's band for a short time during the 1960s. He played in many bluegrass groups both before and after being a Blue Grass Boy, including the Blue Ridge Ramblers, the Virginia Mountain Boys, the Golden State Boys, the Shady Valley Boys, and the Dixie Pals, which later was renamed Del McCoury and His Dixie Pals and renamed again in 1987 as the Del McCoury Band. The band combined the best of traditional bluegrass with interesting song choices and reached a new group of listeners when they accompanied Steve Earle on his album *The Mountain*.[31]

Jim and Jesse McReynolds

From Carfax, Virginia, Jim McReynolds (1927–2002) and Jesse McReynolds (1929–) grew up in a musical family. Their harmony singing was phenomenal, with Jim's clear, high tenor, soaring above Jesse's lead voice. In the mid-1950s they began doing radio programs in Alabama, Georgia, and Florida. Martha White Foods cosponsored some of those programs, making them the number two group promoted by the flour company behind Flatt and Scruggs.[32] Jesse has always been a mandolin stylist, often credited with a method of playing called "cross-picking," which Clarence White also used. Jesse occasionally plays in a "split string" style, where only one of the double strings is fretted and the other is played open. In 1964 Jim and Jesse were inducted into the *Grand Ole Opry*. They are members of the International Bluegrass Music Association Hall of Honor. Since Jim's death in 2002, Jesse has continued performing with their band, the Virginia Boys.

Midnight Jamboree

In 1947 *Grand Ole Opry* star Ernest Tubb opened a record store on Lower Broadway in downtown Nashville, specializing in country music. The Ernest Tubb Record Shop was located within walking distance of the Ryman Auditorium, where the Opry took place. It was a way for Ernest to answer his many fans who kept asking him where they could purchase his records as well as those of other country music stars. WSM quickly started airing a live broadcast at the record shop every Saturday night, right after the Opry. Showcasing both established stars and rising personalities, the program was called the *Midnight Jamboree*. Early performers on the show included Elvis Presley and the Everly Brothers.[33] People would cram themselves into the theater to watch the show, and the crowd often overflowed onto the sidewalk outside. The *Midnight Jamboree* still takes place to this day, though in a different location.

Birch Monroe

Older brother of Bill Monroe, Birch (1901–1982) was an old-time fiddler and occasionally performed with Bill and his other brother Charlie before the latter two became the famous duet the Monroe Brothers. Birch was the manager of the park at Bean Blossom, where Bill Monroe's bluegrass festivals were held. I, along with the rest of the Blue Grass Boys, got to play a few shows with him at Bean Blossom. He recorded an album on which I played banjo: *Brother Birch Monroe Plays Old Time Fiddle Favorites*.[34] Birch had a conservative approach to music in general and fiddle tunes in particular: he played them in the "right" way—according to his own definition—never straying far from the basic melody.[35]

James Monroe

Son of Bill Monroe, James played the bass fiddle in his father's Blue Grass Boys. In 1972 he formed his own band, the Midnight Ramblers. In 1987 James put together a booklet titled *Bill Monroe: 50 Years of Music*, which included a short biography and some photos of his father. He sold space in the booklet for more than thirty endorsements by stars such as Johnny Cash, Conway Twitty, and Jerry Reed.[36]

Sonny Osborne

Born in Hyden, Kentucky, in 1937, Sonny and his family moved to Dayton, Ohio, in the late 1940s. Both he and his brother, Bobby (mandolin), played with the Lonesome Pine Fiddlers for a short while. In 1952, at the early age of fourteen, he became one of Bill Monroe's Blue Grass Boys, appearing on the *Grand Ole Opry* and recording ten sides for Decca records with the Father of Bluegrass. In 1954 Sonny and his brother recorded two classic bluegrass songs with Jimmy Martin: "20–20 Vision" and "Save It." From 1956 to 1958 the two brothers played with Red Allen (guitar/vocals), and in 1958, after Red left, Bobby and Sonny carried on as the Osborne Brothers. They later became members of the *Grand Ole Opry* and achieved lasting fame as one of the leading bluegrass bands of all time.[37] Sonny passed away in 2021.

Ozark Opry

The Ozark Opry was started in 1953 at Lake of the Ozarks, Missouri. It was a live country music stage show that predated and influenced the later Branson, Missouri, country music boom. Started by Lee and Joyce Mace, the Ozark Opry ran for over fifty years, finally closing its doors in 2006.[38]

Don Parmley

Freeman D. "Don" Parmley (1933–2016) was born in Monticello, Kentucky. He began learning the banjo at the age of twelve. As a teenager he played with some of the better-known bluegrass personalities of the day, such as Hylo Brown and Carl Story. In the late 1950s, he moved to Southern California, briefly playing with a band called the Smoggy Mountain Boys, aka the Green Mountain Boys. Parmley's next serious band was the Golden State Boys, which included brothers Vern and Rex Gosdin, who later achieved success in country music and songwriting, respectively. Later on, future Byrds member Chris Hillman was added. The name was changed to the Blue Diamond Boys and after that the Hillmen. Parmley, along with Doug Dillard, provided incidental banjo background passages in some of the later episodes of *The Beverly Hill-*

billies.[39] In 1974 Don formed a band with his son David (guitar/vocals) called the Bluegrass Cardinals. A couple of years later, the family moved to Virginia and continued with the Bluegrass Cardinals group. That band lasted for twenty-five years.

Tony Rice

Raised in Southern California, Tony Rice (1951–2020) has been one of the most esteemed and copied flat-pick guitarists in the world of bluegrass. Playing with bands ranging from traditional to progressive, Tony has been associated with the Bluegrass Alliance, J. D. Crowe and the New South, the David Grisman Quintet, and the Bluegrass Album Band. In the 1970s he founded the bluegrass, progressive bluegrass, and new acoustic group the Tony Rice Unit. He was inducted into the International Bluegrass Music Hall of Fame in 2013. Tony passed away on Christmas Day 2020 at the age of sixty-nine.

Slim Richey

David Michael "Slim" Richey (1938–2015) was born in Atlanta, Texas, and moved to Austin in 1992. He was a jazz guitarist who experimented with crossovers into swing, bluegrass, bebop, and country. In the 1970s and 1980s, he had a mail-order company, Warehouse Music, which sold musical instruments and supplies. He also ran Ridge Runner Records, which specialized in bluegrass and country music from Texas and Oklahoma. Artists he recorded included Marty Stuart, Eddie Shelton, Alan Munde, Joe Carr, Country Gazette, Sam Bush, Richard Bailey, Alison Brown, Stuart Duncan, and Bob Black. In 1977 he produced and recorded *Jazz Grass*,[40] which featured a wide array of musicians including Joe Carr, Ricky Skaggs, Dan Huckabee, Alan Munde, Bill Keith, Richard Greene, and many others. His many bands included the Jazz Pharaohs, Kat's Meow, Back Porch Vipers, Slim Richey's Dream Band, and the Jitterbug Vipers.[41]

Ralph Rinzler

Ralph Rinzler (1934–1994) was an important folklorist and musician. Cofounder of the Smithsonian Folk Life Festival, he made many field recordings of influential folk performers like Bill Monroe, Doc Watson, and Clarence Ashley. He was also a member of the great bluegrass band the Greenbriar Boys, who won first place in the Old-Time Fiddlers' Convention at Union Grove, North Carolina, in April 1960, even though the band played bluegrass, not old-time music.[42]

Mike Seeger

Founding member of the New Lost City Ramblers, Mike Seeger (1933–2009) enjoyed a long and distinguished career in folk music. His parents, Charles Seeger and Ruth Crawford Seeger, studied American folk music, and through them he gained an appreciation for the traditional idiom.[43] Adept at many musical instruments (dulcimer, mouth harp, mandolin, banjo, Dobro, and fiddle), Mike was a collector of field recordings of folk music. Not only was he the director of the Smithsonian Folklife Company, but he was also nominated for three Grammys and won a Guggenheim Fellowship. The New Lost City Ramblers, formed in the late 1950s, was perhaps his best-known legacy.

Jean Shepard

A honky-tonk singer and songwriter, Jean Shepard (1933–2016) was born in Oklahoma and spent the early part of her career in California, where she organized a band called the Melody Ranch Girls. Her first hit was "A Dear John Letter," which included a monologue by Ferlin Husky. The song appealed to families who had men overseas in the Korean War, and it stayed at the top in hillbilly music popularity polls for twenty-eight weeks.[44] She joined the *Grand Ole Opry* in 1955 and called her band the Second Fiddles after a popular recording she made called "Second Fiddle to an Old Guitar."

Jimmie Skinner

Born in Blue Lick, Kentucky, Jimmie Skinner (1909–1979) wrote some of the finest songs in country and bluegrass music. Starting out playing the fiddle and banjo, he performed as a child with his brother Esmer on local radio stations. One of his earliest records included two very well-known standards of today: "Doin' My Time" and "Let's Say Goodbye Like We Said Hello" (which became one of *Billboard*'s top five recordings for

Ernest Tubb in 1948). In the early 1950s, he opened his Cincinnati mail-order and retail record store, the Jimmie Skinner Music Center. Three more of Jimmie's best-known songs are "I Found My Girl in the U.S.A.," "Dark Hollow," and "You Don't Know My Mind" (recorded by Jimmy Martin in 1960).[45]

Bobby Slone

Born in Pike County, Kentucky, Bobby Slone (1936–2013) was an important influence in the world of bluegrass. As a child he taught himself to play the guitar and then the fiddle. By the age of thirteen, Slone was performing on a Pikeville radio station with a band called the Kentucky Ramblers. Later he joined a Bristol, Virginia, band called Buster Pack and the Lonesome Pine Boys. After that Bobby relocated to Chicago and played in country and western swing bands before moving to California. In 1964, after having played with the Golden State Boys and the Kentucky Colonels, Bobby joined J. D. Crowe and the Kentucky Mountain Boys around the Lexington, Kentucky, area. The name of that band was later changed to J. D. Crowe and the New South. He was with Crowe for twenty-four years.[46]

Connie Smith

Born in Indiana, Connie Smith is often named the greatest female singer in country music. "Once a Day," written for her by Bill Anderson, was her first hit in 1964, and she's had many more, including "Then and Only Then" and "I Never Once Stopped Loving You." Though her voice sounds much like Patsy Cline, she stated in 1975 that her favorite country singer was Loretta Lynn.[47] Connie Smith married Marty Stuart in 1997 and has appeared on many shows with him since. Stuart produced Connie Smith's 2011 album, *Long Line of Heartaches*.

Blaine Sprouse

Originally from West Virginia, fiddler Blaine Sprouse is a Kenny Baker protégé. He first started going out to Kenny Baker's farm when he was seventeen years old. Kenny treated him like a son, finding things for him to do like working on fences, mowing pasture, herding cattle, and castrating hogs.[48] A world-class fiddler, Blaine has played with Jimmy Martin, Charlie Louvin, the Osborne Brothers, James Monroe, the Johnson Mountain Boys, Peter Rowan, and Jim and Jesse.

Station Inn

Opening in 1974, the Station Inn was started by Charmaine and Marty Lanham, Bob and Ingrid Fowler, Red and Birdie Smith, and Jim Bornstein. Originally located near Nashville's Centennial Park, it had a coffeehouse atmosphere, and many bluegrass musicians came there to perform and hang out. It moved to 402 Twelfth Avenue South in 1978. In March 1981 the Station Inn was bought by Earl "J. T." Gray (1946–2021), who initiated the practice of hiring name bands along with local bands every night. Gray was a 2020 inductee to the International Bluegrass Music Association Hall of Fame. The Station Inn is now a showcase for many of the top bands in bluegrass, country, and even rock.[49]

Jody Stecher

Jody Stecher was born in 1946 in Brooklyn, New York, to a musical family with no television, no car, but a radio in every room, any of which played bluegrass music when tuned to the right station. His first toy was a turntable. He became a singer and musician, record producer, teacher, songwriter, and tunesmith. He has been a member of the bands Perfect Strangers, Blue Diamond Strings, and the Peter Rowan Bluegrass Band. Jody has had duet partnerships with Hank Bradley, Alasdair Fraser, Bill Evans, Krishna Bhatt, and, for many decades, Kate Brislin, with whom he toured the world and made many influential recordings. His recordings have been Grammy finalists and Indy Award winners. Jody's own songs and tunes comprise the repertoire on his most recent recordings, *Wonders & Signs* and *Dreams from the Overlook*. Reviewers have remarked on Jody's "ability to capture the essence and core of traditional music" and "to crystalize the spiritual essence of a song while making it his own."[50]

Wynn Stewart

Wynn Stewart (1934–1985) was a country singer who played a large part in developing the West Coast Bakersfield sound. His greatest hit was "It's

Such a Pretty World Today." Another one of his hits was "Wishful Thinking." Though never attaining superstar status, Stewart was indisputably an inspiration for such notables as Buck Owen and Merle Haggard. He helped to build a West Coast style of country music that challenged the establishment sounds of Nashville.[51]

Carl Story

Born in Lenoir, North Carolina, Carl Story (1916–1995) played fiddle off and on with Bill Monroe during 1942–1943. After the war, he started his own band, the Rambling Mountaineers, and was one of the first country artists signed by Mercury, a label he remained with until 1953. He returned to Mercury in 1955 after a brief stint with Columbia. In 1957 he went to Nashville and recorded two gospel quartet songs and two instrumentals, one of which was "Mocking Banjo," which featured the Brewster Brothers on mandolin and banjo.[52] Story wrote many classic bluegrass gospel songs.

Stringbean

Musician, singer, and comedian Dave Akeman, better known as "Stringbean" (1915–1973), was a *Grand Ole Opry* regular since 1952, replacing old-time banjo player/singer Uncle Dave Macon, who had passed away. He was the first banjo player to work for Bill Monroe as a Blue Grass Boy. At that time he called himself "Stringbean, the Kentucky Wonder."[53] Earlier in his career he was known as "Stringbeans," and that's what Monroe always called him. He is perhaps best known for his regular appearances on the TV show *Hee Haw*.

Billy Strings

Born in Lansing, Michigan, in 1992, Billy Strings (William Apostol) was steeped in music from the start. He joined his father's bluegrass band at the age of six and was given the nickname Billy Strings by his aunt. He moved to Nashville in 2016 and has been working there as a singer and instrumentalist ever since.[54]

Joe Stuart

A bluegrass singer and all-instrument virtuoso, Joe Stuart was born in Tennessee in 1928 and raised in North Carolina. He played and recorded with some of the greatest names in bluegrass, including Bill Monroe, the Sauceman Brothers, Flatt and Scruggs, the Sullivan Family, and Rual Yarbrough's Dixiemen. In 1957 he appeared on the iconic Folkways album *American Banjo Tunes & Songs in Scruggs Style*,[55] playing "Shortnin' Bread" and "Cacklin' Hen." Although he was a master musician, playing every bluegrass instrument, and worked as both bandleader and quintessential sideman, he was never widely known by the public.[56] He died on September 13, 1987, after an incurable bout with cancer.

Town Hall Party

The *Town Hall Party* began in 1951 as a radio broadcast. It took place in the Town Hall building at 400 South Long Beach Boulevard, Compton, California, and was broadcast over KXLA in Pasadena. One year later it was being televised on KTTV in Los Angeles. It became the most popular country and western program in Southern California and continued successfully all through the 1950s.

Molly Tuttle

Winner of the 2018 Instrumentalist of the Year at the Americana Music Awards, native Californian Molly Tuttle grew up in a musical family, learning to play guitar at an early age. She was a member of a family band, the Tuttles, which included her father, Jack; siblings Sullivan and Michael; and A. J. Lee. She moved to Nashville in 2015. In 2017 she was the first woman to win the International Bluegrass Music Association's Guitar Player of the Year Award. She's been in many groups and won lots of other awards as well. She plays clawhammer banjo, flat-picking guitar, and sings.[57]

Ed Weber

Ed Weber was the banjo player for Pathfinder, a Midwest bluegrass group formed in the 1980s. Later he moved to Nashville and started working for the Gibson Guitar Company, where he worked on banjo necks, pearl inlaying, and other pieces. He is now a freelance scrimshaw artist.

Pete Wernick

Also known as "Dr. Banjo," Pete Wernick is an instructor who organizes a network of "jamming camps" (teaching camps where students learn about bluegrass music jamming). His instructional book *Bluegrass Banjo* has sold close to two hundred thousand copies.[58] He was a founding member of the enormously popular group Hot Rize and its offshoot, Red Knuckles and the Trailblazers.

Kenny Wertz

Kenny Wertz is a West Coast musician who has performed and recorded with many groups, including the Scottsville Squirrel Barkers, Country Gazette, and the Flying Burrito Brothers. On the 1972 live album *The Flying Burrito Brothers: Last of the Red Hot Burritos*,[59] Kenny joins Country Gazette members Byron Berline and Roger Bush for a short set of lively acoustic bluegrass music.[60]

Benny Williams

Horace "Benny" Williams (1931–2007) played many instruments but was perhaps best known as a fiddler. He also played with many bluegrass and country stars and worked in Ernest Tubb's band for a while. He was a bus driver too; in those days, if you drove a bus, you could get a job with anybody. Benny played fiddle and guitar with Bill Monroe, doing many stints with the Blue Grass Boys during the '60s up until early 1968, when Jimmy Martin accidentally shot him in a hunting accident (not fatally). He left the Blue Grass Boys shortly after that.[61]

Bob Wills

Born outside of Kosse, Texas, in 1905, Bob Wills popularized western swing by using an uninhibited, experimental approach that incorporated elements of jazz and blues as well as swing. Starting in the late 1920s, his popularity grew with the public, but his music was often criticized by other hillbilly performers who didn't understand his nontraditional presentation. He composed from his heart and soul and wasn't too concerned with musical propriety. Today he is the best-known proponent of the genre. "San Antonio Rose" is perhaps the most famous of his many compositions. He died in 1975.[62]

Gene Wooten

From North Carolina, Gene Wooten (1953–2001) was a great Dobro player who performed with Wilma Lee and Stoney Cooper, the Osborne Brothers, Del McCoury, Country Gazette, and many others. He was featured on a Patty Loveless album, *Mountain Soul*.[63] He played in a husky, bluesy style reminiscent of Josh Graves and occasionally took jobs with Nashville musical instrument companies repairing and setting up Dobros. He was so good at it that some of the best players around, such as Brother Oswald, would bring their instruments to Gene for setup.[64] In 1989 a German bluegrass band that I was a member of, GroundSpeed, was touring the United States, and when we came to Nashville, Gene Wooten took us under his wing. He was very friendly and helpful, and he arranged a performance for us at the Station Inn, playing his Dobro with us on that show.

Roland White's Family

Mother and Father

Mildred Marie Cyr LeBlanc (White): b. August 3, 1918, Van Buren, Maine; d. January 26, 1992, Lancaster, California

Eric Joseph LeBlanc (White): b. October 27, 1916, Rogersville, New Brunswick, Canada; d. June 1, 1972, Palmdale, California

Mildred and Eric Sr. were married on April 19, 1937, in Madawaska, Maine.

Siblings

Roland Joseph LeBlanc (White): b. April 23, 1938, Madawaska, Maine

JoAnne Marie LeBlanc (White) Bierbrauer: b. September 7, 1939, Lewiston, Maine; d. June 7, 2016, Lancaster, California

Eric Joseph LeBlanc Jr. (White): b. July 9, 1941, Lewiston, Maine; d. June 7, 2012, Lancaster, California

Clarence Joseph LeBlanc (White): b. June 7, 1944, Lewiston, Maine; d. July 15, 1973, Palmdale, California

Rosemarie White: b. April 4, 1955, Burbank, California

First Marriage

Arline Melanson LeBlanc: b. March 1, 1939; d. May 6, 2014

Roland and Arline were married from 1961 to 1986.

CHILDREN

Roline Hodge LeBlanc: b. October 16, 1964
Lawrence White: b. December 24, 1969

Second Marriage

Diane Bouska: b. 1955

Roland and Diane were married in 1989.

Roland White
Instructional Materials

The following instruction materials are available from rolandwhite .com:

Roland White's Approach to Bluegrass Mandolin, by Diane Bouska and Roland White. © 2001, 2013 Diane and Roland Music.

The Essential Clarence White Bluegrass Guitar Leads, by Diane Bouska and Roland White, with Steve Pottier and Matt Flinner. © 2009 Diane and Roland Music.

Roland White's Mandolin Christmas, by Diane Bouska and Roland White. © 2003 Diane and Roland Music.

Roland White's Christmas Chord Book. Two 24-page PDF books.

Notes

Introduction

1. See appendix A, "Banjoy."
2. Bob Black, *Come Hither to Go Yonder: Playing Bluegrass with Bill Monroe* (Urbana: University of Illinois Press, 2005).
3. "Kinross, Iowa, Population 2021," World Population Review, https://worldpopulationreview.com/us-cities/kinross-ia-population (accessed August 31, 2021).
4. See appendix A, "Ed Weber."
5. See appendix A, "Kenny Baker."
6. Woody Platt, interview by Bob Black, March 2015.
7. See appendix A, "Joe Stuart."
8. Bill Monroe, *Knee Deep in Blue Grass,* Decca DL 8731, 1958.

Chapter 1. Doing It for Real

1. Marty Stuart, interview by Bob Black, May 2016.
2. Craig Shelburne, "Rose Maddox: The Remarkable Hillbilly Singer Who Made Bluegrass History," *The Bluegrass Situation*, https://thebluegrasssituation.com/read/rose-maddox-the-remarkable-hillbilly-singer-who-made-bluegrass-history/ (accessed January 2, 2021).
3. See appendix A, "Maddox Brothers and Rose."
4. See appendix A, "Wynn Stewart" and "Jean Shepard."
5. Marty Stuart, interview by Bob Black, May 2016.
6. Vic Jordan and Roland White, interview by Bob and Kristie Black, March 2015.
7. See appendix A, "Station Inn."
8. Mike Compton, interview by Bob Black, December 2, 2020.
9. Marty Stuart, interview by Bob Black, May 2016.
10. Ibid.

Chapter 2. Birth of a Dream

1. Roland White and Diane Bouska, with Steve Pottier and Matt Flinner, *The Essential Clarence White* (Nashville: Diane and Roland Music, 2009), 5–6.

2. Despite never having made a legal name change, Roland was able to get a Social Security number and driver's license in the name of White.

3. White and Bouska, *Essential Clarence White*, 5.

4. Roland White, interview by Bob Black and Kristie Black, March 2015.

5. A tenor banjo has four strings instead of the five-string version favored by most bluegrass and old-time musicians. It also has a shorter neck than a five-string, generally with seventeen to nineteen frets instead of twenty-two. There are many tunings, but the three most often used are jazz tuning, Irish or folk tuning, and guitar tuning (sometimes called Chicago tuning). Jazz tuning, beginning with the fourth string, is C-G-D-A. Being tuned in fifths, similar to the mandolin or fiddle, makes the banjo easier to chord. Irish or folk tuning, beginning with the fourth string, is G-D-A-E. This tuning is an octave below the fiddle, making Irish tunes easy to play, but it has one drawback: the fourth string can sound muddy because it is so low. Another tuning beginning with the fourth string is E-A-D-G—the same as the top four strings of a guitar. This tuning makes for more compact chord positions with easier finger stretches.

6. White and Bouska, *Essential Clarence White*, 6.

7. Roland White, interview by Bob Black and Kristie Black, March 2015.

8. Ibid.

9. White and Bouska, *Essential Clarence White*, 7.

10. Roland White, interview by Bob Black and Kristie Black, March 2015.

11. White and Bouska, *Essential Clarence White*, 6.

12. Ibid., 7.

13. Roland White, interview by Bob Black and Kristie Black, March 2015.

Chapter 3. The Country Boys

1. Roland White and Diane Bouska, with Steve Pottier and Matt Flinner, *The Essential Clarence White* (Nashville: Diane and Roland Music, 2009), 7.

2. Ibid., 8.

3. Ibid.

4. Clarence played that D-18 until 1968, when it was stolen.

5. Ibid., 16.

6. Ibid.

7. Ibid., 9.

8. Douglas B. Green, *Singing in the Saddle: The History of the Singing Cowboy* (Nashville: Country Music Foundation Press/Vanderbilt University Press, 2002), 259.

9. See appendix A, "Bob Wills."

10. White and Bouska, *Essential Clarence White*, 9.

11. Ibid.

12. Ibid., 10.

13. Ibid.

14. See appendix A, *Town Hall Party.*

15. David Vinopal, "Joe Maphis Biography," AllMusic, https://www.allmusic.com/artist/joe-maphis-mn0000141256/biography (accessed May 4, 2020).

16. See appendix A, "Carlton Haney."

17. Robert Shelton and Burt Goldblatt, *The Country Music Story* (Secaucus, NJ: Castle Books, 1966), 50.

18. Bill C. Malone and Judith McCulloh, eds., *Stars of Country Music: Uncle Dave Macon to Johnny Rodriguez* (Urbana: University of Illinois Press, 1975), 428.

19. Roland White, interview by Bob Black and Kristie Black, Nashville, March 2015.

20. White and Bouska, *Essential Clarence White*, 11.

21. Ibid.

22. Roland White, interview by Bob Black and Kristie Black, March 2015.

23. White and Bouska, *Essential Clarence White*, 11.

24. See appendix A, *County Barn Dance Jubilee.*

25. Roland White, interview by Bob Black and Kristie Black, March 2015.

26. Ibid.

27. Malone and McCulloh, *Stars of Country Music*, 407.

28. White and Bouska, *Essential Clarence White*, 13.

29. Ibid., 14.

30. Ibid., 16.

31. Roland White, interview by Bob Black and Kristie Black, March 2015.

32. Ibid.

33. Neil V. Rosenberg and Charles K. Wolfe, *The Music of Bill Monroe* (Urbana: University of Illinois Press, 2007), 301.

34. Roland White, interview by Bob Black and Kristie Black, March 2015.

35. Charlie Cline was hired by Bill Monroe in 1951. He also played the five-string banjo.

36. See appendix A, "Sonny Osborne."

37. Jim Renz, interview by Bob Black, March 2020.

38. "Poison Love" was a popular song originally recorded by Johnny and Jack in 1950.

39. Rosenberg and Wolfe, *Music of Bill Monroe*, 300.

40. White and Bouska, *Essential Clarence White*, 17.

41. Roland White, interview by Bob Black and Kristie Black, March 2015.

42. See appendix A, "Jimmie Skinner."

43. Roland White, interview by Bob Black and Kristie Black, March 2015.

44. Ibid.

45. Ibid.

46. White and Bouska, *Essential Clarence White*, 18.

47. Roland White, interview by Bob Black and Kristie Black, March 2015.

48. Ibid.

49. Liner notes by the Rounder Collective, from talks with Roland White, *The Kentucky Colonels, 1965–1966, Featuring Roland and Clarence White*, Rounder Records 0070, 1976.

50. Chops also helped to differentiate between bluegrass and more traditional mountain music.

51. White and Bouska, *Essential Clarence White*, 18.

52. Roland White, interview by Bob Black and Kristie Black, March 2015.

53. "Clarence White: Innovator, Guitarist, and Pioneer of Country Rock," *Rocks Off* music magazine, https://www.rocksoffmag.com/clarence-white/ (accessed March 10, 2020).

54. See appendix A, "Jim and Jesse McReynolds."

55. Some sources say Billy Ray's last name is spelled "Lathum." It has been listed both ways on various recordings.

56. Roland White, interview by Bob Black and Kristie Black, March 2015.

57. John Lawless, "Billy Ray Latham Passes," *Bluegrass Today*, August 21, 2018, https://bluegrasstoday.com/billy-ray-Latham-passes/ (accessed March 9, 2020).

58. Chris Houchens, "Billy Ray Latham: From Mayberry to Horse Cave," *The Amplifier*, https://bgamplifier.com/music/billy-ray-Latham-from-mayberry-to-horse-cave/article_9aa9fbd2-92df-552e-939c-135425631472.html (accessed March 9, 2020).

59. Lawless, "Billy Ray Latham Passes."

60. Houchens, "Billy Ray Latham."

61. Alan Munde et al., "The Roland White Interview," Mandolin Cafe, June 13, 2010, https://www.mandolincafe.com/news/publish/mandolins_001223.shtml (accessed March 20, 2020).

62. Ibid.

63. Diane Bouska, email correspondence with Bob Black, March 17, 2020.

64. See appendix A, "Don Parmley."

65. Jim Renz, interview by Bob Black, March 2020.

66. White and Bouska, *Essential Clarence White*, 19.

67. Roland White, interview by Bob and Kristie Black, March 2015.

68. See appendix A, "Mike Seeger."

69. Liner notes, *The New Lost City Ramblers, Vol. 4*, Folkways Records FA 2399, 1962.

70. White and Bouska, *Essential Clarence White*, 21.

71. LeRoy McNees, interview by Bob Black, February 2019.

72. Ibid.

73. See appendix A, "Josh Graves."

74. Ibid.

75. LeRoy McNees, interview by Bob Black, February 2019.

76. White and Bouska, *Essential Clarence White*, 21.

77. Ibid., 23.

78. Jim Renz, interview by Bob Black, March 2020.

79. See appendix A, *Midnight Jamboree*; Diane Bouska, email correspondence with Bob Black, March 2020.

80. Guest contributor, "Roland White on Earl Scruggs," *Bluegrass Today*, April 3, 2012, https://bluegrasstoday.com/roland-white-on-earl-scruggs/ (accessed March 29, 2020).

81. Stringbean was also a guest on the show that day. See appendix A, "Stringbean."

82. Green, *Singing in the Saddle*, 219.

83. Jim Renz, interview by Bob Black, March 2020.

84. The Dillards later appeared on several episodes of the *Andy Griffith Show* as the Darling Family, starting in 1963.

85. Floyd, "Two Chairs No Waiting 209: LeRoy Mack," October 9, 2012, Host: Allan Newsome, *Two Chairs No Waiting* Andy Griffith Show Fan Podcast, https://imayberry.com/podcasts/2012/10/two-chairs-no-waiting-209-leroy-mack/.

86. Jim Renz, interview by Bob Black, March 2020.

87. Roland White, interview by Bob and Kristie Black, September 2015.

88. Ibid.

89. "Spring Festival of Music No. 4: Folk Sound, U.S.A.," Paley Center for Media, https://www.paleycenter.org/collection/item/?q=&p=1&item=T84:0155 (accessed November 12, 2020).

90. Roline Hodge, interview by Bob Black, March 2019.

91. Roland White, interview by Bob and Kristie Black, March 2015.

92. Diane Bouska and Roland White, interview by Bob Black, February 2019.

93. Roland White, interview by Bob Black and Kristie Black, Nashville, March 2015.

94. Ibid.

95. Roger Bush, interview by Bob Black, February 2019.

96. Ibid.

97. Ibid.

98. Ibid.

99. Ibid.

100. Ibid.

101. Ibid.

102. Mike Compton, interview by Bob Black, December 2, 2020.

103. See appendix A, "Ralph Rinzler."

104. Roger Bush, interview by Bob Black, February 2019.

105. Jim Renz, interview by Bob Black, March 2020.

Chapter 4. The Original Kentucky Colonels

1. Roland White, interview by Bob and Kristie Black, March 2015.

2. Brooks Otis, interview by Bob Black, December 31, 2020.

3. Guest contributor, "Roland White on Earl Scruggs," *Bluegrass Today*, April 3,

2012, https://bluegrasstoday.com/roland-white-on-earl-scruggs/ (accessed March 29, 2020).

4. Roland White, interview by Bob and Kristie Black, March 2015.

5. Ibid.

6. Roger Bush, interview by Bob Black, February 2019.

7. Ibid.

8. Ibid.

9. Ibid.

10. *Mr. & Mrs. Country Music: Joe and Rose Lee Maphis*, Starday SLP 286, 1964.

11. Douglas B. Green, *Singing in the Saddle: The History of the Singing Cowboy* (Nashville: Country Music Foundation Press/Vanderbilt University Press, 2002), 160.

12. Ibid., 233.

13. The Country Boys, *The New Sound of Bluegrass America*, Briar 109, 1962.

14. Roger Bush, interview by Bob Black, February 2019.

15. Jim Renz, interview by Bob Black, March 2020.

16. From 2004 to 2014, LeRoy McNees traveled and performed as a duet with his wife. During that time he was a volunteer for Habitat for Humanity and SOWERS (Servants on Wheels Ever Ready). He formed the group LeRoy Mack McNees and Gloryland in 2016. He has been featured on recordings with John Denver, Vince Gill, and the Laurel Canyon Ramblers. "The Kentucky Colonels: Biography," Hall of Fame Inductees, Bluegrass Music Hall of Fame and Museum, https://www.bluegrasshall .org/inductees/the-kentucky-colonels/#biography (accessed March 21, 2020).

17. See appendix A, "David Grisman."

18. Roger Bush, interview by Bob Black, February 2019.

19. See appendix A, "Bobby Slone."

20. Roland White and Diane Bouska, with Steve Pottier and Matt Flinner, *The Essential Clarence White* (Nashville: Diane and Roland Music, 2009), 24.

21. Richard S. Ginell, "Django Reinhardt Biography," AllMusic, https://www.allmusic .com/artist/django-reinhardt-mn0000136220/biography (accessed May 4, 2020).

22. Various artists, *Country Music Hootenanny*, Capitol ST 2009, 1963.

23. Tut Taylor and the Folkswingers, *12 String Dobro!*, World Pacific Records 1816, 1964.

24. Originally made on the World-Pacific label with Dick Bock producing, *Dobro Country* is now available on Alcatec Media, AMWP 1829.

25. Louise Scruggs, April 1964, liner notes to Tut Taylor's *Dobro Country* album.

26. John Hartford, *Aereo-Plain*, Warner Bros., WS 1916, 1971.

27. Tut Taylor, *Friar Tut*, Rounder Records, 0011, 1972.

28. Tut Taylor, *The Dobrolic Plectral Society*, Takoma 1050, 1976.

29. See appendix A, "Bill Keith."

30. Blair Jackson, *Garcia: An American Life* (New York: Viking Penguin, 1999), 75.

31. "Sandy Rothman," MusicianBio, https://musicianbio.org/sandy-rothman/ (accessed May 4, 2020).

32. Jackson, *Garcia,* 63.

33. White and Bouska, *Essential Clarence White*, 24.

34. Roger Bush, interview by Bob Black, February 2019.

35. White and Bouska, *Essential Clarence White*, 24.

36. Roger Bush, interview by Bob Black, February 2019.

37. Lester Flatt and Earl Scruggs, *Foggy Mountain Banjo*, Columbia CS 8364, 1961.

38. Thomas Aubrunner, "The Kentucky Colonels, 1962," http://www.burritobrother .com/kentuckycolonels.htm (accessed April 9, 2020).

39. White and Bouska, *Essential Clarence White*, 25.

40. Roland White, interview by Bob and Kristie Black, September 2015.

41. Ibid.

42. Ibid.

43. See appendix A, "Jody Stecher."

44. Jody Stecher, email correspondence with Bob Black, December 4, 2020.

45. Ibid.

46. Roger Bush, interview by Bob Black, February 2019.

47. Jackson, *Garcia*, 76.

48. Bruce Eder, "Scotty Stoneman Biography," AllMusic, https://www.allmusic .com/artist/scotty-stoneman-mn0000837808/biography (accessed May 5, 2020).

49. Various artists, *The Beverly Hillbillies*, Columbia CL 2402, 1965.

50. Lester Flatt and Earl Scruggs, *Hard Travelin'*, Columbia CL 1951, 1963.

51. The Kentucky Colonels, "That's What You Get for Lovin' Me"/"The Ballad of Farmer Brown," World Pacific 427, 1965.

52. Mike Duffy and Jeff Owens, "How Clarence White's B-Bending Telecaster Bridged Country and Rock," n.d., Fender, https://www.fender.com/articles/gear/ how-clarence-whites-b-bending-telecaster-bridged-country-and-rock/ (accessed December 22, 2020).

53. White and Bouska, *Essential Clarence White*, 25–26.

54. Ibid., 26.

55. Ibid.

56. See appendix A, "Ozark Opry."

57. Bob Warford played as a guest for Bill Monroe two times—first at the Ash Grove in 1967 and later that same year at a folk club called Penny University in San Bernardino. Warford later switched to electric guitar and toured with the Everly Brothers. Richard Thompson, "I'm Going Back to Old Kentucky #291," *Bluegrass Today*, July 18, 2011, https://bluegrasstoday.com/im-going-back-to-old-kentucky-291/ (accessed March 19, 2020).

Chapter 5. The Blue Grass Boys

1. Tom Ewing, "Thirty Years Ago This Month," *Bluegrass Unlimited*, May 1997, 8.

2. See appendix A, "Doug Green."

3. Byron Berline with Jane Frost, *Byron Berline: A Fiddler's Diary* (Stillwater, OK: New Forums Press, 2013), 63.

4. Tom Ewing, *Bill Monroe: The Life and Music of the Bluegrass Man* (Urbana: University of Illinois Press, 2018), 223.

5. The G-run, played at the end of many measures, is probably the most often used guitar lick in bluegrass. It punctuates the important lines and ties the music together.

6. Roland White, interview by Bob and Kristie Black, March 2015.

7. Ewing, *Bill Monroe*, 293.

8. Roland White, interview by Bob and Kristie Black, March 2015.

9. See appendix A, "James Monroe."

10. Berline, *Byron Berline*, 37.

11. Neil V. Rosenberg, *Bluegrass: A History* (1985; Champaign: University of Illinois Press, 1993), 241.

12. Berline, *Byron Berline*, 36–37.

13. Roland White, interview by Bob and Kristie Black, March 2015.

14. Bob Black, *Come Hither to Go Yonder: Playing Bluegrass with Bill Monroe* (Urbana: University of Illinois Press, 2005), 118.

15. Jim Renz, interview by Bob Black, March 2020.

16. Roland White, interview by Bob and Kristie Black, March 2015.

17. Berline, *Byron Berline*, 64–65.

18. Roland White, interview by Bob and Kristie Black, March 2015.

19. Ibid.

20. Jim Renz, interview by Bob Black, March 2020.

21. See appendix A, "David Grier."

22. David Grier, email correspondence with Bob Black, April 24, 2019.

23. See appendix A, "IBMA."

24. "2017 IBMA Hall of Fame Members Conversation Part 1—Alice Gerrard and Roland White," October 4, 2017, https://youtube/-qJnrf5vpOM (accessed December 23, 2020).

25. Roland White, interview by Bob and Kristie Black, March 2015.

26. Goo Goo Cluster, "What a Cluster!," "How We Started," https://googoo.com/pages/about (accessed January 3, 2021).

27. Goo Goo Cluster, "About That Great Name," https://googoo.com/pages/about (accessed January 3, 2021).

28. Ewing, *Bill Monroe*, 173–74.

29. Thomas A. Adler, *Bean Blossom: The Brown County Jamboree and Bill Monroe's Bluegrass Festivals* (Urbana: University of Illinois Press, 2011), 93.

30. Roland White, interview by Bob and Kristie Black, March 2015.

31. See appendix A, "Birch Monroe."

32. Roland White, interview by Bob and Kristie Black, March 2015.

33. Roland White, quoted in Adler, *Bean Blossom*, 99.

34. Ibid., 98.

35. Roland White, interview by Bob and Kristie Black, March 2015.

36. Neil Rosenberg and Charles Wolfe, *The Music of Bill Monroe* (Urbana: University of Illinois Press, 2007), 184.

37. Decca DL 75213, 1970 (see "Roland White Recordings Cited").

38. Virginia Stauffer (1940–2011) had written several songs that Bill recorded, including "I Live in the Past," "Body and Soul," "Show Me the Way," and "The Road of Life."

39. See appendix A, "Benny Williams."

40. Ewing, *Bill Monroe*, 297.

41. Rosenberg, *Bluegrass: A History*, 306.

42. Richard Thompson, "Vic Jordan Remembered," *Bluegrass Today*, September 23, 2016, https://bluegrasstoday.com/vic-jordan-remembered/ (accessed December 23, 2020).

43. Doug Green, interview by Bob Black, February 21, 2019.

44. Ibid.

45. Rosenberg, *Bluegrass: A History*, 57.

46. Roland White, interview by Bob and Kristie Black, March 2015.

47. *Sweetheart of the Rodeo*, Columbia, CS 9670, 1968. John Hartford, banjo/guitar; Roy M. Huskey, bass; Chris Hillman, bass/mandolin; Jon Corneal, drums; Kevin Kelley, drums; Clarence J. White, guitar; Gram Parsons, guitar; Earl P. Ball, piano; Jay Dee Maness, pedal steel guitar; Lloyd Green, pedal steel guitar; Roger McGuinn, guitar/banjo.

48. David N. Meyer, *Twenty Thousand Roads* (New York: Villard Books, 2008), 231.

49. See appendix A, "Lloyd Green."

50. Roger McGuinn, "Random Most Interesting Facts about Byrds' 'Sweetheart of Rodeo,'" https://www.bestrandoms.com/get-random-most-fascinating-facts-about-byrds-sweetheart-of-rodeo (accessed August 16, 2021).

51. Meyer, *Twenty Thousand Roads*, 232.

52. Roland White, interview by Bob Black, February, 2019.

53. Roland White, interview by Bob and Kristie Black, September 2015.

54. Roland's parents were both heavy smokers too. Jim Renz, interview by Bob Black, March 2020.

55. Roland White, interview by Bob and Kristie Black, September 2015.

56. Roland White, interview by Bob Black, February 2019.

57. Bill Monroe, *Uncle Pen*, MCA-500, 1972.

58. Jim Renz, interview by Bob Black, March 2020.

59. Ibid.

60. Diane Bouska, email correspondence with Bob Black, June 11, 2020.

61. See appendix A, "Vassar Clements."

62. Rosenberg and Wolfe, *Music of Bill Monroe*, 184.

63. Ibid., 184–85.

64. James Rooney, *Bossmen: Bill Monroe and Muddy Waters* (New York: Dial Press, 1971), 92.

65. Vic Jordan and Roland White, interview by Bob and Kristie Black, March 2015.

66. Adler, *Bean Blossom*, 101.

67. Ewing, *Bill Monroe*, 298.

68. Ewing, "Thirty Years Ago This Month," *Bluegrass Unlimited*, April 1997, 8.

69. Vic Jordan and Roland White, interview by Bob and Kristie Black, March 2015.

70. Roland White, interview by Tom Ewing, August 2011.

71. Ibid.

72. Vic Jordan and Roland White, interview by Bob and Kristie Black, March 2015.

73. Roland White, interview by Tom Ewing, August 2011.

74. Roland White, interview by Bob and Kristie Black, March 2015.

75. Kenny Baker, *Portrait of a Bluegrass Fiddler*, County 719, 1969.

76. See appendix A, "Del McCoury."

77. Roland White, interview by Tom Ewing, August 2011.

78. See appendix A, "Tex Logan."

79. Vic Jordan and Roland White, interview by Bob and Kristie Black, March 2015.

80. Ibid.

81. Ibid.

82. Ibid.

83. Ewing, *Bill Monroe*, 303.

84. See appendix A, "Lance LeRoy."

85. Roland White, interview by Bob and Kristie Black, March 2015.

86. *Will the Circle Be Unbroken* (United Artists Records UAS-9801) was the Nitty Gritty Dirt Band's seventh album. Released in 1972, the three-record collection was a landmark event in the history of country and bluegrass music. Pioneering country performers such as Mother Maybelle Carter, Roy Acuff, and Merle Travis were featured. Doc Watson, Earl Scruggs, and Jimmy Martin also participated, along with many others. Young city audiences were introduced to the music of these greats as a result of the album's release. Rosenberg, *Bluegrass: A History*, 317–18.

87. Sandra Brennan, "Paul Warren Biography," AllMusic, https://www.allmusic.com/artist/paul-warren-mn0000752976/biography (accessed May 5, 2020).

88. "Cousin Jake Memorial Bluegrass Festival," Etowah Arts, http://www.etowaharts.org/bluegrass/cousin-jake/ (accessed May 5, 2020).

89. "2017 IBMA Hall of Fame Members Conversation Part 1—Alice Gerrard and Roland White," October 4, 2017, https://youtube/-qJnrf5vpOM (accessed December 23, 2020).

Chapter 6. The Nashville Grass

1. Tom Ewing, "Thirty Years Ago This Month," *Bluegrass Unlimited*, January 2000, 6.

2. Ibid., March 2000, 6.

3. Ibid., January 2000, 6.

4. Ibid., April 2000, 6.

5. Neil V. Rosenberg, *Bluegrass: A History* (Urbana: University of Illinois Press, 1985), 319.

6. Ibid., 318.

7. The phrase "lined out" was often used by Lester Flatt. By this he meant "planned" (usually only in his head).

8. Roland White, interview by Bob and Kristie Black, March 2015.

9. Lester Flatt, *Flatt Out*, Columbia CS 1006, 1970.

10. "Lester Flatt Setlist," Toronto Island Park, July 26, 1969, Setlist.fm, https://www.setlist.fm/setlist/lester-flatt/1969/toronto-island-park-toronto-on-canada-4bf043be.html (accessed January 4, 2021).

11. Ewing, "Thirty Years Ago This Month," September 1999, 6.

12. Ibid., October 1999, 6.

13. Ibid., November 1999, 6.

14. Vic Jordan and Roland White, interview by Bob and Kristie Black, March 2015.

15. Ewing, "Thirty Years Ago This Month," June 2000, 10.

16. Ibid., August 2000, 6.

17. Ibid., September 2000, 7.

18. Ibid., October 2000, 6.

19. Bluegrass Music Hall of Fame and Museum, "Lance LeRoy," Hall of Fame Inductees, https://www.bluegrasshall.org/inductees/lance-leroy/ (accessed March 23, 2020).

20. Vic Jordan and Roland White, interview by Bob and Kristie Black, March 2015.

21. Jim Renz, interview by Bob Black, March 2020.

22. Ewing, "Thirty Years Ago This Month," August 2000, 6.

23. See appendix A, "Carl Story."

24. Vic Jordan and Roland White, interview by Bob and Kristie Black, March 2015.

25. Jon Weisberger, "Bobby Thompson, 1937–2005," Nashville Scene, June 2, 2005, https://www.nashvillescene.com/arts-culture/article/13011840/bobby-thompson-19372005 (accessed December 28, 2020).

26. Ibid.; Lester Flatt, *The One and Only Lester Flatt*, Nugget NRLP 104, 1970.

27. Rosenberg, *Bluegrass: A History*, 267.

28. Bobby Thompson, "Mocking Banjo," Mercury 71088, March 21, 1957.

29. Rosenberg, *Bluegrass: A History*, 267.

30. Lester Flatt and Earl Scruggs, *Changin' Times,* Columbia CS9596, 1968, and *Nashville Airplane*, Columbia CS9741, 1968.

31. Ewing, "Thirty Years Ago This Month," November 2000, 6.

32. Alan Munde, interview by Bob Black, March 2015.

33. Lester Flatt, *Flatt on Victor*, RCA LSP-4495, 1971.

34. Lester Flatt, "The Good Old-Fashioned Way," on *Foggy Mountain Breakdown*, RCA 4789, 1972.

35. Vic Jordan, *Pickaway*, Atteiram API 1027, 1973.

36. Vic Jordan and Roland White, interview by Bob and Kristie Black, March 2015.

37. Roland White, interview by Bob Black, February 2019.

38. Tom Ewing, *Bill Monroe: The Life and Music of the Bluegrass Man* (Urbana: University of Illinois Press, 2018), 302.

39. Lester Flatt and Mac Wiseman, *Lester 'N' Mac*, RCA LSP-4547, 1971; Vic Jordan and Roland White, interview by Bob and Kristie Black, March 2015.

40. See appendix A, "Howdy Forrester."

41. Ewing, "Thirty Years Ago This Month," July 2001, 6.

42. Ibid., October 2001, 6.

43. Ewing, *Bill Monroe*, 325.

44. Red and Birdie Smith were two of the founders of the Station Inn.

45. Seth Stephen Bate, *Coming Home to Winfield: The History of the Walnut Valley Festival*, dissertation, Wichita State University, 2018, 23, https://soar.wichita.edu/handle/10057/15473 (accessed March 31, 2020).

46. Rusty Russell, "Clarence," The Granddaddy of Bender Guitars, MartyStuart.com, http://www.martystuart.com/zArt-VintageGuitar4-04.htm (accessed December 25, 2020); originally published in *Vintage Guitar*, April 2004.

47. Marty Stuart, interview by Bob Black, May 2016.

48. Lester Flatt, *Kentucky Ridgerunner*, RCA LSP-4633, 1972.

49. Lester Flatt and Mac Wiseman, *On the Southbound*, RCA LSP-4688, 1972.

50. "Salty Dog," or "Salty Dog Blues," is a public domain folk song from the early 1900s. It has been recorded in many different styles, including ragtime, jazz, blues, country, and, of course, bluegrass. Flatt and Scruggs recorded it in the late 1940s under the title "Old Salty Dog Blues." In the early days of the song's existence, off-color verses were often sung.

51. Double stops are two notes played simultaneously. On fiddle and mandolin, a double stop consists of picking or bowing two adjacent strings. On banjo, triple stops are often played using three fingers to pick three strings simultaneously.

52. Lester Flatt, *Country Boy*, RCA APL1-0131, 1973.

53. Diane Bouska, email correspondence, April 15, 2020.

54. The original members of the Byrds—Roger McGuinn, Gene Clark, David Crosby, Chris Hillman, and Michael Clarke—did record a reunion album in 1973 that was titled *Byrds*.

55. After leaving Lester Flatt, Marty Stuart played for six years with Johnny Cash's band. Beginning in 1985, he focused on his solo career. In the early 1990s, he toured and recorded with Travis Tritt. By the mid-1990s, he was recording duets with Steve Earle, Willie Nelson, and B. B. King. In 2002 he formed his own backup band, the Fabulous Superlatives.

Chapter 7. The New Kentucky Colonels

1. Muleskinner, *A Potpourri of Bluegrass Jam*, Warner Bros. BS-2787, 1974.
2. Roland White, interview by Bob Black and Kristie Black, March 2015.
3. Ibid.
4. The Dillards, *Wheatstraw Suite*, Electra EKS-74035, 1968, and *Copperfields*, Elektra EKS-74054, 1970.
5. Stephen K. Peeples, "Herb Pedersen Q&A on Earl Scruggs," March 31, 2012, https://stephenkpeeples.com/news-and-reviews/spotlight-qa-with-herb-pedersen-on-earl-scruggs/ (accessed November 17, 2020).
6. Jason Ankeny, "Artist Biography: Herb Pedersen," AllMusic, https://www.allmusic.com/artist/herb-pedersen-mn0000677128/biography (accessed May 4, 2020).
7. Roland White, interview by Bob Black and Kristie Black, March 2015.
8. Byron Berline with Jane Frost, *Byron Berline: A Fiddler's Diary* (Stillwater, OK: New Forums Press, 2013), 138.
9. Ibid.
10. Ibid., 139.
11. Roland White, interview by Bob Black and Kristie Black, March 2015.
12. *The New Kentucky Colonels, Live in Holland*, Roland White 0001, 2013.
13. A couple of Johnny Rivers's hits were "Mountain of Love" and "Secret Agent Man."
14. *The White Brothers: Live in Sweden*, Rounder Records 0073, 1976.
15. *The New Kentucky Colonels: Live in Sweden 1973*, Roland White RW0003, 2016.
16. Alan Munde, liner notes to *The New Kentucky Colonels: Live in Sweden 1973*, Roland White RW0003, 2016.
17. See appendix A, "John Kaparakis."
18. See appendix A, "Jack Hicks."
19. Roland White, interview by Bob Black and Kristie Black, March 2015.
20. "Never Ending Love," "Last Thing on My Mind," "Alabama Jubilee," and "Why You Been Gone So Long?" were released by Sierra Records on the album *Silver Meteor*.
21. Berline, *Byron Berline*, 141–42.
22. Roland White, interview by Bob Black and Kristie Black, March 18, 2015.
23. Diane Bouska and Roland White, with Matt Flinner and Steve Pottier, *The Essential Clarence White* (Diane and Roland Music, 2009), 4.
24. See appendix A, "Norman Blake" and "Dan Crary."
25. See appendix A, "Tony Rice"; Jim Renz, interview by Bob Black, March 2020.

Chapter 8. Country Gazette

1. David N. Meyer, *Twenty Thousand Roads* (New York: Villard Books, 2008), 409.
2. Ibid.
3. Byron Berline with Jane Frost, *Byron Berline: A Fiddler's Diary* (Stillwater, OK: New Forums Press, 2013), 145.

4. Clarence's mother, Mildred M. White, (1918–1992), is also buried in Joshua Memorial Park, next to Clarence and her husband. After her death in 2016, Roland's sister JoAnne was cremated; her remains are in a columbarium in that same cemetery.

5. Berline, *Byron Berline*, 145.

6. Ibid.

7. Country Gazette, *Traitor in Our Midst*, United Artists, UAS-5596, 1972, and *Don't Give Up Your Day Job*, United Artists, UA-LA090-F, 1973.

8. Berline, *Byron Berline*, 109.

9. Peter Vacher, "Kay Starr Obituary," *The Guardian*, https://www.theguardian.com/music/2016/nov/06/kay-starr-obituary (accessed December 27, 2020).

10. Berline, *Byron Berline*, 112.

11. See appendix A, "Kenny Wertz."

12. Scottsville Squirrel Barkers, *Bluegrass Favorites*, Crown Records CLP 5346, 1963.

13. Berline, *Byron Berline*, 142.

14. Byron Berline, interview by Bob Black, April 23, 2019.

15. Ibid.

16. Steve, LeRoy, and Brother Dave, *Bluegrass Gospel According to Steve, LeRoy, and Brother Dave*, Manna Records MS-2023, 1974.

17. Country Gazette, *Country Gazette Live*, Antilles AN-7014, 1976.

18. Berline, *Byron Berline*, 162.

19. See appendix A, "Dave Ferguson."

20. Country Gazette, *Out to Lunch*, Flying Fish FF027, 1976.

21. Alan Munde, interview by Bob Black, March 2015.

22. The Dillards, *Pickin' and Fiddlin'*, Elektra EKL-285, 1965.

23. Kenny Wertz, email correspondence with Bob Black, April 17, 2019.

24. See appendix A, "Slim Richey."

25. Bob Black, *Ladies on the Steamboat*, Ridge Runner RRR 0018, 1979.

26. Alan Munde, *Banjo Sandwich*, Ridge Runner RRR 0001, 1975.

27. Doc Hamilton played the fiddle with Buck White and the Down Home Folks while I was in that band (1977–1979).

28. Dave Ferguson, *Dave Ferguson: Somewhere Over the Rainbow*, Ridge Runner RRR 0003, 1976.

29. Roland White, *I Wasn't Born to Rock'n Roll*, Ridge Runner RRR 0005, 1976.

30. The 1976 National Dobro Champion, Dan started producing music instruction recordings in 1973 and now has over two thousand instructional products available in his Musician's Instruction Company.

31. Dan Huckabee, *Why Is This Man Smiling?*, Ridge Runner RRR 0004, 1976.

32. Steve, LeRoy, and Brother Dave, *Life's Railway to Heaven*, Crown Sound CS-004, 1976.

33. See appendix A, "Connie Smith."

34. Country Gazette, *What a Way to Make a Living*, Ridge Runner RRR 0008, 1977.

35. See appendix A, "Jim Lauderdale."

36. Jim Lauderdale, interview by Bob Black, October 2015.

37. Ibid.

38. Ibid.

39. See appendix A, "Gene Wooten."

40. Jim Lauderdale, interview by Bob Black, October 2015.

41. *Jim Lauderdale & Roland White*, Yep ROC Records YEP-2597, 2018.

42. Jim Lauderdale, interview by Bob Black, October 2015.

43. Country Gazette, *All This and Money Too*, Ridge Runner RRR 0017, 1979.

44. Slim Richey, *Jazz Grass*, Ridge Runner RRR0009, 1977.

45. See appendix A, "Pete Wernick."

46. Alan Munde, *Festival Favorites, Vol. 1*, Ridge Runner RRR 0026; and *Festival Favorites, Vol. 2*, Ridge Runner RRR 0027, 1980.

47. Country Gazette, *American and Clean*, Flying Fish FF 253, 1981.

48. Roland White, interview by Bob Black and Kristie Black, March 2015.

49. Country Gazette, *America's Bluegrass Band*, Flying Fish FF 295, 1982.

50. Tom Ewing, *Bill Monroe: The Life and Music of the Bluegrass Man* (Urbana: University of Illinois Press, 2018), xviii-xix.

51. Alan Munde, *Festival Favorites: Nashville Sessions*, Ridge Runner RRR 0031, 1982.

52. See appendix A, "Sam Bush."

53. See appendix A, "Blaine Sprouse."

54. From a live recording given to me by my friend Ron Stafford.

55. Alan Munde, *Festival Favorites: Southwest Sessions*, Ridge Runner RRR 0032, 1983.

56. The Dreadful Snakes, *The Dreadful Snakes: Snakes Alive*, Rounder CD 0177, 1982.

57. See appendix A, "Charmaine Lanham."

58. Alan Munde, *Alan Munde: In the Tradition*, Ridge Runner RRR 0035, 1986.

59. Country Gazette, *Bluegrass Tonight*, Flying Fish FF 383, 1986.

60. See appendix A, "Ingrid Fowler."

61. William (Billy) Smith, email correspondence, May 12, 2020.

62. Ibid.

63. Country Gazette, *Strictly Instrumental*, Flying Fish FF 446, 1987.

64. See appendix A, "Kathy Chiavola."

65. Alan Munde, interview by Bob Black, March 2015.

66. Alan Munde, liner notes to Country Gazette, *Hello Operator . . . This Is Country Gazette*, Flying Fish 70112, 1991.

67. Ewing, *Bill Monroe*, 418.

68. David Grier, *Freewheeling*, Rounder Records 0250, 1988.

69. Roland White, interview by Bob and Kristie Black, March 2015.

Chapter 9. The Nashville Bluegrass Band

1. Dolly Parton, Linda Ronstadt, Emmylou Harris, *Trio*, Warner Brothers 925491-1, 1-25491, 25491-1, 1987.

2. Nashville Bluegrass Band, "Alan O'Bryant," http://nashvillebluegrassband.net/alanobryant.html (accessed May 4, 2020).

3. Béla Fleck, *Crossing the Tracks*, Rounder Records 0121, 1979.

4. Nashville Bluegrass Band, "Pat Enright," http://nashvillebluegrassband.net/patenright.html (accessed May 3, 2020).

5. Mike Compton, "A Modern American Mandolin Master," https://mikecompton.net/bio (accessed May 3, 2020).

6. Tom Ewing, *Bill Monroe: The Life and Music of the Bluegrass Man* (Urbana: University of Illinois Press, 2018), 375; Bill Monroe, *Master of Bluegrass*, MCA Records, MCA-818, 1981.

7. Nashville Bluegrass Band, *My Native Home*, Rounder Records 0212, 1985.

8. Nashville Bluegrass Band, http://nashvillebluegrassband.net (accessed November 29, 2020).

9. Penny Parsons, "Reaching for the Gold: The Nashville Bluegrass Band," *Bluegrass Unlimited*, July 1992.

10. Stuart Duncan, "Bio," http://www.stuart-duncan.com/bio/ (accessed May 3, 2020).

11. Now called the Grey Fox Bluegrass Festival, the Winterhawk Bluegrass Festival began in 1984, near Ancramdale, New York, on the site of on older festival that began in 1976 called the Berkshire Mountain Bluegrass Festival. The site was moved to Oak Hill, New York, in 2008.

12. "The History of NBB . . . 1984–1989," The Nashville Bluegrass Band, http://nashvillebluegrassband.net/history.html (accessed May 4, 2020).

13. Parsons, "Reaching for the Gold."

14. Steve Garner, "Alan O'Bryant: The Executionist," *Banjo Newsletter*, June 1992, 6.

15. Parsons, "Reaching for the Gold."

16. Alan Munde, phone conversation with Bob Black, November 30, 2020.

17. Tamara Best, "How the Grammy Awards Are Made: 4 Craftsmen and 'Grammium,'" *New York Times*, February 7, 2017, https://www.nytimes.com/2017/02/07/arts/music/grammy-award-maker-john-billings.html (accessed November 20, 2020).

18. "Roland White—Mandolin," AcousticMusicCamp, https://acousticmusiccamp.com/roland-white/ (accessed March 28, 2020).

19. Homer and Jethro, *Playing It Straight*, RCA Victor LPM-2459, 1962; *It Ain't Necessarily Square*, RCA Victor LSP-3701, 1967.

20. Robert Shelton, *The Country Music Story: A Picture History of Country and Western Music* (Secaucus, NJ: Castle Books, 1966), 120.

21. Nashville Bluegrass Band, *The Boys Are Back in Town*, Sugar Hill SH-CD-3778, 1990.

22. The Earl Scruggs Revue, *The Earl Scruggs Revue Vol. II*, Columbia PC 34090, 1976.

23. Hat tip to Thomas Goldsmith.

24. Nashville Bluegrass Band, *Home of the Blues*, Sugar Hill SH-CD-3793, 1991.

25. midlifefanclub, "The Fairfield Four," Biography, *last.fm.*, January 20, 2016, https://www.last.fm/music/The+Fairfield+Four/+wiki (accessed May 2, 2020).

26. Nashville Bluegrass Band, *Waitin' for the Hard Times to Go*, Sugar Hill SH-CD-3809, 1993.

27. "Roland White—Mandolin," AcousticMusicCamp, https://acousticmusiccamp .com/roland-white/ (accessed March 28, 2020).

28. Jody Stecher, email correspondence with Bob Black, December 4, 2020.

29. Roland White, *Trying to Get to You*, Sugar Hill SH-CD 3826, 1994.

30. Diane Bouska, interview by Bob Black, February 2019.

31. Nashville Bluegrass Band, *Unleashed*, Sugar Hill SHCD-3843, 1995.

32. LeRoy McNees, *LeRoy Mack and Friends of the Kentucky Colonels*, Rebel Records C-1729, 1996.

33. Nashville Bluegrass Band, *American Beauty*, Sugar Hill SHCD 3882, 1998.

Chapter 10. The Roland White Band

1. Richard Bailey, interview by Bob Black, February 2019.

2. The SteelDrivers, *The SteelDrivers*, Rounder Records, 11661-0598-2, 2008.

3. The SteelDrivers, *The Muscle Shoals Recordings*, Rounder Records 11661-9180-2, 2015.

4. Roland White Band, *Jelly on My Tofu*, Copper Creek CCCD-0211, 2002.

5. Mike Compton, interview by Bob Black, December 2, 2020.

6. Roland White and Diane Bouska, interview by Bob and Kristie Black, September 2015.

7. See appendix A, "Gatemouth Brown."

8. Bob Black, *Come Hither to Go Yonder: Playing Bluegrass with Bill Monroe* (Urbana: University of Illinois Press, 2005), 81.

9. Roland White Band, *Straight Ahead Bluegrass*, Roland White and Diane Bouska, 2014.

10. "Not Fiddlin' Around: Alumni Brian Christianson Shines in Music City," MSC Southeast, December 23, 2013, https://www.southeastmn.edu/alumni/alumni .aspx?id=4605 (accessed January 5, 2021).

11. Richard Bailey, interview by Bob Black, February 2019.

12. Ibid.

13. Ibid.

14. Ibid.

Chapter 11. Roland's Family Ties

1. Rosemarie Johnson, email correspondence with Bob Black, March 25, 2019.
2. Ibid.
3. Jim Renz, interview by Bob Black, March 2020.
4. Performers at the 2016 Huck Finn Jubilee included David Grisman, Peter Rowan, Rhonda Vincent, Balsam Range, Special Consensus, the Mountain Faith Band, the Soggy Bottom Boys, Leftover Salmon, the Cleverlys, Dan Tyminski, Doyle Lawson and Quicksilver, Della Mae, the Boxcars, the Church Sisters, the Punch Brothers, the Infamous Stringdusters, Elephant Revival, Mountain Heart, Dailey and Vincent, the Sweetwater String Band, and Flatt Lonesome.
5. Rosemarie Johnson, email correspondence with Bob Black, March 25, 2019.
6. Ibid.
7. Roline Hodge and Lawrence LeBlanc, interview by Bob Black, March 29, 2019.
8. Ibid.
9. Ibid.
10. Ibid.

Chapter 12. A Visit with Roland and Diane

1. Nitty Gritty Dirt Band, *Will the Circle Be Unbroken*, United Artists Records, UAS-9801, UAS 9801, 1972.
2. Diane Bouska and Roland White, interview by Bob and Kristie Black, March 2015.
3. Often singers and musicians form music publishing companies as a means of getting their own material copyrighted in order to protect the use of their songs and to collect royalties when their songs are used. Licensing for film, TV, ads, and so forth is undertaken by the publishing company.
4. George Jones and Tammy Wynette, *One*, MCA Records, MCAD-11248, 1995.
5. Roland White and Diane Bouska, *Roland White's Approach to Bluegrass Mandolin* (2001; Nashville: Diane and Roland Music, 2013).
6. See appendix A, "Laurie Lewis."

Chapter 13. Back to Where It All Started

1. Marty Stuart, interview by Bob Black, May 2016.
2. Created in 1991, the IBMA Hall of Fame was called "Hall of Honor" through 2006, thereafter becoming dubbed "Hall of Fame." Managed by the International Bluegrass Music Association, the hall is located at the Bluegrass Music Hall of Fame and Museum in Owensboro, Kentucky.
3. The text on the plaque reads: "ROLAND WHITE / Born April 23, 1938 / Bandleader, mandolin and guitar player, and vocalist Roland White has performed and recorded some of the most influential bluegrass music of the past six decades. A

native of northernmost Maine and early transplant to southern California, Roland organized family members and friends into a group known as the Country Boys and reached millions through appearances on Andy Griffith's network television show in 1961. The band evolved into the Kentucky Colonels who were part of a wave of young urban bands that brought bluegrass to new audiences on both coasts during the folk revival. After moving to Tennessee in 1967, Roland played with bluegrass pioneers Bill Monroe for two years and Lester Flatt for four years. He reconnected with brothers Eric and Clarence as the New Kentucky Colonels until Clarence's untimely death in 1973. Roland then performed with award-winning acts Country Gazette for thirteen years and the Nashville Bluegrass Band for ten years. A true mandolin stylist and a kind and generous mentor, he began the Roland White Band in 2000, and continued as a stalwart carrier of bluegrass music traditions."

4. Roland White, *Roland White and Friends: A Tribute to the Kentucky Colonels*, Mountain Home Music Company MH17242, 2018.

5. See appendix A, "Billy Strings."

6. See appendix A, "Molly Tuttle."

7. "Listen to the Mocking Bird," Traditional, Songfacts, https://www.songfacts .com/facts/traditional/listen-to-the-mocking-bird (accessed October 21, 2020).

8. Scotty Stoneman did the comic bird whistles with his family's band as well.

9. See appendix A, "Brittany Haas."

10. See appendix A, "Justin Hiltner."

11. See appendix A, "Kristin Scott Benson."

12. Jon Weisberger, interview by Bob Black, February 18, 2019.

13. Lamar Grier.

14. David Grier, email correspondence with Bob Black, April 24, 2019.

Afterword

1. David Grier, email correspondence with Bob Black, April 24, 2019.

Appendix A. People, Bands, and Venues

1. Tom Ewing, *Bill Monroe, the Life and Music of the Bluegrass Man* (Urbana: University of Illinois Press, 2018), 214; Bill Monroe, *Bill Monroe's Uncle Pen*, MCA-500, 1972.

2. Kristin Scott Benson, "Biography," https://www.ksbbanjo.com/bio (accessed May 3, 2020).

3. Neil Rosenberg, *Bluegrass: A History* (Urbana: University of Illinois Press, 1985), 291.

4. Bill Dahl, "Clarence 'Gatemouth' Brown Biography," AllMusic, https://www.allmusic .com/artist/clarence-gatemouth-brown-mn00001129547 (accessed May 3, 2020).

5. Craig Harris, "Sam Bush Biography," AllMusic, https://www.allmusic.com/ artist/sam-bushmn0000286662 (accessed May 3, 2020).

6. "About Kathy . . .," Kathy Chiavola, https://www.kathychiavola.com/bio.html (accessed May 6, 2020).

7. Ewing, *Bill Monroe*, 452.

8. "Bert Foreman Phillips," Hillbilly dawt com, http://www.hillbilly-music.com/artists/story/index.php?id=13883 (accessed May 3, 2020).

9. Eugene Chadbourne, "Dave Ferguson Biography," AllMusic, https://allmusic.com/artist/dave-ferguson-mn0001594214/biography (accessed May 3, 2020).

10. Ewing, *Bill Monroe*, 118–19.

11. "Fowler, Bob," Alabama Music Office, http://www.alabamamusicoffice.com/artists-az/f/780-fowler-bob (accessed May 17, 2020).

12. Ed Bain, "Ingrid and Bob Fowler—Anyone Remember Them?," alt.music.bluegrass, https://groups.google.com/forum/m/#!topic/alt.music.bluegrass/x5meSC4Acwc (accessed May 17, 2020).

13. Rosenberg, *Bluegrass: A History*, 107.

14. Bill C. Malone and Judith McCulloh, eds., *Stars of Country Music* (Urbana: University of Illinois Press, 1975), 420.

15. Blair Jackson, *Garcia: An American Life* (New York: Viking Penguin, 1999), 202.

16. Brittany Haas, "About," https://www.brittanyhaas.com/biopress (accessed May 3, 2020).

17. Rosenberg, *Bluegrass: A History*, 206.

18. James Stiltner, "An Interview with Jack Hicks," *Banjo Hangout*, February 9, 2014, https://www.banjohangout.org/blog/31505 (accessed May 3, 2020).

19. Bill and James Monroe, *Father and Son*, MCA Records, MCA 310, 1973.

20. Justin Hiltner, "Justin Hiltner: Banjoist/Songwriter/Journalist/Activist," https://www.justinhiltner.com (accessed May 4, 2020).

21. The Lonesome River Boys, *Raise a Ruckus*, Riverside Records RLP 7535, 1961, LP (Rick Churchill, banjo; Dick Stowe, bass; James Buchanan, fiddle; John Kaparakis, guitar; Jack Tottle, mandolin).

22. Guest contributor, "John Kaparakis Passes," *Bluegrass Today*, April 20, 2020, https://bluegrasstoday.com/john-kaparakis-passes/ (accessed December 6, 2020).

23. Tony Trischka and Pete Wernick, *Masters of the 5-String Banjo* (New York: Oak Publications, 1988), 175; Earl Scruggs, *Earl Scruggs and the 5-String Banjo* (New York: Peer International Corp, 1968).

24. "Meet Charmaine," Charmaine Lanham, http://charmainelanham.com/about/ (accessed May 5, 2020).

25. *Jim Lauderdale and Ralph Stanley and the Clinch Mountain Boys: I Feel Like Singing Today*, Rebel, REB-CD-1755, 1999 CD; *Jim Lauderdale and Ralph Stanley: Lost in the Lonesome Pines*, Dualtone—80302-01125-2, 2002, CD.

26. John Lawless, "Lance Leroy Passes," *Bluegrass Today*, December 17, 2015, https://bluegrasstoday.com/lance-leroy-passes/ (accessed May 4, 2020).

27. Brenda Hough, "Skipping and Flying with Laurie Lewis," Bluegrass Breakdown, March 2012, https://laurielewis.com/interviews.html (accessed May 4, 2020).

28. Ewing, *Bill Monroe*, 276.

29. Craig Shelburne, "Rose Maddox: The Remarkable Hillbilly Singer Who Made Bluegrass History," *The Bluegrass Situation*, March 30 2020, https://theblue grasssituation.com/read/rose-maddox-the-remarkable-hillbilly-singer-who-made -bluegrass-history/ (accessed January 2, 2021).

30. Malone and McCulloh, *Stars of Country Music*, 312.

31. Sandra Brennan, "Del McCoury Biography," AllMusic, https://www.allmusic .com/artist/del-mccoury-mn0000234488 (accessed May 4, 2020).

32. Rosenberg, *Bluegrass: A History*, 314.

33. Malone and McCulloh, *Stars of Country Music*, 232.

34. Birch Monroe with the Blue Grass Boys, *Brother Birch Monroe Plays Old Time Fiddle Favorites*, Atteiram API-L-1516, 1975, LP (Bill Monroe, mandolin; Bob Black, banjo; Ralph Lewis, guitar; Randy Davis, bass).

35. Rosenberg, *Bluegrass: A History*, 237.

36. Ewing, *Bill Monroe*, 415.

37. Trischka and Wernick, *Masters of the 5-String Banjo*, 111.

38. Joshua Heston, "Lee Mace's Ozark Opry," StateoftheOzarks.net, January 15, 2010, http://stateoftheozarks.net/culture/music/ozarkopry.php (accessed May 4, 2020).

39. Rosenberg, *Bluegrass: A History*, 261.

40. Various artists, *Jazz Grass*, Ridge Runner RRR0009, 1977, LP (reissued 2001, Ridge Runner RRR0009, CD). Alan Munde, banjo; Bill Keith, banjo; Gerald Jones, banjo; Dan Huckabee, Dobro; Richard Greene, fiddle; Ricky Skaggs, fiddle; Sam Bush, fiddle; Slim Richey, guitar; Joe Carr, mandolin; Kerby Stewart, mandolin; Jerry Case, rhythm guitar; Sumter Bruton, rhythm guitar.

41. Kevin Curtin, "Slim Richey 1938–2015: Austin's Jazz Maverick Peaces Out," *Austin Chronicle*, June 1, 2015, https://www.austinchronicle.com/daily/music/2015-06-01/ slim-richey-1938-2015/ (accessed May 4, 2020).

42. Rosenberg, *Bluegrass: A History*, 158.

43. D. K. Wilgus, liner notes, *Mike Seeger*, Vanguard VRS-9150, 1964.

44. Jack Hurst, *Nashville's Grand Ole Opry* (New York: Harry N. Abrams, 1975), 258.

45. Steve Kurutz, "Jimmie Skinner Biography," AllMusic, https://www.allmusic .com/artist/jimmie-skinner-n0000347351 (accessed May 5, 2020).

46. Richard Thompson, "Bobby Slone: A Bluegrass Life," *Bluegrass Today*, August 5, 2013, https://bluegrasstoday.com/bobby-slone-a-bluegrass-life/ (accessed May 5, 2020).

47. Hurst, *Nashville's Grand Ole Opry*, 276.

48. John Lawless, "Blaine Sprouse Remembers Kenny Baker," *Bluegrass Today*, August 11, 2011, https://bluegrasstoday.com/blaine-sprouse-remembers-kenny-baker-2/ (accessed May 5, 2020).

49. "History," Station Inn, https://www.stationinn.com/history/ (accessed May 5, 2020).

50. Jody Stecher & Kate Brislin, https://jodyandkate.com/ (accessed August 27, 2021).

51. Malone and McCulloh, *Stars of Country Music*, 420.

52. Rosenberg, *Bluegrass: A History*, 137.

53. Hurst, *Nashville's Grand Ole Opry*, 128.

54. Mark Deming, "Billy Strings Biography," AllMusic, https://www.allmusic.com/artist/billy-strings-mn0003292359/biography (accessed May 5, 2020).

55. Various artists, *American Banjo Tunes & Songs in Scruggs Style*, Folkways Records FA 2314, 1957, LP (reissued Smithsonian Folkways SF 40037, CD).

56. Richard Thompson, "I'm Going Back to Old Kentucky #130," *Bluegrass Today*, February 7, 2011, https://bluegrasstoday.com/im-going-back-to-old-kentucky-130/ (accessed May 5, 2020).

57. "About," Molly Tuttle, https://www.mollytuttlemusic.com/about (accessed May 5, 2020).

58. Trischka and Wernick, *Masters of the 5-String Banjo*, 319.

59. Flying Burrito Brothers, *Last of the Red Hot Burritos*, A&M Records, SP 4343, 1972, LP (Kenny Wertz, guitar/banjo; Chris Hillman, bass/mandolin; Michael Clarke, drums; Roger Bush, bass; Byron Berline, fiddle; Al Perkins, pedal steel guitar; Rick Roberts, rhythm guitar).

60. "Flying Burrito Brothers, The," *Nostalgia Central*, https://nostalgiacentral.com/music/artists-a-to-k/artists-f/flying-burrito-brothers/ (accessed May 5, 2020).

61. Ewing, *Bill Monroe*, 297.

62. Malone and McCulloh, *Stars of Country Music*, 157.

63. Patty Loveless, *Mountain Soul*, Jahaza Records, Epic, EK 85651, 2001, CD. (Gene Wooten, Dobro; Alan O'Bryant, banjo; Clarence "Tater" Tate, bass; Rob Ickes, Dobro; Deanie Richardson, fiddle; Stuart Duncan, fiddle/mandolin; Emory Gordy, Jr., guitar; Butch Lee, banjo; Tim Hensley, mandolin; Ricky Skaggs, mandolin; Jon Randall, guitar; Travis Tritt, guitar; Earl Scruggs, banjo; Biff Watson, guitar; Darrell Scott, banjo; Tom Britt, slide guitar; Jeff White, guitar.)

64. Eugene Chadbourne, "Gene Wooten Biography," AllMusic, https://www.allmusic.com/artist/gene-wooten-mn0000198597/biography (accessed May 5, 2020).

Roland White
Recordings Cited

Alan Munde: In the Tradition. Ridge Runner RRR 0035, 1986, LP. Alan Munde, banjo; Roland White, mandolin; Billy Joe Foster, fiddle/bass/guitar; Bubba Ray Bodart, guitar; Joe Carr, guitar/mandolin; Gene Wooten, Dobro; Craig Fletcher, mandolin; Bill Evans, banjo.

All This and Money Too. Ridge Runner RRR 0017, 1979, LP. Country Gazette (Roland White, mandolin/vocals; Alan Munde, banjo/guitar; Michael Anderson, bass/vocals; Joe Carr, guitar/vocals). Also featured: Slim Richey, guitar; Tommy Spurlock, pedal steel guitar; Dave Ferguson, fiddle; Michael McCarty, drums; Michael J. Dohoney, drums.

American and Clean. Flying Fish FF 253, 1981, LP. (Portions reissued 1999, Flying Fish FF 70112, CD) Country Gazette (Roland White, mandolin/vocals; Alan Munde, banjo/guitar; Michael Anderson, bass/vocals; Joe Carr, guitar/vocals). Also featured: Tommy Spurlock, pedal steel guitar; Slim Richey, guitar; Dave Ferguson, fiddle; Mike McCarty, drums; Dahrell Norris, drums.

American Beauty. Sugar Hill SHCD-3882, 1998, CD. The Nashville Bluegrass Band (Roland White, mandolin/vocals; Pat Enright, guitar/vocals; Alan O'Bryant, banjo/vocals; Stuart Duncan, fiddle/vocals; Gene Libbea, bass/vocals).

America's Bluegrass Band. Flying Fish FF 295, 1982, LP. (Portions reissued 1999, Flying Fish FF 70112, CD) Country Gazette (Bill Smith, bass/vocals; Roland White, mandolin/vocals; Joe Carr, guitar/mandolin/vocals; Alan Munde, banjo/guitar).

Appalachian Swing! World Pacific 1821, 1964, LP. (Reissued by Rounder SS 31, 1993, CD, cass.) The Kentucky Colonels (Clarence White, guitar; Roland White, mandolin; LeRoy McNees, Dobro; Roger Bush, bass; Billy Ray Latham, banjo; Bobby Slone, fiddle).

"The Ballad of Farmer Brown"/"That's What You Get for Lovin' Me." 45 rpm single. World Pacific 427, 1965. The Kentucky Colonels (Clarence White, guitar; Roger Bush, bass; Billy Ray Latham, banjo).

Banjo Sandwich. Ridge Runner RRR 0001, 1975, LP. (Reissued 2005, Ridge Runner RRR 0001, CD.) Alan Munde, banjo; Roland White, mandolin; Roger Bush, bass; Dave Ferguson, fiddle; Doc Hamilton, guitar.

The Beverly Hillbillies. Columbia CL 2402, 1965, LP. Roland White, mandolin; Lester Flatt and Earl Scruggs and the Foggy Mountain Boys, Buddy Ebsen, Donna Douglas, Irene Ryan, Max Baer, Nancy Kulp, Raymond Bailey.

Bluegrass Gospel According to Steve, LeRoy, and Brother Dave. Manna Records MS-2023, 1974, LP. LeRoy McNees, Dobro; Steve Hatfield, banjo/guitar/vocals; Dave Hatfield, bass/vocals; Roland White, mandolin; Byron Berline, fiddle; Roger Bush, bass; John Hickman, banjo.

Bluegrass Tonight. Flying Fish FF 383, 1986, LP. (Portions reissued 1999, Flying Fish FF 70112, CD) Country Gazette (Alan Munde, banjo/guitar/vocals; Roland White, mandolin/guitar/vocals; Gene Wooten, Dobro/guitar/vocals; Billy Joe Foster, electric bass/fiddle/guitar/vocals).

The Boys Are Back in Town. Sugar Hill SH-3778, 1990, LP; also Sugar Hill SH-CD-3778, 1990, CD. The Nashville Bluegrass Band (Roland White, mandolin/vocals; Pat Enright, guitar/vocals; Alan O'Bryant, banjo/vocals; Stuart Duncan, fiddle/vocals; Gene Libbea, bass/vocals).

Country Boy. RCA APL1-0131, 1973, LP. Lester Flatt and the Nashville Grass (Lester Flatt, guitar; Roland White, mandolin; Charles Nixon, Dobro; Billy Linneman, bass; Paul Warren, fiddle; Marty Stuart, fiddle; Howard "Johnny" Johnson, guitar; Jerry Shook, guitar; Ray Edenton, guitar; Hargus Robbins, piano; Robby Osborne, drums).

Country Gazette Live. Antilles AN-7014, 1976, LP. (Reissued 2013, Sierra Records SXCD 6034, CD) Country Gazette (Byron Berline, fiddle/mandolin; Roland White, guitar; Alan Munde, banjo; Roger Bush, bass).

Country Music Hootenanny. Capitol ST 2009, 1963, LP. The Kentucky Colonels, Buck Owens, Bob Norris, Rose Maddox, Buddy Cagle, Johnny Bond, Joe and Rose Lee Maphis, Tommy Collins, Glen Campbell, Jean Shepard, Roy Nichols, Merle Travis, Roy Clark, Cousin Herb Henson.

"Crossing the Cumberlands." 45 rpm single, Decca 32502, Side B, recorded 1968, released 1969. Bill Monroe and the Blue Grass Boys (Bill Monroe, mandolin; Roland White, guitar; Vic Jordan, banjo; James Monroe, bass; Kenny Baker, fiddle). Side A: "I Haven't Seen Mary in Years," recorded 1969 (after Roland White left the Blue Grass Boys). Bill Monroe and the Blue Grass Boys (Bill Monroe, mandolin; James Monroe, guitar; Rual Yarbrough, banjo; Joe Zinkan, bass; Kenny Baker, fiddle; Joe "Red" Hayes, fiddle).

David Grier: Freewheeling. Rounder Records 0250, 1988, LP; also Rounder Records CD 0250 1991, CD. David Grier, guitar; Roland White, mandolin; Stuart Duncan, fiddle; Billy Joe Foster, banjo; Wyatt Rice, guitar; Mark Schatz, banjo/bass.

Dobro Country. World Pacific 1829, 1964, LP. (Reissued by Alcatec Media AMWP 1829, 2008, CD) Tut Taylor, Dobro; Clarence White, guitar; Roland White, mandolin; Victor Gaskin, bass; Gary Carlson, rhythm guitar.

Don't Give Up Your Day Job. United Artists UA-LA090-F, 1973, LP. Country Gazette (Clarence White, guitar; Roger Bush, bass/vocals; Byron Berline, fiddle/mandolin/vocals; Alan Munde, banjo/guitar). Also featured: Herb Pedersen, guitar/vocals; Kenny Wertz, guitar/vocals; Leland Sklar, electric bass; Al Perkins, pedal steel guitar.

Festival Favorites: Nashville Sessions. Ridge Runner RRR 0031, 1982, LP. (Portions reissued 1993, Rounder CD 0311, CD) Alan Munde, banjo; Roland White, mandolin; Sam Bush, fiddle; Jerry Douglas, Dobro; Marty Stuart, lead guitar; Joe Carr, rhythm guitar; Blaine Sprouse, fiddle; Larry Wexer, harmonica; Bob French, banjo.

Festival Favorites: Southwest Sessions. Ridge Runner RRR 0032, 1983, LP. (Portions reissued 1993, Rounder CD 0311, CD) The Southwest Society of String Sizzlers (Alan Munde, banjo; Roland White, mandolin; Jim "Texas Shorty" Chancellor, fiddle; Robert Bowlin, fiddle; Bob French, banjo; Mark Land, guitar; Bob Clark, mandolin).

Festival Favorites, Vol. 1. Ridge Runner RRR 0026, 1980, LP. (Portions reissued 1993, Rounder CD 0311, CD) The Texcohomanewmexiline Ramblers (Alan Munde, banjo; Roland White, mandolin; Robert Bowlin, fiddle; Joe Carr, guitar; Mike Anderson, bass).

Festival Favorites, Vol. 2. Ridge Runner RRR 0027, 1980, LP. (Portions reissued 1993, Rounder Records CD 0311, CD) The Texcohomanewmexiline Ramblers (Alan Munde, banjo; Roland White, mandolin; Robert Bowlin, fiddle; Joe Carr, guitar; Mike Anderson, bass).

Flatt on Victor. RCA LSP-4495, 1971, LP. Lester Flatt and the Nashville Grass (Lester Flatt, guitar; Roland White, mandolin; Josh Graves, Dobro; Vic Jordan, banjo; Jake Tullock, bass; Paul Warren, fiddle).

Flatt Out. Columbia CS1006, 1970, LP. Lester Flatt, guitar; Roland White, mandolin; Josh Graves, Dobro; Vic Jordan, banjo; Jake Tullock, bass; Paul Warren, fiddle.

"The Gold Rush"/"Virginia Darlin." 45 rpm single. Decca 32404, recorded 1967, released 1968. Bill Monroe and the Blue Grass Boys (Bill Monroe, mandolin; Roland White, guitar; Byron Berline, fiddle; Vic Jordan, banjo; James Monroe, bass).

Home of the Blues. Sugar Hill SH-CD-3793, 1991, CD. The Nashville Bluegrass Band (Roland White, mandolin; Alan O'Bryant, banjo; Pat Enright, guitar; Stuart Duncan, fiddle; Gene Libbea, bass). Also featured: the Fairfield Four, vocals.

"Is The Blue Moon Still Shining?" Decca 32245, recorded 1967, released 1970. Bill Monroe and the Blue Grass Boys (Bill Monroe, mandolin; Roland White, guitar; Vic Jordan, banjo; James Monroe, bass; Benny Williams, fiddle; Vassar Clements, fiddle).

"I Want to Go with You." Recorded 1967. Bill Monroe, mandolin; Roland White, guitar; Vic Jordan, banjo; James Monroe, bass; Kenny Baker, fiddle.

I Wasn't Born to Rock'n Roll. Ridge Runner RRR 0005, 1976. (Reissued 2010, Tompkins Square TSQ 2400, CD) Roland White, mandolin/vocals; Alan Munde, banjo; Roger Bush, bass/vocals; Kenny Wertz, guitar/vocals; Dave Ferguson, fiddle.

Jelly on My Tofu. Copper Creek CCCD-0211, 2002, CD. The Roland White Band

(Roland White, mandolin/vocals; Diane Bouska, guitar/vocals; Richard Bailey, banjo; Todd Cook, bass/vocals). Also featured: Stuart Duncan, fiddle; Alan Munde, banjo; Andy Leftwich, fiddle; Mark Howard, vocals; Kenny Malone, brushes.

Jim Lauderdale & Roland White. Yep ROC Records YEP-2597, 2018, CD. Jim Lauderdale, guitar/vocals; Roland White, mandolin/guitar/vocals; Gene Wooten, Dobro; Johnny Warren, fiddle; Stan Brown, banjo; Terry Smith, bass; Marty Stuart, guitar.

Kentucky Bluegrass. Decca DL 7-5213, 1970, LP Compilation. Bill Monroe and the Blue Grass Boys. ("Sally Goodin" recorded 1967; Bill Monroe, mandolin; Roland White, guitar; Byron Berline, fiddle; Vic Jordan, banjo; James Monroe, bass).

The Kentucky Colonels, 1965–1966, Featuring Roland and Clarence White. Rounder Records 0070, 1976, LP. The Kentucky Colonels (Clarence White, guitar; Roland White, mandolin; Roger Bush, bass; Billy Ray Latham, banjo). Also featured: Scotty Stoneman, fiddle; Bob Warford, banjo; Dennis Morris, rhythm guitar.

The Kentucky Colonels Onstage. Rounder Records 0199, 1984, LP. The Kentucky Colonels (Clarence White, guitar; Roland White, mandolin; Roger Bush, bass; Billy Ray Latham, banjo). Also featured: Sandy Rothman, rhythm guitar; Scotty Stoneman, fiddle.

"Kentucky Hills"/"Head Over Heels in Love with You." 45 rpm single. Sundown SD 45-131, ca. 1959. The Country Boys (Clarence White, guitar; Roland White, mandolin; LeRoy McNees, Dobro; Roger Bush, bass; Billy Ray Latham, banjo).

"Kentucky Mandolin." Recorded 1967; Bill Monroe, mandolin; Roland White, guitar; Vic Jordan, banjo; James Monroe, bass; Benny Williams, fiddle.

Kentucky Ridgerunner. RCA LSP-4633, 1972, LP. Lester Flatt and the Nashville Grass (Lester Flatt, guitar; Roland White, mandolin; Josh Graves, Dobro; Vic Jordan, banjo; Haskell McCormick, banjo; Jake Tullock, bass; Don Smith, bass; Junior Huskey, bass; Paul Warren, fiddle; Howard "Johnny" Johnson, guitar; Hargus Robbins, piano; Jerry Smith, piano; Jerry Carrigan, drums; Jim Isbell, drums; Ralph Gallant, drums; Dale Sellers, electric guitar).

LeRoy Mack and Friends of the Kentucky Colonels. Rebel Records C-1729, 1996, CD. Leroy Mack, Dobro/vocals; the Nashville Bluegrass Band, Josh Graves, Byron Berline, Mike Stevens, Laurel Canyon Ramblers, Born Again Bluegrass Band.

Lester 'N' Mac. RCA LSP-4547, 1971, LP. Lester Flatt, guitar; Mac Wiseman, guitar; Roland White, mandolin; Josh Graves, Dobro; Vic Jordan, banjo; Haskell Mc-Cormick, banjo; Jake Tullock, bass; Paul Warren, fiddle; Howdy Forrester, fiddle; Howard "Johnny" Johnson, guitar; Hargus Robbins, piano; Jerry Carrigan, drums.

Life's Railway to Heaven. Crown Sound CS-004, 1976, LP. LeRoy McNees, Dobro; Roland White, mandolin; Steve Hatfield, bass/vocals; Dave Hatfield, banjo/guitar/vocals; Byron Berline, fiddle; Roger Bush, bass; Al Perkins, pedal steel guitar; John Hickman, banjo.

Live in Holland 1973. Roland White 0001, 2013, CD. The New Kentucky Colonels (Roland White, mandolin; Clarence White, guitar; Eric White, bass; Herb Pedersen, banjo).

Livin' in the Past. Briar Records BT-7202, 1975, LP. (Reissued by Sierra Records

HS 67003, 1997, CD, and by Rural Rhythm Records RHY 1020, 2003, CD) The Kentucky Colonels (Clarence White, guitar; Roland White, mandolin; LeRoy McNees, Dobro; Roger Bush, bass; Billy Ray Latham, banjo). Also featured: Scotty Stoneman, fiddle; Bobby Slone, fiddle.

Long Journey Home. Vanguard VCD 77004, 1991, CD. The Kentucky Colonels at the Newport Folk Festival, 1964 (Clarence White, guitar; Roland White, mandolin; Roger Bush, bass; Billy Ray Latham, banjo). Also featured: Bill Keith, banjo; Doc Watson, guitar.

The Muscle Shoals Recordings. Rounder Records 11661-9180-2, 2015, CD. The Steel-Drivers (Richard Bailey, banjo; Gary Nichols, guitar/vocals; Tammy Rogers, fiddle/vocals; Brent Truitt, mandolin; Mike Fleming, bass/vocals).

My Native Home. Rounder Records 0212, 1985, LP. (Reissued 1991 Rounder CD 0212, CD) The Nashville Bluegrass Band (Alan O'Bryant, banjo/vocals; Mike Compton, mandolin/vocals; Pat Enright, guitar/vocals; Mark Hembree, bass/vocals). Also featured: Blaine Sprouse, fiddle.

The New Kentucky Colonels: Live in Sweden (Reissue of Rounder 0073 with added tracks). Roland White RW0003, 2016, CD. The New Kentucky Colonels (Roland White, mandolin/vocals; Clarence White, guitar/vocals; Eric White, bass/vocals; Alan Munde, banjo/guitar).

The New Sound of Bluegrass America. Briar 109, 1962, LP. The Kentucky Colonels (Clarence White, guitar; LeRoy McNees, Dobro; Roger Bush, bass; Billy Ray Latham, banjo).

1965 Live in LA. Sierra Briar Records SBR 4206, 1978, LP. (Reissued by Rural Rhythm Records, Sierra Records RHY 1017, 2002, CD; Sierra Records SXCD 6029, 2009, CD) The Kentucky Colonels (Roland White, mandolin; Clarence White, guitar; Roger Bush, bass; Billy Ray Latham, banjo; Scotty Stoneman, fiddle).

The One and Only Lester Flatt. Nugget NRLP 104, 1970, LP. Lester Flatt, guitar; Roland White, mandolin; Josh Graves, Dobro; Vic Jordan, banjo; Jake Tullock, bass; Paul Warren, fiddle.

"On the Mountain (Stands My Love)"/"The Valley Below." 45 rpm single. Republic Records 45-R-1055, ca. 1959. The Country Boys (Clarence White, guitar; Roland White, mandolin; LeRoy McNees, Dobro; Roger Bush, bass; Billy Ray Latham, banjo).

On the Southbound. RCA LSP-4688, 1972, LP. Lester Flatt, guitar; Mac Wiseman, guitar; Roland White, mandolin; Josh Graves, Dobro; Vic Jordan, banjo; Haskell McCormick, banjo; Jake Tullock, bass; Don Smith, bass; Paul Warren, fiddle; Howdy Forrester, fiddle; Howard "Johnny" Johnson, guitar; Hargus Robbins, piano; Jerry Carrigan, drums.

Out to Lunch. Flying Fish FF027, 1976, LP. (Reissued 2013, Sierra Records SXCD 6034, CD) Country Gazette (Roger Bush, bass; Alan Munde, banjo; Roland White, mandolin; Kenny Wertz, guitar). Also featured: Dave Ferguson, fiddle; Al Perkins, pedal steel guitar.

Portrait of a Bluegrass Fiddler. County 719, 1969, LP. Kenny Baker, fiddle; Roland White, mandolin; Doug Green, bass; Del McCoury, guitar.

A Potpourri of Bluegrass Jam. Warner Bros. Records BS2787, 1973, LP. (Reissued on Ridge Runner, RRR 00016, 1978, LP) Muleskinner (Clarence White, guitar/vocals; Bill Keith, banjo; Richard Greene, fiddle; David Grisman, mandolin/vocals; Peter Rowan, guitar/vocals; John Kahn, bass; John Guerin, drums).

Roland White and Friends: A Tribute to the Kentucky Colonels. Mountain Home Music Company MH17242, 2018, CD. Roland White, mandolin/vocals; Billy Strings, guitar/vocals; Molly Tuttle, guitar; Brittany Haas, guitar; Justin Hiltner, banjo; David Grier, guitar; Kristin Scott Benson, banjo; Gina Furtado, banjo; Jeremy Darrow, bass; Jeremy Garrett, fiddle; Drew Matulich, guitar; Darin and Brooke Aldridge, vocals; Russ Carson, banjo; Jon Weisberger, bass; Patrick McAvinue, fiddle; Darren Nicholson, vocals; Jon Stickley, guitar; Josh Haddix, guitar; Aaron Bibelhauser, banjo; Nick Dauphinais, vocals; Lindsay Pruett, fiddle; Kimber Ludiker, fiddle; Lindsay Lou, vocals.

Snakes Alive. Rounder Records 0177, 1983, LP. (Reissued 1995, Rounder CD 0177, CD) The Dreadful Snakes (Roland White, mandolin; Béla Fleck, banjo; Blaine Sprouse, fiddle; Mark Hembree, bass; Jerry Douglas, Dobro; Pat Enright, guitar).

Somewhere Over the Rainbow. Ridge Runner RRR 0003, 1976, LP. Dave Ferguson And His Friends (Roland White, mandolin; Alan Munde, banjo/guitar; Roger Bush, bass; Stephen Bruton, guitar).

The SteelDrivers. Rounder Records, 11661-0598-2, 2008, CD. The SteelDrivers (Richard Bailey, banjo; Mike Fleming, bass/vocals; Tammy Rogers, fiddle/vocals; Chris Stapleton, guitar/vocals; Mike Henderson, mandolin).

Straight Ahead Bluegrass. Roland White and Diane Bouska, 2014, CD. The Roland White Band (Roland White, mandolin/vocals; Diane Bouska, guitar/vocals; Richard Bailey, banjo; Jon Weisberger, bass/vocals; Brian Christianson, fiddle/vocals).

Strictly Instrumental. Flying Fish FF 446, 1987, LP. (Portions reissued 1999, Flying Fish FF 70112, CD) Country Gazette (Alan Munde, banjo; Roland White, mandolin; Kathy Chiavola, electric bass; David Grier, guitar; Gene Wooten, Dobro/banjo).

Sweetheart of the Rodeo. Columbia CS 9670, 1968, LP. (Reissued many times.) The Byrds (Clarence J. White, guitar; Lloyd Green, pedal steel guitar; John Hartford, banjo/guitar; Roy Huskey, bass; Chris Hillman, bass/mandolin; Jon Corneal, drums; Kevin Kelly, drums; Gram Parsons, guitar; Roger McGuinn, guitar/banjo; Earl P. Ball, piano; Jay Dee Maness, pedal steel guitar).

"Train 45 (Heading South)"/"Is the Blue Moon Still Shining." 45 rpm single, Decca 32245, recorded 1967, released 1968. Side A: Bill Monroe and the Blue Grass Boys (Bill Monroe, mandolin; Roland White, guitar; Benny Williams, fiddle; Vassar Clements, fiddle; Vic Jordan, banjo; James Monroe, bass).

Traitor in Our Midst. United Artists UAS-5596, 1972, LP. Country Gazette (Byron Berline, fiddle/mandolin/vocals; Roger Bush, bass/vocals; Alan Munde, banjo/guitar; Kenny Wertz, guitar/vocals). Also featured: Skip Conover, Dobro; Chris Smith, guitar.

Treasures Untold. Vanguard VCD 77001, 1991, CD. Doc Watson and Family, Clarence White field recording, 1964.

Trying to Get to You. Sugar Hill SH-CD 3826, 1994, CD. Roland White, mandolin/ vocals; Diane Bouska, vocals; David Grier, guitar; Stuart Duncan, fiddle/vocals; Gene Wooten, Dobro/vocals; Richard Bailey, banjo; Gene Libbea, bass; Alan O'Bryant, vocals; Pat Enright, vocals.

Unleashed. Sugar Hill SHCD-3843, 1995, CD. The Nashville Bluegrass Band (Roland White, mandolin/vocals; Alan O'Bryant, banjo/vocals; Gene Libbea, bass/vocals; Pat Enright, guitar/vocals).

Waitin' for the Hard Times to Go. Sugar Hill SH-CD-3809, 1993, CD. The Nashville Bluegrass Band (Roland White, mandolin/vocals; Alan O'Bryant, banjo/vocals; Pat Enright, guitar/vocals; Gene Libbea, bass/vocals; Stuart Duncan, fiddle/vocals). Also featured: Jerry Douglas, Dobro.

"Walls of Time." Recorded 1968, first released 1994, MCA, *The Music of Bill Monroe from 1936 to 1994*, MCAC/D4–11048, disc 3, CD. Bill Monroe and the Bluegrass Boys (Bill Monroe, mandolin; Roland White, guitar; Vic Jordan, banjo; James Monroe, bass; Kenny Baker, fiddle).

What a Way to Make a Living. Ridge Runner RRR 0008, 1977, LP. (Reissued 2013, Sierra Records SXCD 6034, CD) Country Gazette (Roland White, mandolin; Byron Berline, fiddle; Skip Conover, Dobro; Slim Richey, guitar; Richard Greene, fiddle; Bill Bryson, bass).

The White Brothers (The New Kentucky Colonels) Live in Sweden, 1973. Rounder Records 0073, 1976, LP. The New Kentucky Colonels (Roland White, mandolin/vocals; Clarence White, guitar/vocals; Eric White, bass/vocals; Alan Munde, banjo/guitar).

Why Is This Man Smiling? Ridge Runner RRR 0004, 1976, LP. Dan Huckabee, Dobro; Roland White, mandolin; Roger Bush, bass; Dave Ferguson, fiddle; Joe Carr, guitar.

Index

White, Buck, 137, 149, 163, 261
White, Bukka, 34
White, Clarence, ix, x, 7, 12, 13, 16, *19*, *23*,
27, 36, *39*, *42–44*, 47, 55–67, *60*, *64*,
73, 92, 118, *122*, 133, 149, 151, 168, 175,
177, 194, *199*, 200, 211, 213, 225, 253–57;
Appalachian Swing!, 201–2; appearance
in *The Farmer's Other Daughter*,
65; audition at Riverside Rancho,
24–25; Bob Baxter's *Guitar Workshop*,
119; beginning lead solos, 34; bird
dropping, 62; Bluegrass Hall of Fame,
193; the Byrds, 106; cross-picking, 54;
death of widow, Julia, 142–43; East
Coast tour and workshop with Doc
Watson, 59–61; *The Essential Clarence
White Bluegrass Guitar Leads*, 227; first
time playing guitar, 18; funeral, 128–29;
on the G-run, 69; guitar players
emulated by, 195–98; guitar style
development, 51–52; harmony singing,
29; and Roline Hodge, 183; influenced
by Joe Maphis and Mac Wiseman, 24,
52; influenced by Django Reinhart,
56; influenced by Earl Scruggs, 30;
influenced by Arnold Terry, 31;
influence on Jerry Garcia, 58; influence
on David Grier, 72, 148, 208; influence
on Marty Stuart, 113; influence on
Roland White, 156, 157–58; introducing
Arline Melanson to Roland White, 43;
invention of the Parsons/White Pull-
String, StringBender, or B-Bender, 66;
"Laughing Guitar," 132; *Muleskinner*,
117; with Muleskinner band, 155; not
smiling, 37; performing at Indian
Springs, Maryland bluegrass festival,
123; picking with Doug Green, 79;
plans to revive the Kentucky Colonels,
115–17; playing to metronome, 51;
"Powder Creek," 136; recording for
Warner Brothers in LA, 124; recording
of *Appalachian Swing!*, 57; recording
of *Dobro Country* (with Tut Taylor),
58; recording of *Don't Give Up Your
Day Job*, 129; recording of *Sweetheart
of the Rodeo*, 80; recording of *The New

Kentucky Colonels: Live In Holland,
120–21; recording of *The New Kentucky
Colonels: Live In Sweden*, 121–23;
relationship to brothers Eric and
Roland, 44; Roland pressing mandolin
peghead on Clarence's guitar, 61–62;
scheduled to perform at Winfield,
Kansas, 127; session work from James
Burton, 67; and sister Rosemarie,
178–79; smashed guitar, 61; stage
demeanor, 63; struck by car and killed
in Lancaster, California, 125–27
White, Eric Jr., *19*, *23*, *27*, 39, *42–44*, *122*,
124, 173, 177, 193, 194, 225, 254, 255,
257; burning of shoes by Roland, 45
White, Eric Sr., 127, 128, 177, 178–79, 184,
194, 225
White, (Hodge) Roline, x, 59, 61, 65, 77,
99, *101*, 114, 177, 179–85, *181*, 226
White, JoAnne, 16–18, *19*, *23*, 225
White, Lawrence, 177, 180–85, *181*, 226
White, Martha, 5, 40, 91, 97–99, 109, 110,
112, 115, 213
White, Mildred Cyr, 14–17, *19*, 25, 30, 33,
37, 65, 125, 127, 177, 179, 184, 225
White, Roland, ix, x, *19*, *23*, *27*, *38*, *39*,
42, *43*, *51*, 54, *64*, *78*, *100–102*, 110,
122, *124*, *132*, *137*, 148–50, *162*, *167*,
175, 176, *193*, *199*, 200; account of
Clarence's death, 125–26; *Appalachian
Swing!*, 201–2; appearance on *The
Andy Griffith Show*, 41–43; appearing
in *The Farmer's Other Daughter*, 65;
appearing with Clarence White on Bob
Baxter's *Guitar Workshop*, 119; in the
army, 48–50; baseball with Monroe,
79; becoming a Blue Grass Boy, 70–71;
bent nails confrontation with Birch,
88; birth of Roline, 61; Bluegrass Boys
reunion on *Prairie Home Companion*,
172–73; burning Eric White's shoes,
45; Joe Carr introduction of Roland
White at Smithsonian Institution,
144; clearing trees and building stage
at Brown County Jamboree, 85–86;
co-founding the Nashville Bluegrass
Music Association, 145–46; Mike

Compton's observations of Roland White's playing, 171–72; coping with the Monroe work ethic, 75–76; The Country Boys practice sessions, 31–32; country rock tour, 124–25; decision to leave the Nashville Grass, 115–16; disbanding The Kentucky Colonels, 67; distributing posters for Birch, 88; divorce from Arline, 146; drafted, 47; driving tour bus for Bill Monroe, 150; driving tour bus for Lester Flatt, 102–3, recording of *The One and Only Lester Flatt*, 104–5; "Dusty Miller" and "Rawhide" rhythm challenge, 76; entry into Country Gazette, 131; European tour, 119–23; family, 177–85; family and musical background, 14–19; first Bill Monroe record purchases, 27–29; first East Coast tour, 58–59; first Flatt and Scruggs record purchases, 29–30; first *Grand Ole Opry* show with Monroe, 72–74; first meeting and hiring of Roger Bush, 45–47; first meeting with and hiring of LeRoy NcNees, 35–37; first meeting with Bill Monroe, 33; first meeting with Billy Ray Latham, 32–33; formation of The Roland White Band, 169–70; David Grier tribute, 202; getting job with Lester Flatt, 95–97; guests of Roland at the *Grand Ole Opry*, 1, 3–4; Indian Springs bluegrass festival, 123; induction into the Bluegrass Hall of Fame, 192–94; influence of Sam Tester, 30–31; influence on Marty Stuart, 6–7, 12, 109; interview with Roland and Alan O'Bryant, 152, 155–60; interview with Roland White and Vic Jordan, 84–90; introduction of Marty Stuart to Lester Flatt, 109; invitation to join Country Gazette, 129; jamming with Jethro Burns, 163; on leaving The Nashville Bluegrass Band, 169; life story at the Red Roof Inn, 2; life with Diane Bouska, 187; listening to Monroe play on the bus, 82–83; mandolin techniques, 155–58; meeting

and jamming with Alan Munde, 106; meeting and marrying Arline Melanson, 43–44; meeting Richard Bailey, 174; Monroe's mandolin and learning from Bill, 83; moving to California, 20–21; music video with the Steep Canyon Rangers, 3–4; Nashville jam sessions, 11; the need to have a book written about, 2, 4; observing old Brown County Jamboree stage, 75; origin of "Chee Chee" nickname, 107–8; passion for music, 5–10, 13; performance jobs at other venues, 40; performing at The Ash Grove, 33–35; performing in Japan, 172; performing "Midnight on the Stormy Deep" at the *Grand Ole Opry*, 80–81; performing with Gatemouth Brown, 172; philosophical description of playing music, 11; pictured in Lester Flatt souvenir booklet, 99; plans to form The New Kentucky Colonels, 117–18; playing as extension of personality, 11–12; playing at bowling alley, 66–67; playing at drive-in theaters, 107; playing at first Bean Blossom bluegrass festival, 74–75; playing with Bill Monroe at The Ash Grove, 68–70; playing with the Nashville Bluegrass Band, 3; playing with Marty Stuart in the Nashville Grass, 112–14; reading of *Come Hither to Go Yonder: Playing Bluegrass with Bill Monroe*, 2; recording in LA, 124; recording of *All This and Money Too*, 141–42; recording of *American and Clean*, 142; recording of *American Beauty*, 168; recording of *America's Bluegrass Band*, 143–44; recording of *Appalachian Swing!*, 57; recording of *Bluegrass Tonight*, 146–47; recording of *Country Boy*, 114–15; recording of *Country Gazette Live*, 132–33; recording of *Country Music Hootenanny*, 56–57; recording of *David Grier: Freewheeling*, 150–51; recording of *Dobro Country* with Tut Taylor, 58; recording of *Flatt on Victor*,

BOB BLACK played banjo in Bill Monroe's Blue Grass Boys and recorded with Monroe on the *Weary Traveler* album. Black later played with Buck White and the Down Home Folks and has performed with Ricky Skaggs, Ralph Stanley, Rhonda Vincent, Marty Stuart, and many others. He is the author of *Come Hither to Go Yonder: Playing Bluegrass with Bill Monroe.*

Music in American Life

The University of Illinois Press
is a founding member of the
Association of University Presses.

———————————————

Composed in 11/14 Adobe Minion Pro
with Avenir display
by Jim Proefrock
at the University of Illinois Press
Manufactured by Sheridan Books, Inc.

University of Illinois Press
1325 South Oak Street
Champaign, IL 61820-6903
www.press.uillinois.edu